PARKER & HULME

PARKER & HULME

HULME

A LESBIAN VIEW

Julie Glamuzina and Alison J. Laurie

Introduction
by B. Ruby Rich

Firebrand
Books
Ithaca, New York

Parker & Hulme: A Lesbian View was originally published in New Zealand by New Women's Press.

Copyright © 1991 by Julie Glamuzina and Alison J. Laurie
Introduction to the U.S. Edition Copyright © 1995 by B. Ruby Rich
All rights reserved.

This book may not be reproduced in whole or part, except in the case of reviews, without permission from Firebrand Books, 141 The Commons, Ithaca, New York 14850.

Cover design by Debra Engstrom

Printed in the United States on acid-free paper by McNaughton & Gunn

10 9 8 7 6 5 4 3 2 1

Library of Congress Cataloging-in-Publication Data

Glamuzina, Julie, 1954-
     Parker & Hulme: a lesbian view / Julie Glamuzina & Alison J.
Laurie ; introduction by B. Ruby Rich.
     p. cm.
Originally published: Auckland : New Women's Press, 1991.
Includes bibliographical references and index.
     ISBN 1-56341-066-4 (alk. paper). — ISBN 1-56341-065-6 (pbk. :
alk. paper)
     1. Murder—New Zealand—Case studies. 2. Parricide—New
Zealand—Case studies. 3. Lesbians—New Zealand—Case studies.
4. Lesbianism—New Zealand—Case studies. I. Laurie, Alison J. II.
Title.
HV6535.N46G53   1995
364.1'523'099383—dc20
                                                      95-25420
                                                          CIP

Contents

People gather outside the Supreme Court, Christchurch, 1954. (N.Z. Truth)

Introduction to the U.S. Edition/ B. Ruby Rich

The investigation undertaken in New Zealand in the 1980s by lesbian historians Julie Glamuzina and Alison J. Laurie arrives in the U.S. at a moment as thoroughly auspicious as it must have been unforeseeable at the time of its inception. Two singular events in 1992—the trial and conviction of lesbian sex worker Aileen Wuornos (FBI-and tabloid-dubbed "America's first woman serial killer") and the politically controversial but commercially successful launch of Sharon Stone as the ice-pick killer of *Basic Instinct*—bestowed upon the 1990s a new image of the lesbian murderer.

For all the prevalent stereotypes of lesbians that dominated popular imagination and subcultural fantasy over the years, lesbo-murderess has never been central. On-screen lesbians have been more often prone to suicide or depression, infantile neurosis or sadistic dominance, with the occasional vampire thrown in for good measure. Their victims were most often themselves or other women. Now, however, the Wuornos-Stone mix has been thickened by the interplay of media attentions, cinematic representations, and political reclaimings, resulting in an unprecedented synergy of disparate activities that coalesce into a brand-new figure of dyke as killer--a figure that's equal parts heroine or villain, promise or threat, depending on viewer identification. Manifestations have ranged from the giant banner supporting Wuornos at the 1992 March on Washington for Lesbian and Gay Rights to such Wuornos-inspired creations as the theatre production *Lesbians Who Kill* staged by Deb Margolin, Peggy Shaw and Lois Weaver in New York City.

Lesbian audiences turned out, too, for the 1995 re-release of the bisexual-killer cult classic, *Faster Pussycat, Kill! Kill!*, as well as for two recent independent films that used true stories as the basis for exploring their lesbian killer-couples: *Fun* and *Sister My Sister.* New short films with killer heroines attracted huge audiences on the lesbian/gay film festival circuit in spring 1995.

In academic circles during the same period, the vampire as lesbian icon has been staked out by theorist Sue-Ellen Case and film historian Andrea Weiss. They are building new critical structures upon the foundations laid originally in the 1970s by scholars Richard Dyer and Bonnie Zimmerman, a direction long left dormant even when

The Hunger might have been expected to spark a Sarandon/Deneuve-fueled revival. (Instead, according to a recent account in the gay weekly, the *Advocate, The Hunger* may be credited with sparking the lesbian-chic phenomenon of the 1990s or, at the very least, with landing Deneuve a dedicated lesbian following that rivals the accolytes Delphine Seyrig collected for her role in *Daughters of Darkness,* an earlier lesbian-vampire cult classic.) In literature, too, the lesbian vampire has experienced a renewal, from Jewelle Gomez's groundbreaking *The Gilda Stories* (Firebrand Books) to recent anthologies like *Daughters of Darkness* (Cleis Press). Some combination of lust and bloodlust has undeniably animated interest in this new figure and her emergent narratives, spawning a vibrant cultural territory-in-formation in which this volume dedicated to Parker and Hulme now finds itself.

And all of the above is merely the start of the back-story. It's doubtful that ten or fifteen years ago many Americans had ever heard of a locally sensational New Zealand case from 1954 involving two young women, Pauline Parker and Juliet Hulme, who together killed Parker's mother, were then tried and convicted, imprisoned and released and exiled, never to be heard from again. Riveting as the case and its lore may have been to New Zealanders, there was nothing about the long-ago event to attract U.S. notice. (Even in Britain, their case was so little present that an anthology on women and murder [*Moving Targets: Women, Murder and Representation* from Virago] that included other figures from down under omitted their mention entirely.)

Ah, but that was before a certain film based upon the case loomed into view. Popular culture being what it is, there are likely to be few readers of this volume who do not come to it informed and misinformed by *Heavenly Creatures,* the dramatic feature film directed by New Zealander Peter Jackson and written by Jackson and his wife Frances Walsh, purporting to tell in fictionalized form the true story of Parker and Hulme, their friendship, their home life in distinctly different families, their fantasy life, and of course, the *pièce de résistance,* their act of murder.

The uproar that surrounded the release of *Heavenly Creatures* in the U.S. (which included the attendant identification by an alert international reporter of best-selling mystery novelist Anne Perry as none other than the former Juliet Hulme, teenage murderer, now alive and well and a Mormon, living one village over from Mum in Scotland) has performed a simultaneous service and disservice to the text at hand. Certainly the movie has upstaged this serious work of historical analysis which—please take note—actually preceded the film chronologically. Furthermore, while there is no way of knowing whether the book at hand was an unacknowledged source for any filmic details, the movie has planted a distorted view of the girls and the case in a U.S. public previously ignorant of the material.

Interestingly, this very notoriety and distortion replicate the effect originally produced on the case by the New Zealand press, thereby providing modern readers with a personal experience of media representations, misrepresentations, and their consequences. Our contemporary experience therefore reverberates with the story offered here and makes its telling all the more relevant. Thanks to the publicity machine set in motion by the Miramax distribution company's considerable resources, by newspaper wire services, and by the film's wide release and resultant access to a general audience, we too have a stake in the fate of "Juliet" and "Pauline," whoever or wherever they happen to be. We have, that is, a vested interest in following Glamuzina and Laurie down memory lane in search of clues to the society and circumstances that made these two girls of legend what they were—and, in turn, as cycles of reception repeat themselves, make of us, in relation to them, what we are today.

The recuperation of popular memory has long been a motivating force in feminist history projects. While lesbian historiography often has been more occupied with projects of retrieval, legitimacy, and reclamation than with paying attention to the questions of representational effects occasioned by the specifics of such a singular incident as the original Parker and Hulme case, the release of *Heavenly Creatures* presents just such a challenge to our understanding of how representations enter popular consciousness. It offers an unprecedented opportunity to reconsider the interplay between popular culture, individual identity, and societal prescription. If the film can be credited in part for Parker and Hulme's finding a readership in the U.S. at this time, it has also given its mission even more urgency than it had in 1986, when Glamuzina and Laurie first rescued the Parker-Hulme case from obscurity and began to explore the links it suggests between the 1950s and the present—in Christchurch, in New Zealand, and in communities everywhere where lesbianism is as taboo as matricide.

Heavenly Creatures opens with a hallucinatory scene of two giddily excited teenage girls running onto a posh estate, covered with blood, then backtracks to the story of the two girls, their families, their passionate friendship. The film employs a barrage of technical special effects to visualize the girls' shared fantasies and interior world, ranging from plasticine models of imaginary royals to fanciful encounters with saints, Orson Welles, and Mario Lanza in baroque scenarios. The film's handling of the actual murder scene, by contrast, is peculiarly devoid of the mannered subjectivity and visual splash that run rampant elsewhere, as though imagination failed the filmmaker when faced with the act itself. The film's success seems to be due to two main factors: first, the fascination of the story itself, virtually unknown outside of New Zealand though fabled within, and second, the audience's equal fascination with the cinematic effects utilized to literalize the girls' invented universe.

My own view of *Heavenly Creatures* failed to incorporate either the praise of mainstream critics or the applause of lesbian audiences. Was I enacting the role of self-styled spoilsport, the unpopular cinematic expert who breaks up the party by shining a bright light on the revellers and ruins the fun by informing audiences that they don't understand what appears so plainly before their eyes? It wasn't just the Ninja-turtle styling of the fantasy kingdom that irked me. I couldn't help but notice that the film's withholding of its signature style at the key juncture of the murder effectively supplied the film with a moral message, retroactively, to its story. The message is one of disapproval, with the filmmaker weighing in, like it or not, with the Christchurch elders at the point when push came to shove and matricide loomed. Further, Jackson's abandonment of all identification with his characters at the fateful moment of murder is decisive, for he inevitably takes the audience with him.

Luckily, the stories and histories contained in this volume provide more than sufficient evidence to support and amplify my misgivings regarding the film and its script. I am not alone: Glamuzina and Laurie perform an adept deconstruction of the film despite the fact that it didn't exist at the time of their investigation. It accomplishes this debunking by means of the simple elaboration of factual materials and perspectives which, in their veracity, pierce the purported verisimilitude of the characters and shatter the coherence of the narratives so painstakingly created on-screen.

This study, conducted as an intensive collaboration between two historians who clearly identify the extent to which they themselves are implicated in the histories they present, is a work of recovery. It's a pioneering expedition into the ruins of social structures and the tracks of identity formations, one that pieces together the clues as convincingly as any archaeologist or crime-scene detective. Glamuzina and Laurie utilize materials from period newspapers, trial transcripts, diary entries, and interviews with surviving participants (excepting the two principals, whom they decided not to try to track down, on principle.)

There are a number of areas in which Glamuzina and Laurie literally redefine how we see Juliet and Pauline by virtue of recontextualizing their lives in the time of Kinsey on the one hand and teenagedom on the other. Detailing Juliet's mother's work as a marriage counsellor, her extramarital affair, divorce and remarriage, and Pauline's father's previous marriage and adulterous relationship to her mother, Glamuzina and Laurie show the extent to which both families had "secrets" related to sexual behavior that violated social norms. When the date of the murder is matched to the date of Juliet's "primal scene" of witnessing her mother in bed with Walter Perry (a passage of three days, by my reckoning), the effect of social taboos upon the girls becomes even more significant. Did the girls become, perhaps, scapegoats for their families? Were they human lightning rods, providing an extreme reaction to events that demanded some kind of response but had otherwise received none at all?

As U.S. readers in the age of O.J. Simpson or Sharon Smith well know, only those trials that offer the public an entry into horror or fascination, beauty or glamor, class privilege or taboo rupture, and which combine a potent mix of such unique factors with a public moral (a lesson that an unstoppable force of public interest seems to want to learn, or that some elements within the society want the public to unlearn) are the ones with which the public imagination cathects and which stay with us, seemingly forever. What, then, did New Zealanders want to learn from Juliet and Pauline's crime and punishment? What was at stake with that lesson, who was administering it, and why?

The owners and editors of the media in New Zealand in the 1950s were conservative and, according to Glamuzina and Laurie, committed to the notion that their readership "was, or ought to be, white, heterosexual, anti-communist, and firm supporters of fixed gender roles and the nuclear family." Certainly Juliet and Pauline were exceptional protagonists for a murder case. They were treated with uncommon interest for a variety of reasons, including Juliet's class position, Pauline's relative exoticism, their youth, their unusual imaginations, their family histories, and, of course, the nature of their crime. Nevertheless, the extent to which the trial and media coverage sought to perform a "monsterisation" and "eccentrification" of the two remains striking. New Zealand seemed to want to seal Pauline and Juliet off, away from the rest of society, perhaps to create a foolproof barrier that would guarantee the rest of society remain uncontaminated by their example and, therefore, (arguably) normal.

To this end, the defense strategy of arguing that the murder was the result of a *folie à deux* assumes great significance. This version of an insanity plea, supported by testifying defense psychiatrist Reginald Medlicott though disputed by prosecution psychiatrists, contended that the two girls, although seemingly sane individually, actually were changed by each other's company so as to assume a joint madness precipitated by their shared fantasies. Their defense attorneys invented the *folie à deux* plea as the only available back-up once the two had confessed. The concept was discredited at the trial by prosecution psychiatrists, while the court concurred by finding the girls rational and therefore guilty. Yet its attractiveness as a theory implicitly collecting lesbianism under the banner of criminal pathology was so powerful that defense psychiatrist Medlicott held to the *folie à deux* for the rest of his professional life, the media continued to promote it, and *Heavenly Creatures* returned it to the screen as central narrative and character base, undamaged by decades of psychoanalytic and legal skepticism.

There's also a history to this psychiatric strategy, traceable to two other cases from the 1930s: one in Chicago, the other in Le Mans, France. At the time of Honora Mary Parker's murder, the New Zealand press referred to Pauline and Juliet as the country's own Leopold and Loeb. Nathan Leopold and Richard Loeb were the pair of wealthy young Chicagoans who, united by homoeroticism and a taste for crime, kidnapped and murdered a young boy. Clarence Darrow, their defense attorney, tried to save them by arguing the pathologizing effects of homosexuality; he succeeded, at least, in averting the death penalty.

There's also the 1933 French case of the Papin sisters, a pair of maids who savagely killed their mistresses and then starred in a particularly spectacular trial at which the prosecution speculated that an incestuous and homosexual love for one another figured as motivation and explanation. The trial was made notorious by the famous writers and intellectuals who wrote about it: Jean Genet (whose *The Maids* is based upon the case), Jean-Paul Sartre, Simone de Beauvoir, and Jacques Lacan. It was Lacan who employed the term *délire à deux* to offer a psychoanalytic explanation of the drives that produced the horrific act. And it was this Lacanian reading, I suspect, that formed the basis of Medlicott's own diagnosis.

All three murder cases under discussion here involved a pair of killers of the same gender bound by ties of love or affection. All three couples were young and attractive. All three killed directly and brutally, with hands or brick, without knife or gun. All three, despite the insanity which their societies felt compelled to project upon them, were consigned to prison rather than mental asylums. Finally, all three cases have become the basis of dramatic films in the past five years: *Swoon* by Tom Kalin, one of the first of the New Queer Cinema hits; *Sister My Sister* by Nancy Meckler, a British theater director turned filmmaker, who was surprised by the film's enthusiastic reception at gay and lesbian film festivals; and *Heavenly Creatures,* the biggest crossover hit of the three, thanks to its Miramax distribution, visual style, and real-life tie-in to Anne Perry. Only *Swoon* was made by a gay filmmaker. It's also the only one to eroticize the murder, using the filmmaker's memories of his Chicago boyhood and his fascination with the case to create something that was less a *folie* or a *délire* than the constructed organization of a range of pathologies once deemed abhorrent by mainstream society: Jewishness, Blackness, Gayness, Drag, etc.

Like Kalin's script, Glamuzina and Laurie's study insists on displacing totally individualized notions of murder and motivation by revealing the full context within which crime and punishment transpired. Key to their strategy is the interrogation of informants not recognized as "experts" by the society in which the trial transpired, the fifties class-based Anglophiliac world of Christchurch: namely, Maoris and lesbians. It is here that they've made their most startling discoveries.

The Port Levy house where the Hulme family vacationed had been in Maori hands for six centuries until its sale to a white family a decade earlier. More importantly, it was located in a spiritually charged Maori area, where concepts of a "fourth world" that could be entered with the proper keys still retained a vital force. The Maori elder whom Glamuzina and Laurie consulted felt that Pauline and Juliet could very possibly have come under the influence of such spiritual forces, pointing out their use of the numbers seven and ten, the saints, and frequent bathing as elements in concordance with these spirit-forces. Bolstered by the revelation that such spirits could be placated by a blood sacrifice from within one's own kinship group, as well as by their discovery that Pauline spent some of her prison years studying the Maori language, the authors contend that this link remains an important unexplored aspect of the murder. Outside New Zealand, where Maori culture is so little known and little understood, it's particularly important to emphasize this connection.

Glamuzina and Laurie go on to conduct in-depth interviews with New Zealand lesbians who lived through the time of the trial, and to survey others who grew up or became lesbians in the years that followed. This is the kind of work that everyone talks about doing but seldom does: historically and theoretically grounded, it is empirical work in the service of charting new territory. As such, these interviews serve as a model of how new advances might be made in lesbian theory and historiography and how blindly we proceed without them. Numerous revelations emerge from their extraordinary research, pinpointing the disparate uses of the trial as immunization, shock therapy, advertisement, or wish fulfillment.

Mothers throughout New Zealand, almost without exception, used the case as the dominant "cautionary tale" for their pubescent daughters. In this sense, the trial's virtue must have been its inclusion of substantial self-interest to motivate mothers to pass on the moral (the set-up is obvious: tell your daughter this or die!). Teachers used it as well, sometimes with a double message intended to seduce as much as warn. The most poignant memories belong to those girls who policed themselves with the case: one woman remembers recognizing herself in the description of the girls' relationship and immediately breaking off her relations with another girl at school, returning to women only after terminating a twenty-year marriage. Woman after woman echoes her story of trauma by newspaper—stories of being scared out of incipient feelings by their horror at such a consequence.

For all the tragedy of these stories, however, there are other (albeit fewer) stories of girls who recognized their feelings for the first time with pleasure or excitement, realized they weren't the "only" ones, were reassured that lesbianism was an option in the world (and a legal one, not being criminalized until the following decade). Some girls even celebrated Juliet's and Pauline's example, admitting that they, too, as adolescents, felt like killing their mothers. These interviewees believed the pair had gotten away with it, since they drew only five years in prison and obtained a university education while there.

Hence, an important lesson in the working of subcultural resistance: that a campaign aimed at the curtailing of "lesbian relationships and of 'permissive' family life," as the authors have it, could backfire and strengthen the resolve of its intended victims.

It is tempting to imagine a new generation of historians conducting a similar study, sometime in the next century, of American adolescent girls' reactions to the wave of killer-couple films and murderess-heroine movies of the 1990s. The difference, of course, immediately and unmistakeably, is the distance between the unremitting repression of Christchurch in the 1950s and the U.S. today.

Heavenly Creatures was launched in the heyday of independent gay and lesbian cinema, with upwards of seventy-five gay and lesbian film festivals worldwide and a vigorous niche market awaiting each new release. It was preceded by *Claire of the Moon,* the much-reviled lesbian drama that nevertheless had such box office success with its target audience that it established a new commercial benchmark for lesbian product, and by *Go Fish,* the first lesbian independent film in many years to win critical praise and box office success on the art house/festival circuit. It's more likely, though, that Miramax was equally influenced by the response to crossover films like *Fried Green Tomatoes* or *Thelma and Louise* when it decided to take on *Heavenly Creatures* for distribution.

Heavenly Creatures won its audience appeal through strategies that may be of dubious value to the lesbian historian. Its *folie à deux* narrative line, as well as its inability to allow the viewer to experience the act of murder subjectively, effectively prevent our return to a temporal or regional landscape that could make Pauline and Juliet's story comprehensible. Thankfully, this volume substitutes a meditative pace, governed by logic and investigation, for the euphoric but deceptive breakneck pace of the special-effects movie. It allows us to slow down the myth machine and reexamine the dynamics that palpably governed the girls' decisions, fears, desires, and consequences. In so doing, Glamuzina and Laurie succeed in returning the girls' story once again to its era, a context which in no way robs them of their particular individualism, but which finally helps us, in our world, make sense of its unusual expression through the materials of fantasy and murder.

Finally, and hardly incidentally, Glamuzina and Laurie offer this retrospective analysis at a time when its truths can be pressed into immediate service. As the lesbian murderess is amongst us at this very moment, haunting the pages and screens of our fantasy lives and entertainment industries, we consumers of popular culture are sorely in need of all the help we can get in sorting out the relative benefits and malevolences of such an image. Here, in *Parker and Hulme*, we finally have the research and the data we require to argue the uses of such representations without falling into the usual traps. Unlike the influential Frankfurt School philosophers, who came to the United States during the rise of Nazism and popularized a reflexive refusal of popular culture and its mass-market products, unlike the Catherine McKinnon line of thought likely to damn such reclaimings and celebrations of lesbian villainy as inherently delusional if not oppressive or outright evil, unlike the subcultural mystification of such figures as "invert-heroines" reversing the usual moral order to score points against the literal bodies representative of a paternalistic society, we can utilize the histories gathered herein to assess the function of such figures in our society and to attempt to fathom the appeal of their contemporary resurgence.

What this study demonstrates is that all such representations transport contradictory meanings onto a battlefield which, engaged anew by each successive generation, carries no built-in victories or defeats, merely implications of help or harm for those who manage to survive. Were those girls "mad" or "bad"? That was the central question asked by the media and by the court, which provided the answer in the end by ruling for the prosecution: they were bad. Thus were Juliet and Pauline judged criminal and bundled off to separate prisons for five years, instead of winning a judgment of madness and a lifetime of confinement in mental institutions.

The 1990s are a very different era. Freed of the unitary values of 1950s Christchurch, young lesbians today have a considerably wider range of choices than the separation-or-murder chasm that faced Pauline and Juliet. Or do they? Recent news stories on cyberspace assignations, the murder of a young cross-dressing woman in a midwestern small town, and an unexplained double-suicide of a pair of "best friends" in a California town all beg the question of progress on the front of adolescent sexuality and the policing of its parameters. While happy-ending movies for lesbians have finally become a fact of life in the multiplexes of the metropolises, with the popular lesbian date movie *The Incredibly True Adventure of Two Girls in*

Love dominating the 1995 press, their arrival has been accompanied by a renewed interest in true-story movies about pairs of best friends (lovers, sisters, schoolgirls, or maids) who bond their affections with the spilling of blood and then pay for their crimes. Lucky coincidence or sinister parallel? Thanks to Glamuzina and Laurie, we now have the tools to understand one chapter of the past. May it help us to understand our own present and future as well.

© B. Ruby Rich, 1995

Acknowledgements

We acknowledge the assistance of the Social Sciences Research Fund Committee for a grant during 1987 and the Stout Research Centre for a small grant and accommodation during 1987.

We want to thank all of the people who helped us during our research, including:

Arohata Women's Prison: Fleur Grenfell; *Broadsheet*: Pat Rosier; Cherry Farm: Julia Faed; *Christchurch Star:* Graham Kilty; Department of Justice: John Meek; Department of Social Welfare Library: Porleen Simmonds; Lesbian and Gay Archives of NZ: Phil Parkinson; Lincoln University: Manawaroa Gray; Ministry of Defence: Stephanie Tyler-Wright; Ministry of Women's Affairs Library: Frances Austin; Dictionary of NZ Biography: Professor W. H. Oliver; *NZ Truth*: Edward Rooney, Hedley Mortlock, Cynthia Shaw; Police College, Porirua: Sherwood Young; Stout Research Centre: Valerie Jacobs, Dr Jock Phillips; University of Auckland: Dr Ngahuia Te Awekotuku; University of Waikato: Janie Bedggood, Lynne Gifford; Victoria University of Wellington: Chris Atmore, Phillida Bunkle, Dr Les Cleveland, Barbro Harris, Prue Hyman, Jackie Matthews, Jan Jordan Robinson, Barbara Taylor; General: Frances Cherry, Bronwyn Dean, Pat Donovan, Brian Easton, Anne Else, Anna Hoffman, Katie Hogg, Rachel McAlpine, Dr R. W. Medlicott, Mrs N. Medlicott, Irihapeti Ramsden, Hugh Young.

We would also like to thank all the people who were directly involved with the case and who were prepared to talk with us but did not wish to be named. We appreciate the insights they gave.

Thanks also to staff of Christchurch Girls High School – the Principal, school secretary and those teachers we interviewed in 1987; and the staff of the Christchurch Marriage Guidance Council.

Thank you to all the lesbians who spoke with us and took the time to answer a questionnaire. Thank you also to the gay men who spoke with us about the 1950s.

We would like to acknowledge the assistance given to us by both library and clerical staff at Alexander Turnbull Library, Archives Connexional Office of the Methodist Church,

Broadcasting Reference Library, Canterbury Public Library, Department of Education, Department of Health, Department of Internal Affairs, Department of Justice, General Assembly Library, High Court Christchurch, Lands and Deeds Office (Christchurch), National Archives, New Zealand Library Association, Office of the Chief Film Censor (Lower Hutt), State Services Commission, and Victoria University of Wellington Law Library.

Thanks to Kaye Wilkinson for transcribing tapes and to Rosemary Curb and Bette Tallen for editorial assistance. Daphne Brasell encouraged us and gave us important feedback and editorial assistance at the beginning of our project. Linda Evans has provided ongoing editorial assistance and valuable feedback. Debbie Jones edited the manuscript and compiled the index.

Helen Mitchell reproduced the cover photograph, the excerpt from the *NZ Woman's Weekly*, and designed and photographed the newspaper collage. The photographs of Christchurch were supplied courtesy of the Alexander Turnbull Library; those of people involved in the case courtesy of *N.Z. Truth* and the *Christchurch Star*.

We thank all copyright holders for permission to reproduce photographs and texts. Every effort has been made to contact copyright holders. We regret any omissions and extend our thanks to everyone who helped produce this book, in particular Wendy Harrex of New Women's Press.

Above: *Brian McLelland, assistant to Counsel for Juliet Hulme, with Mrs Hulme and Walter Perry.* (N.Z. Truth)
Left: *Dr Hulme, Juliet's father.* (N.Z. Truth)

Preface

'I've been waiting thirty years for this phone call . . . '

'When you rang up and asked if you could interview us about our part in the case we thought you were those two girls coming back to get us! . . . '

'It seems to us that it is not in the best interests of lesbians worldwide to emphasise that unfortunate aberration in the world of lesbian relationships . . . after all, most lesbians are greatly superior to the people around them . . . we tend to make the world better, not worse . . . '

'Why do you want to dig all this up again? Why write about a murder? Why write about lesbians who did a murder? . . . '

'Why bring it all up again? They were completely mad, you know – they must have been. Normal lesbians like us don't behave like that . . . '

'You seem to be really interested in murders, don't you? . . . '

'How come you wanted to write a book about this? . . . '

'We don't want to have anything to do with your book because we don't believe in violence! . . . '

'I think it's really bad that you didn't contact Juliet Hulme and Pauline Parker. Don't you think that they should have a say in your book? Why haven't you contacted them . . . '

'I think it's really bad that you are thinking of contacting Juliet and Pauline. What do you think will happen if you do reach them? Why would they want to talk to you? What's in it for them? It'll only disrupt their lives and upset them. You don't know what effect you will have on them – it could be disastrous! . . . '

'You have no right to do a book on other lesbians' lives – especially without their permission! I don't think you should do the book at all without their permission. By the way do you know what happened to them, or where they are now? . . . '

'I've decided not to publish your book because of the diary – I think its unethical to use someone's diary without their permission. I kept a diary myself when I was a teenager . . . '

'Why don't you write about something nice, Julie?'

'The trouble with you, Alison, is that you're so academically limited and narrowly focussed on one topic – you seem obsessed with lesbians.'

'If you put the word "lesbian" on the cover of your book, people will think that it's only for lesbians.'

'When's your book coming out?'

We started to write this book in 1986. The process has been long and difficult. First, we had to learn to work together. Then we found that there were difficult ethical issues which we had to resolve.

Who were we to say which was the best solution to the question of whether or not to contact Juliet Hulme and Pauline Parker? We argued with each other and with ourselves about it, each of us changing our minds several times during the process. In the end we did what we felt was best. We decided to limit our project to considering what happened at the time and not to intrude into the new identities of Pauline Parker and Juliet Hulme in the present. We hope they will, sometime, write their own accounts.

Then there was the question of who else we should contact. There were family members and friends of both Juliet and Pauline. Some of the people we contacted did not want to be interviewed or to be reminded of the case at all. We had to proceed without the information they could have added to this account.

We also contacted some people less immediately connected to Juliet and Pauline. Some of these were willing to be interviewed but most did not want to be named. For some, it was the first time they had felt free to talk about the case since 1954. Others were unwilling to talk to us.

Most of the people directly involved with the case were still alive in 1986. Some have since died. We were fortunate in being able to interview Reginald Medlicott, the defence psychiatrist, before his death but were unable to interview Peter Mahon, assistant prosecutor, before he died.

We also interviewed a number of lesbians about the impact the case has had on them. This group was self-selected and drawn from our personal networks. Almost all of these women did not want their names used.

To be consistent, we decided to make all interviews anonymous. We felt this would not detract from the value of the information which had been given to us.

An important source of information was Pauline Parker's diaries for 1953 and 1954. We obtained the transcribed versions used at the trial. These contain a number of omissions (words which the typist could not decipher) and errors (typing mistakes and guesses). We noticed this because in a few cases we were able to compare published photographs of original diary entries with the transcripts. We were not able to locate the original diaries but are satisfied that the transcripts are reasonably accurate.

We were concerned about using the private diaries of someone without their express permission. However, Pauline Parker's diaries had been made available publicly at the trials and had been extensively – but selectively – quoted. Many of these selections highlighted the planning of the murder or were used out of context. We decided to include diary entries which would give a more balanced picture of Pauline Parker and would give her a voice in the book.

It was more difficult to give Juliet a voice – all we had of her writing was a short poem she wrote while at Christchurch Girls' High School. Other than that we had to rely on what others said about her and what they relayed as her words.

We were given access to the Department of Justice prison files for Juliet and Pauline. These included transcripts of the Supreme Court trial. Special conditions, outlined in Chapter 7, were placed on our use of these files.

We also worried that writing about lesbians in the context of a murder case would simply be another instance of associating lesbians with criminality, insanity, and murder. And would we be doing the same as most of the other articles and books about the case – writing sensationally about the lives of two girls, despite our best intentions, especially since we would be including material which had not previously been published? This was hard, but we decided it was important to revise the main accounts of the case and to give a different perspective – one which was from a pro-lesbian, feminist point of view. We decided to present this point of view as an alternative to the sensational and distorted versions of the case which were published in the 1950s and which continue to appear, even as late as the 1980s. We found one of these versions on the walls of a bar in the Ramada Inn, Christchurch, in 1987. It was included in the display of newspaper front pages which give an historical perspective of Christchurch. The Parker-Hulme case was preserved behind the varnish, for hotel patrons to read while they socialised.

The question of using illustrations was another difficult area. Previous accounts of the case have used photographs of Juliet and Pauline, as well as Pauline's diary, as an accompaniment to their sensational stories. But we wanted to emphasise the context. For this reason we decided to include contemporary photographs of Christchurch. We also provide a collage of media headlines to illustrate the visual impact of the media accounts. On the cover, we have placed a contemporary photograph of Juliet and Pauline. This was a photograph which had been telegraphed to media outside Christchurch and then touched up so that it could be satisfactorily reproduced. The reworked photograph distorts Juliet's and Pauline's features and the lines crossing the prison bars further obscure their faces. We thought this was representative of the way in which they were depicted at the time and suggests how observers focussed mainly on Parker and Hulme while ignoring the social context in which the murder had occurred.

We had become interested in this case separately . . .

Alison

I was thirteen and in the third form at a girls' school when the murder happened. I remember reading about the case in the newspapers – probably the *Evening Post* which my parents bought and possibly *NZ Truth*, though I don't remember how I got access to that. There may have been some discussion with schoolfriends too. For me, at thirteen, this case provided definite confirmation that there were other girls who fell in love and had relationships with each other.

I was fascinated by the fact that the two girls were in love and had a close friendship. I fell in love with girls and had a rich fantasy life full of romance and passion – limited by my sexual ignorance, however. I don't recollect that I was particularly shocked by the murder. I was fond of love poetry and influenced by the romantic art of Hollywood and the grand tragic passions of novels. Death and love did seem to be connected in some way in my teenage mind. I lived in a world without television and without the realistic portrayals of violence common in later years. Saturday matinees at the pictures had brought stories of Wild West heroines rescued from certain death and of passionate romantic love which overcame all obstacles.

I think the fact that Pauline and Juliet had murdered Honora was simply unreal for me – the whole episode was like a romantic story in which lovers die and conquer obstacles for their great love. Though this story held a fascinating difference – the lovers were both girls, and they felt for one another as I felt for a number of girls.

I came out as a lesbian in 1957 at the age of sixteen and began a long search for others like myself. In 1958 I visited Christchurch briefly. While I was there, I thought about the Parker-Hulme case and went to the newspaper library where I read the old newspaper reports from 1954. I went out to the Ilam house, dark and deserted. I walked around the outside of the house in the dusk, thinking about the temple to Minerva and moonlit escapades reported in the newspapers. I found this all very scary and frightened myself, hurriedly returning to town. By the age of seventeen I was aware of the finality of death and the horror of murder. Nonetheless I sympathised with the girls and thought that they must have had some stronger provocation for committing such a deed than was apparent from the newspaper stories.

I did meet other lesbians and through the next thirty years the story of 'the two Christchurch girls' would be mentioned from time to time. I remember heterosexual people exclaiming when I told them I was a lesbian: 'Oh, you're like those two Christchurch girls who killed the mother then!' And other lesbians would often refer to the case too. During the late 1950s and through the 1960s until gay liberation we were all aware that the medical profession saw homosexuality as a sickness.

I'd often thought about the case over the years and felt that it was important that the Parker-Hulme case and its implications for lesbians be written about by lesbians from a lesbian perspective. I was pleased to find that Julie was also keen to write about this case. We teamed up and I now feel that a part of our New Zealand lesbian past has been recorded.

Julie

Because of my family background, I had always been very interested in history and politics. So, when I came out as a lesbian in Auckland in late 1973, I wondered how other lesbians had survived prior to then. To me it was more than simply interesting to learn about your roots – I thought it was necessary. I knew about my Yugoslav heritage. I had to know about my lesbian predecessors.

I had followed the start of gay liberation from a distance so knew about that, but I wanted to know about the 1960s and before. So I asked the lesbians I met about those times. According to them there had been nothing organised, apart from the lesbian club which existed at that time and which had started relatively recently in late 1970. This was for Auckland, anyway. What about other cities? What about in the country? No one knew. Hardly anyone seemed to know of any older lesbians – well, just one or two. While studying history at Auckland University from 1971 to 1974 I had never come across anything about lesbians in New Zealand, pre-gay liberation.

When I moved to Wellington, I went to the Alexander Turnbull Library and, searching through the archives there, tried to prove that there had been women who lived as lesbians in New Zealand in the nineteenth and early twentieth centuries. I got little further than the case of Amy Bock who pretended to be a man. I gave up, but knew that I would come back to this.

One weekend in 1982, my parents visited me in Wellington and I went walking with them up to Mount Victoria, near where I was living. As we enjoyed the view, my mother mentioned that this was where a murder had happened years before. She couldn't remember exactly but she thought that a woman had been beaten to death with a brick in a stocking by her teenage daughter and her daughter's friend. I was immediately interested and questioned her further. She couldn't remember any more, she said. I decided to follow this up.

Later, after they had gone, I looked up a section on notable trials in a New Zealand encyclopaedia and found the case my mother had mentioned. I discovered that the murder had been in Victoria Park, Christchurch, not Mount Victoria, Wellington. As I suspected, it seemed that the two girls were having a lesbian relationship. I wanted to find out more, but didn't do anything about this until 1985. Going back to the Turnbull library, I found newspaper accounts of the trial of Juliet Hulme and Pauline Parker and decided to write about it.

I mentioned that I was doing this to some friends and found out that Alison had been interested in the case too, when she had come out in the 1950s. It seemed a good idea to team up and combine our skills, resources and contacts.

Alison: I am a lesbian of mainly Pakeha and some Maori ancestry. I come from a working-class background and grew up in Island Bay, Wellington. I have been active in lesbian, gay and feminist politics both here and overseas since the 1960s. At present I am a lecturer in women's studies at Victoria University of Wellington

Julie: I am of Yugoslav background and was born in Auckland in 1954. My parents ran a fish shop there. I have been active in gay, feminist, and lesbian politics in New Zealand since 1974 and have published articles on New Zealand social history. Currently I work as a tutor in information technology.

TWO New Zealand schoolgirls shocked the
...d 15 years ago. After cold, deliberate plan-
...g, they committed a brutal murder with half a
...ck in a stocking. International criminologists
...r rate the murder as one of the most horrify-
... this century. In this article, part of a Sunday
...es series, top British crime writer CHARLES
...ANKLIN looks into the young killers' minds,
...xamines their motives and the fantasies which
...o their crime, then outlines their sensational

TEEN PASS...
• MOTHER H...

THE WORLD'S WORST MURDERERS

● PAULINE'S mother lay still as the two girls hurried away . . .

CHRISTCHURCH,
Parker

Girls 'wrote novels full of murder'
STORY OF BLACKMAIL ATTEMPT

CHRISTCHURCH, Tuesday.—Two girls accused of
murder of the mother of one of them together wrote
... full of murder, suicide, imprisonment and blood-
...w and today

24 AUG 1954

ONE GIRL HAS NO...
Pauline of the teen-age murder trial—

GIRL IS NOW SORRY FOR MURDER
A bold experiment

...in psychiatry by New Zealan...
...remade the personality of...
...dme.

...Gaunt, haunt-
...ly, tall

GIRLS "INCUR... CASE PUT BY CROWN

CHRISTCHURCH, Saturday. — The
...girls charged with the Christchurch
...were "not incurably insane, but
...d," the Crown Prosecutor

FLARES —
TO DIE •

● THE ACCUSED: Pauline Parker Gaff... and Juliet Hulme
...k into the Supreme Court
at Christchurch for their sen-
...ational murder trial

MURDER TRIAL JURY HEARS OF DEATH IN A PARK AND IS TOLD—

Dirty-minded girls plotted to kill mother

24 AUG 1954

WELLINGTON, Monday—Two "dirty-minded"
little girls plotted to kill the mother of one
...em, a New Zealand murder trial jury...

PART FOUR

MURDER
THE WOMEN WHO DI...

JULIET AND PAULINE

'ARE BOTH CRACKERS'

Last speeches put—
jury retires

28 AUG 1954

...RAM JONES: Christchurch, Saturday
...speeches for the defence and th...
...in the teenage murder trial w...
...of 12 men when the sixth...

BAD —

JUDGE SUMS UP

Pity Must Not Sway The Jury

...CHRISTCHURCH, Saturday...
...his summing up Mr. Justice...
Adams said that the crime...
the two schoolgirls had committed
was dreadful, but the jury must
not be swayed by any feelings of
pity.

"Next time I write in my...
will be dead: how odd, h...

PINK STONE

Introduction

On 22 June 1954, in Christchurch, Juliet Hulme and Pauline Parker, killed Honora Parker, Pauline's mother. They were aged fifteen and sixteen.

A sensational court case followed, with extensive local and international media coverage and a resulting association of lesbianism with 'evil', 'insanity' and murder. This reinforced negative attitudes about lesbians and contributed to an already large volume of derogatory and stereotyped material.

Accounts of the case simplistically portrayed Pauline and Juliet as either 'mad' or 'bad'. They made little attempt to place the events within a social context. The murder victim herself received little media attention. For the readers of these articles, she remained an incomplete figure, murdered apparently as a whim of diseased or criminal minds.

The simplistic suggestion that Pauline killed her mother because in either her 'madness' or her 'badness' she decided to remove an 'obstacle' in her path, does not explain the killing, in our view. Further, the idea that Juliet acted solely from a desire to 'help' Pauline remove an 'obstacle' because she too was either 'mad' or 'bad' does not take into account her own position and expectations within her own family.

All events happen in a social and political context. We think that reducing the motive for murder to a single individual expression of violence ignores the context in which it occurred. Our account includes a description of the time and place in which the murder occurred – Christchurch, New Zealand in the early 1950s. We use a pro-lesbian, feminist view to illuminate the case. This viewpoint is particularly helpful when considering issues of sexuality and gender.

We start with a reconstruction of the killing itself. In the next chapters we discuss the context which includes the two family backgrounds, the circumstances surrounding the killing and the relationships between all of the people involved. In the chapter on diaries we consider Pauline Parker's diaries in the light of adolescent girls' diary writing. Then we discuss the trial in some detail and consider the treatment received by Parker and Hulme while they were in prison in Auckland and Wellington.

We review accounts of the case and criticise how medical and popular crime writers have used the case and examine the media presentations. We refute in some detail the notion of *folie à deux* because, although rejected at the trial, it has continued to be promoted by some writers.

We found feminist perspectives on women who kill particularly useful in discussing the murder of Honora Parker. We also found Maori interpretations helpful in providing a dimension lacking in previous accounts of the case.

Although we are aware of the problematic nature of much medical, sociological and criminological research because of its sexist and heterosexist assumptions, we nevertheless found some of this useful when we considered children who kill. It enabled us to compare the Parker-Hulme case to other murders carried out by children.

The chapter on lesbians in New Zealand provides some background from which to assess the impact the case had on lesbians. The consequences of this case were felt long after 1954 and have had a strong impact on the lives of many women, including lesbians. We describe and discuss this impact by including interviews with a small self-selected number of lesbians.

The private worlds of the Parker/Riepers and the Hulmes exploded into the public domain because of the murder of Honora Parker. In the process the facade of conformity was torn away, exposing contradictions to the prescribed morality of the time. In part, this helps explain the wide interest in the case which pulled together a range of key issues. Adultery, divorce, lesbianism, women and children apparently out of control, were some of the central elements in this public drama. We interpret these as forms of resistance, whether conscious or otherwise, to established codes of sexuality and gender.

The Killing

We based this reconstruction on the Supreme Court trial transcripts, the Coroner's report, entries in Pauline Parker's diary and on interviews with some of the participants.

Early morning, 22 June 1954
Pauline made the following entry in her diary:
> ' "The Day of the Happy Event".I am writing a little of this up on the morning before the death. I felt very excited and "the night before Christmas-ish" last night. I did not have pleasant dreams though. I am about to rise.'

After breakfast, Pauline helped her mother about the house. Her father and sister had already left for work.

10:30 am
At the Hulmes' house, Juliet prepared for her day out with her friend Pauline and Honora Rieper, Pauline's mother. She took a half brick from the garage near her house, wrapped it in newspaper and put it in her bag. Her mother, Hilda Hulme, noticed how 'radiantly happy' she seemed. Henry Hulme, her father, drove Juliet in his car and dropped her near the Riepers' home in Gloucester St. Juliet walked from there, doing some shopping on the way.

11:00 am
Juliet arrived at the Rieper house. She and Pauline chatted to Honora. While Honora prepared lunch, they went upstairs to Pauline's bedroom. Juliet gave Pauline the half-brick, which Pauline took and put inside one of her old lisle stockings. She tied a knot in the stocking to keep the brick in place.

Pauline put this into her shoulder bag, ready for the outing with Juliet and Honora that afternoon. Juliet had in her pocket a small pink stone which had been taken from a brooch.

11:45 am
Herbert Rieper, Pauline's father, arrived home from work and spent some time in the backyard working in his garden.

Midday

Pauline and Juliet sat down to lunch with Herbert, Honora and Wendy, Pauline's sister. It was a happy meal. At the trial, Herbert Rieper explained how Pauline and Juliet had laughed and joked throughout lunch. After the meal, Herbert and Wendy went back to work, leaving the girls and Honora to clean up the dishes.

1:30 pm

Honora, Juliet and Pauline left the house for Cathedral Square where they took a bus to Victoria Park in the Cashmere Hills. The day was cool, but sunny and clear.

2:35 pm

They arrived at the bus terminus and walked the short distance to the tea kiosk further uphill. As was usual for a weekday there were not many visitors to the park. There were only two other customers in the kiosk where Honora ordered afternoon tea. She drank tea and Juliet and Pauline had soft drinks. They all ate cakes and scones and chatted to Agnes Ritchie who ran the tea kiosk.

3:05 pm

They left the kiosk, turned right through a gap in the stone wall and walked down a long steep path surrounded by trees. About 450 metres down the path, they crossed a little bridge. Here, taking care not to be seen by Honora, Juliet placed the pink stone on the path. They walked on a little further and then turned back. As they approached the bridge again, Pauline pointed out the pink stone to her mother. Honora bent down to look.

Pauline took the brick in the stocking from her shoulder bag and hit her mother who was still bending to examine the stone. Honora raised her hand towards her head to protect herself. Pauline continued hitting her and was joined by Juliet who took the brick in the stocking from Pauline and hit Honora too. They hit her a number of times around the head and then one of them held her down by the neck while the other continued hitting her. There was a great deal of blood which splattered onto their clothing and also ran down the path for a metre or two.

Honora lost consciousness quickly and died within minutes.

3:30 pm

As Agnes Ritchie looked out from the tea kiosk she saw Pauline and Juliet running towards her. Their clothes were covered in blood and Pauline had blood on her face. They asked her to help them and said that there had been an accident and that Honora had slipped, hitting her head on a rock.

Agnes sat the girls down and sent one of the other customers to get her husband, Kenneth Ritchie who was the caretaker at the park. She went outside and looked down the path but could not see Honora. She went back and asked the girls where the accident had happened. They begged her not to make them go back down again and indicated that Honora was further down in the park. Kenneth arrived and went to investigate while Agnes phoned for a doctor and an ambulance. Then she ran water so that Juliet and Pauline could wash off some of the blood.

Both girls asked for their fathers. Agnes phoned Pauline's father but he was out of the fish shop on business. She left a message for him to call her back. She called Juliet's father who said he would come immediately.

After this she brought the girls cups of tea. She remarked later that Pauline gulped down the boiling tea without any milk and did not seem to be aware of the temperature. She seemed to be in a state of shock.

3:40 pm
Meanwhile, Kenneth Ritchie and his assistant Eric McIlroy followed the path taken by the group, down 450 metres into the park. They found Honora lying on her back and saw at once that she was dead. Blood streamed from her head and her mouth was blocked with vomit. One shoe lay some distance from her body and other articles lay strewn nearby. Her lower dentures lay on the ground just below her chin. She was smeared with mud and bloodstains. They noticed a half brick and a stocking near her body and realised that Honora could not have died accidentally.

She was lying with her feet pointing up the hill so Kenneth pulled down her dress which had fallen up around her thighs. He told Eric to stay with the body while he ran back to the kiosk.

3:45 pm
Kenneth reached the kiosk. An ambulance had just arrived. He phoned the police.

4:00 pm
Henry Hulme arrived at the kiosk. He told Agnes to tell the police that he was taking Pauline and Juliet to the Hulmes' home at Ilam.

4:10 pm approx

Dr Donald Walker arrived in response to Agnes' call. After talking to Kenneth and learning that someone was dead he decided to wait at the kiosk for the police.

4:20 pm

Sergeant Robert Hope and Constable Donald Molyneaux from Christchurch finally arrived, having first gone to Victoria Lake instead of Victoria Park. Kenneth Ritchie took them together with Dr Walker and the ambulance driver to where Honora lay. Dr Walker confirmed that Honora was dead and did not disturb the body. Sergeant Hope told Constable Molyneaux to stay at the scene and to make sure that no one approached the body or the area. The others returned to the kiosk and Sergeant Hope radioed the Central Police Station from the patrol car.

5:00 pm

Senior Detective McDonald Brown of the Criminal Investigation Branch received Sergeant Hope's message and sent Detective Sergeant Archie Tate and Detective Gordon Gillies to the park.

Having finally received Agnes Ritchie's message Herbert Rieper got a friend to drive him to the park. Agnes had told him that Honora had met with an accident and an ambulance had been called. But when he arrived Sergeant Hope questioned him as to his whereabouts during the afternoon. Clearly Herbert, at this point, was regarded as a principal suspect. He was not taken to Honora's body but was told to wait at the kiosk. He paced anxiously up and down outside.

5:20 pm

Detectives Tate and Gillies arrived with a woman constable, Audrey Griffiths. Sergeant Hope took them to the body where Constable Molyneaux waited. They examined the body and the area thoroughly, noting the blood-stained half brick and a short distance away, the torn stocking.

Meanwhile at Ilam, Hilda, Juliet's mother, ran a bath for Pauline and Juliet, treated them for shock and gave them a meal before putting them to bed. Hilda washed their underclothes while Walter Perry, her friend who lived at Ilam, took the rest of their blood-stained clothes to Wicks' Drapery, dry cleaning agents in Fendalton Road.

6:00 pm

Detective Sergeant Tate returned to the kiosk and reported back to Senior Detective Brown who then contacted Inspector McKenzie of the C.I.B. Meanwhile Tate arranged for the coroner, a pathologist and the police photographer to come to the park.

7:00 pm

Inspector McKenzie and Senior Detective Brown joined pathologist E. B. Taylor, the city coroner Dr Colin Pearson and the police photographer William Ramage, at Victoria Park. Together with the other detectives and working by flash-lamps in the dark, they examined the body and the surrounding area carefully and took detailed photographs.

Inspector McKenzie then instructed Brown and Tate to interview Juliet and Pauline. Brown interviewed Herbert Rieper and got his permission to interview Pauline. The detectives left for Ilam.

8:00 pm

Detectives Brown and Tate arrived at Ilam where they saw Hilda Hulme, Henry Hulme and Walter Perry. Tate and Brown, accompanied by Hilda, interviewed Pauline, who was in bed. She told them that her mother had fallen accidentally. The detectives invited Walter Perry into the bedroom about half-way through their interview. The half brick and the stocking were discussed.

The detectives then went downstairs where Juliet was interviewed in a sitting-room. Hilda, Henry and Walter were present. At first Juliet told the same story as Pauline had done. But when Brown told her that they did not believe that she was present when Honora had died she hesitated. Walter then asked if he could speak to Juliet alone. The detectives thought this was a good suggestion and left him with her. A little later Walter said that Juliet wanted to make another statement. While Tate took this down in writing Brown returned to Pauline's bedroom and told her that they believed that Juliet had not been present when Honora died. He then accused Pauline of murdering her mother. She agreed to answer questions put to her by Brown. He took a statement from her which she then signed. In this she admitted killing her mother and said that Juliet had not been involved.

Juliet, meanwhile, told Tate that she had been walking ahead of Pauline and Honora, but that when she heard voices calling she went back to find Honora lying on the ground with blood all around her. She seemed to be unconscious. Juliet said she had not noticed a stocking with

a knot in it nor had she taken any particular notice of a brick. She said
that Pauline had told her that her mother had slipped and banged her
head against a stone. Juliet admitted that she had supported Pauline's
story when they went back to the kiosk.

   The detectives decided to arrest Pauline. As they were leaving the house
with her, they asked her where she got the half brick. Before she could reply
Hilda quickly asserted that she had not obtained it from Ilam. They took
Pauline to the Christchurch Central police station.

Later that evening

Detectives Tate and Brown went with Herbert Rieper to the Riepers' house
in Gloucester Street where they obtained his permission to search Pauline's
room. They found fourteen exercise books including Pauline's diaries
lying openly on furniture in the bedroom. They read the diary entry for
that day as well as earlier entries planning the murder. They took
possession of all the written material.

   Detective Gillies, Sergeant Hope and Constable Griffiths helped take
Honora's body to the Christchurch Hospital mortuary. Griffiths removed
Honora's clothing and her belongings which Gillies took away as
evidence.

   Meanwhile, at the police station Pauline sat in Detective Tate's office.
She wrote a diary note on a piece of scrap paper:

'I find myself in an unexpected place . . . after having committed my
murder. All the Hulmes have been wonderfully kind and sympathetic
(anyone would think I had been good). I had a pleasant time with the
police, talking nineteen to the dozen and showing as though I hadn't a
care in the world . . . I have not had a chance to talk to Deborah [her
name for Juliet] properly but I am taking the blame for everything.'

   The police confiscated this note and Tate put it into an envelope.
Pauline spent the night in the police cells.

   At Ilam Juliet spent the night sleeping in her mother's arms after Hilda
had read aloud Juliet's favourite poetry.

23 June 1954

Detective Gillies took Herbert Rieper to the mortuary to identify Honora's
body.

   Gillies also went to Wicks' Drapery, the dry cleaning agent, to retrieve
the girls' clothes as evidence. They were still blood-stained as they had not
yet been cleaned.

10:00 am

Pauline was taken to the courthouse where she was charged before magistrate Rex Abernethy with the murder of her mother. She was charged as Pauline Yvonne Parker because the police had discovered that Herbert Rieper and Honora Parker were not legally married. From then on Honora Rieper was referred to in the media as 'Mrs Parker', and Pauline Rieper as 'Pauline Parker'.

After her court appearance Pauline was taken back to the police station where Brown and Tate interviewed her again. They questioned her about the diary note she had written the night before. She told them that she would tell them the truth if she could see Juliet. She also asserted that Juliet would agree with whatever she said. The detectives then left to go to Ilam, the envelope containing the note remaining on Tate's desk.

Pauline was left with police matron Margaret Felton. They sat in Tate's office by the fire as it was a cold morning. Pauline went over to Tate's desk and managed to grab the envelope and throw it into the fire. Felton successfully rescued the note which was later presented as evidence at the trial.

Late morning

Detectives Tate and Brown arrived at Ilam. Later they went upstairs to Juliet's bedroom. She apologized to them for having lied to them and said that she would now tell the truth. This time she made a different statement confessing that she had known that Pauline was carrying a brick in her bag and that Honora Rieper might be attacked. She said that when she went back up the path, she saw Honora in a sort of squatting position. She saw Pauline hit her mother with the brick and admitted that she had hit her too. 'I was terrified,' she continued in her statement. 'I thought one of them had to die. I wanted to help Pauline.' Juliet said that she did not know what would happen when they went to Victoria Park but she thought they might be able to frighten Pauline's mother with the brick. The police arrested Juliet.

24 June 1954

The body of Honora Parker was cremated after a funeral service at Bromley Methodist cemetery, Christchurch. Meanwhile, Juliet appeared before magistrate Raymond Ferner, charged with her murder.

Both girls were kept in Paparua prison to await their trial in the Magistrate's Court on 14 July. In Paparua, they were examined by doctors and psychiatrists for both the defence and prosecution. At the same

*time, the police continued to assemble prosecution evidence. The half
brick, the stocking, the clothes, and Pauline's diaries which were to be
transcribed, were prepared for the court.*

*An inquest into the death of Honora Parker was held and at the
hearing in mid-July it was established that there was sufficient evidence
for a Supreme Court trial. After this Pauline was sent to Mount Eden
prison in Auckland. Unknown to her, this was done at her own lawyer's
request so that defence psychiatrists could observe what effect a separation
would have on her relationship with Juliet.*

*The Supreme Court trial of Pauline Parker and Juliet Hulme for the
murder of Honora Parker was scheduled to begin in late August 1954 in
Christchurch.*

CHAPTER ONE

The Place

'. . . who before today, would have thought that society needed protection against two sixteen-year-old girls?'[1]

The murder of Honora Parker happened in Christchurch, a conservative and class-conscious city in the South Island of New Zealand. It occurred during the early 1950s, when conservative social and political interests dominated the country.

We decided to look more closely at what Christchurch was like at the time of the murder. We wanted to understand the values and the culture in which the events of 1954 took place, and in which they were interpreted. We wanted to understand the impact the case had on people and what the murder meant to them.

The Mayor of Christchurch, writing in 1950 for a booklet celebrating the city's centennial, had proudly stated that Christchurch was:

> 'A little bit of England transplanted to the Southern seas – such was the dream of those who dared the hazards of colonization to build the foundation of the city we inherit . . . The dream has come true. The swamplands have been transformed into parks and busy highways . . . the happy garden homes of 140,000 people and the modern streamlined factories where they work to produce their contribution to the needs of the growing nation.'[2]

The city had been founded in 1850 with the arrival of the first main group of Pakeha settlers, the so-called 'pilgrims', though Europeans had acquired land from the Maori owners and had settled in the area twenty years earlier. It was named after Christ Church College, at Oxford in England. During the following decades, many thousands of English migrants settled in Christchurch. Most of these people received assisted passages, either from the government or from private employers. Pauline O'Regan in her book *Aunts and Windmills* discusses the fears of the Canterbury Company that activists who talked about 'a world where everyone was equal' or worse still, Irish immigrants, might slip through the screening process.[3] As Canterbury historian Stevan Eldred-Grigg points out, eventually there were enough

English settlers to 'give Canterbury a distinctive Anglican tone'.[4]
The buildings and houses throughout the city and along the
banks of the small river they had called the Avon all reflected the
'Englishness' planned by the founders.

By the 1950s Christchurch had a wide reputation for this
English character. A reporter from a British newspaper,
accompanying the 1953-54 Royal Tour by Queen Elizabeth II,
wrote 'They say that Christchurch is the most English city outside
England', a statement which pleased the city officials who
regarded 'Englishness' as a desirable quality.[5] However, the kind
of Englishness which it tried to achieve was certainly not a
working-class, Cockney or northern style. As a Pakeha creation
set up to be English, Anglican and conservative, Christchurch
developed a special identity where the cultural values of a middle
and upper-class elite were promoted. The founders had
attempted to create a genteel market town which would
appropriately serve the developing landed gentry of the
Canterbury plains. The class structure, the patterns of life and the
physical environment itself all followed from these origins. The
Christchurch Cathedral, for example, was a symbol of these ideas.
It dominated the city centre, situated in the middle of a cathedral
square around which the main business and retail areas
developed. According to a guide produced by the Friends of
Christchurch Cathedral Association in 1954, the building was
constructed in the 'Early English Gothic style' and although they
admitted that it was small compared with the cathedrals of the
'Old Country', they reassured readers that its shortness prevented
'any impression of squatness which greater length would tend to
give'.[6]

The names of the streets also reflected a desire for Englishness.
The main streets ran outwards from the square in long straight
lines, many of them named after Anglican bishoprics, such as
Gloucester in England and Colombo in what was then Ceylon.

The University College was a particularly English institution.
John Godley, founder of the city, had wanted a university college
like his own Christ Church in the new settlement. A high church
Tory, he insisted that 'only leaders imbued with such ideals could
restore confidence in the established order' which he feared had
been shaken by the social upheavals of the 1840s in Europe.[7] A
school system was developed in the settlement to further these

aims at a junior level. Christ's College, a private school founded in 1850, helped supply suitable undergraduates for the university. Until 1949 the University College administered both Christchurch Girls High School (founded in 1877), where Juliet Hulme and Pauline Parker were to meet, and Christchurch Boys High School (founded in 1881). A 1950s publication for tourists unquestioningly stated:

> 'In this city there are a large number of public and private schools, catering for all classes . . . The school and colleges, in Christchurch, are founded on the lines of the English Public Schools and uphold the highest ideals of these schools.'[8]

The University College, where Henry Hulme was to become the first full-time rector, the schools and the Anglican Church were important institutions within the structure of the settlement, and perpetuated English class distinctions. During the nineteenth century Canterbury had become, as Eldred-Grigg puts it '. . . one of the most steeply stratified societies in New Zealand . . .'[9] This stratification persisted into the twentieth century and was still evident in the 1950s.

The myth of class equality was, however, widely believed at that time. An article in *Landfall*, a literary magazine, pointed out in 1952 that:

> ' . . . the ruling idea of post-war society was that "everybody acts the same, receives the same amount of the world's goods, everyone moves in the same direction." '[10]

Because class differences in New Zealand functioned in a different way from the 'Old Country', the presence of class distinctions could be denied or trivialised. Certainly there was more movement between social classes than was possible in Britain, and the distinctions were less extreme. However, Christchurch, because of its particular origins, developed a more rigid and openly acknowledged class system than did other New Zealand cities.[11]

Writing in the 1980s, historian Graeme Dunstall said that even though class consciousness may have diminished during the 1950s and 1960s, this did not imply that 'social inequalities (or social strata) were not present in post-war New Zealand.'[12]

People were strongly aware of these class differences, as Maude Eaton, a researcher for the Department of Scientific and

Industrial Research, explained in 1947:

'Even in a country such as New Zealand, where there are fewer extremes
of poverty and wealth than in most countries, the occupational and class
strata tend to be rigid. People almost invariably gravitate to their own
income-level. A professional man or woman will mix with other doctors,
lawyers, teachers, and scientific workers. Office workers will meet other
office workers. Factory employees, skilled artisans, and labourers will
rarely meet clerks or stockbrokers. Factory girls will see other factory
girls, not typists or teachers.'[13]

One Christchurch resident of the time said that 'people
certainly knew who was who and where they fitted on the social
scale'[14] while another commented that:

'Everybody in Christchurch was classist, absolutely. Whoever I
mentioned from the whole school class to my grandmother, she'd say
"oh that would be the so and so's and their parents used to live in
Merivale Lane" . . . there was nobody she didn't know . . . there were
those who were all right and those who weren't.'[15]

By the 1950s, suburbs linked by public transport to the centre
had developed around Christchurch city, with observable
differences between the elite areas such as the Cashmere Hills
and the poorer sections around industrial developments.

While there were obvious class differences in Christchurch
during the 1950s there was scarcely any racial diversity – it was
almost completely a 'white' city. The Christchurch inhabitant of
1954 was typically a white person who had limited experience of
or contact with other racial groups. The population of
Christchurch, including Maori, in 1956 was 193,367[16] and while it
was the second largest urban area in the country after Auckland[17],
there were fewer than 700 people classified in the census as 'other
races'.[18]

As Christchurch was clearly a 'white city', the entire Te Wai
Pounamu, known to Pakeha inhabitants as the South Island, had
become a 'white island'. The total population of the island during
the period grew from 625,603 in 1951, including only 4164 Maori,
to 676,698 in 1956, which included only 5257 Maori.[19] Pauline
Parker was unusual in that she had contact with a group of male
students from Ceylon (now Sri Lanka) who were studying at
Canterbury University College, and whom she'd met through the
Hulmes.

By the early 1950s, Christchurch had become the major market centre for the Canterbury plains, with extensive business and commercial developments. With its international airport, established in 1950, good road and rail transport and a deep-water port about eleven kilometres away at Lyttelton, the city was an important distribution and industrial centre. It had a variety of established industries, including tanning, footwear, clothing, rubber, steel production, and engineering. The city was also the point of departure for the province's meat and wool exports, shipped mainly to Great Britain.[20]

Recreational activities were diverse and there were many public domains and parks including the 200 hectare Hagley Park in the centre of the city. This contained rugby, soccer, hockey and baseball grounds as well as tennis courts, bowling greens and a public golf course. Numerous suburban parks had similar facilities, including Lancaster Park, which was used for major rugby football and cricket matches. The rugby match between Canterbury and Waikato at this park on the last day of the trial attracted a crowd of almost 40,000 people.[21] There were racecourses for flat racing, hurdle events, trotting and pacing.[22]

Christchurch people also took trips to New Brighton and Sumner beaches, as Pauline Parker's family did in 1953, or took walks through the city parks or along the Port Hills, or had picnics in places like Victoria Park, the scene of the murder.

As elsewhere in New Zealand at this time, churches provided facilities for a number of social activities, such as church socials, bible class camps and church picnics. Pauline Parker attended the East Belt Methodist Church regularly, but does not record having attended any social functions.[23]

Often dances were held at public halls. The upper classes sometimes held their own events. During the 1950s private and highly select dances were still held at the homes of the wealthy, for their sons and daughters attending elite boarding schools.[24] Such exclusive events ensured that the young landed classes would meet appropriate partners, with a view to desirable marriages in the future. Debutante balls were also attended by this class for the same purpose. As in the rest of the country, family parties were held by all social classes.

There were few organised social activities for children and teenagers. There were milk-bars where young people could meet – there were over twenty milk-bars in the Christchurch area in

1953 – but frequenting these was not considered 'respectable'.[25]

Other forms of recreation included listening to the three radio stations: 3ZB, the only commercial station, which broadcast the Top Ten, avidly followed by Pauline Parker and her school-friends[26]; 3YA and 3YC, the non-commercial stations, over which Hilda Hulme broadcast advice to parents on a panel with other prominent local women. Surveys of 'leisure-time activities' carried out in two provincial North Island towns in 1954 suggested that the most popular activities of the period were gardening, reading novels and magazines, visiting friends and relatives, going to the pictures (there were fourteen picture theatres in Christchurch in 1954), playing cards, going to the races, attending local drama productions, and working at various hobbies, such as knitting, stamp collecting, sewing or carpentry. The activities most enjoyed varied according to age and gender.[27]

Local non-professional drama groups such as the Christchurch Repertory Society put on performances from time to time, as did the Royal Musical Society. Small local groups held amateur concerts and other functions. Overseas performers of various kinds visited the country regularly. Theatre director and writer Ngaio Marsh, who lived in Christchurch, attracted overseas actors to the country and helped develop drama in the city.

The New Zealand National Orchestra, as it was called in 1954, and the Alex Lindsay String Orchestra toured the main centres and gave concerts. There were also small string quartets and chamber music groups which gave occasional performances. Although there was no national ballet or opera company at the time, dance teachers gave annual recitals at which their pupils performed for the public. The Christchurch Competitions were held in the school holidays, when private pupils who learnt music, dancing, singing or elocution from assorted teachers in the district could compete for prizes and awards. Pauline Parker's mother and sister attended the local Competitions in 1953.[28]

Drinking at the local hotel was a 'frequently mentioned' activity by the 30-49 year age group in the 1954 survey. Sixty-one per cent of the men but only fourteen per cent of the women listed this as a leisure-time activity. Few 'respectable' women in Christchurch would have gone to hotel bars for a drink.[29] Public bars usually did not serve women at all and few hotels at this time even had the

The Ilam homestead occupied by the Hulmes. Photo: L.H. Hahn, ATL.

so-called 'lounge bar' for 'ladies and escorts'. One contemporary noted:

> 'It isn't only wowserism that keeps women out of the bars: when a woman enters a bar . . . the men stop in their talk like surprised culprits. The bar is their stronghold and they want a place where they can swear loudly and boast without being held to their word.'[30]

Hotel bars closed at six o'clock, though guests staying in the 'house' could continue to drink in the house bar.[31]

By the 1950s, Christchurch had established a name as the 'Garden City'. The cultivation and presentation of gardens became something of a cult, with competitions for the street with the best array of gardens. One such competition attracted fifty-nine entries, each entry being submitted by a committee which represented that street.[32] One enthusiast wrote:

> 'We get the results and have the organisation from the Canterbury Horticultural Society, a very lively body, which . . . yearly [awards] trophies for the best gardens in Christchurch . . . Devoted children of the Horticultural Society are the unique garden clubs, who look to their parent body for help, guidance and assistance. Being a member of a Christchurch garden club is quite a privilege as there are long waiting lists for entry.'[33]

The gardens of the Ilam homestead occupied by the Hulmes were one of the tourist attractions of Christchurch.

As we have shown, during the early 1950s Christchurch had a special character, reflecting its origins as a white, class-conscious, Anglican settlement. It was here then, on the day following Tuesday, 22 June 1954, that Christchurch residents learned that a middle-aged woman had been battered to death the previous day in beautiful Victoria Park. They were even more shocked when they learnt that her daughter was charged with her murder. And a day later they were told that the daughter of the Rector of the University and of a woman prominent in the local Marriage Guidance Council and on local radio was also implicated. For many people it was beyond comprehension. Social commentator, Ian Hamilton, expressed his perception of the reaction in October 1954:

'These girls lived in Christchurch . . . and they eked out their existence in a respectable high school . . . Then suddenly all these veils are torn apart and we're faced with bloody murder and no remorse. It's shocking, there's no other word; and if only somebody would explain.'[34]

For other people, the events were not as surprising. Writer Fay Weldon, reported in a 1987 interview, said of her early years in Christchurch that:

'It didn't surprise her to learn shortly after her departure that two girls from her old school . . . had taken one of their mothers . . . and battered her to death . . . Weldon [recalled] post-war New Zealand as "repressive and repressed." '[35]

Clearly, for some observers, much lay under the surface of the apparently 'respectable' Christchurch.

CHAPTER TWO

The Families

The Parker/Rieper and the Hulme families were very different from each other. They lived in Christchurch in 1954 under contrasting circumstances. Who were these families?

The Parker/Rieper Family

Pauline Parker's father, Herbert Detlev Rieper, was born on 22 October 1894 in Strahan, Tasmania.[1] His father, Claude Detlev Rieper, a shop assistant, was of German origin. His mother was Katie Thurza Stubbings. He also had a sister, Rhoda Katie Rieper, who died in Christchurch in 1973. Herbert Rieper died on 5 May 1981 in Christchurch, of pneumonia after a long illness.

In 1910, at the age of sixteen, Herbert came to New Zealand. When World War I began he enlisted in the army and was eventually stationed at Cairo. There he met Louise McArthur (nee Mackrie), an Englishwoman born in India who had been married previously. Louise was thirty-four and Herbert twenty-one when they married in Cairo in 1915, returning to New Zealand after the war.

They settled in Napier, but by 1922 had moved to Raetihi where Herbert worked as a bookkeeper for a local firm. They had two children, the first born in Napier in 1919, the second in 1924 in Raetihi when Louise was forty-three.

Honora Mary Parker, almost fifteen years younger than Herbert, worked for the same firm as he did in Raetihi. A relationship developed between them and Herbert left Louise and the children.

Herbert and Honora moved from Raetihi and by 1936 had re-established themselves in Christchurch. They lived in Mathesons Road, which was in an industrial area of the city.

Honora Parker was born in Birmingham, England, and came to New Zealand at the age of eighteen. Her mother was Amy Lilian Parker and her father, Robert William Parker, was a chartered accountant.

Herbert and Louise did not divorce and although Herbert paid some maintenance to his first family he had on the whole very little contact with them.[2] Honora and Herbert lived together as though legally married and it seems that until the murder when the family circumstances became public knowledge, only Honora's mother, Amy Parker, was aware that they were not married. [We refer to Honora and Herbert as 'the Riepers' because that was the way they described themselves. We refer to Honora as 'Honora Parker' when we are discussing her alone.]

One contemporary described Herbert as quiet, polite and a 'dapper little man.'[3] Honora, described at the trial as of medium height and going grey, must have seemed very like any other ordinary middle-aged woman to outside observers.[4]

Herbert and Honora had four children in their twenty-three years together. Their first child, a boy, died shortly after birth. He was a so-called 'blue baby'[5] (a baby with cardiac difficulties). A girl, Wendy Patricia, was born in March 1937 and on 26 May 1938, Pauline Yvonne was born.

In March 1949, another girl was born. This child, Rosemary, had Downs Syndrome.[6] Honora was forty and Herbert fifty-five years at the time of her birth.

The girls were known as Wendy, Pauline and Rosemary Rieper. They were not aware of their legal status, or of Herbert's previous family.[7]

In 1946 the family purchased a house at the top of Gloucester Street. This was registered in Honora's name as the 'wife of Herbert Rieper'[8] and was a two-storeyed structure in the inner city, with an enclosed back yard, overlooked by Christchurch Girls High School. The area had once been popular among the wealthier classes, but by 1946 many of these people had moved to the suburbs and a quarter-acre lifestyle. The large houses in the inner city were being converted to flats for rental accommodation, or used as rooming or boarding houses.[9] One observer, commenting on the 'dinginess of the centre of the city', noted that 'Like other New Zealand cities the heart of Christchurch has had virtually no new buildings since before the war . . . the inner city area . . . now looks dingy, faintly seedy – almost, in places, decrepit'.[10] As in other cities throughout the country, the people left behind in the inner city were not only generally poorer but were perceived to be of a lower social class.[11] A former classmate of Pauline's said of Honora Parker that 'She would have been . . . completely different . . . to the suburban matrons. Socially she wouldn't have fitted in . . . she wouldn't be like other people's mothers, meeting them down at the store . . . in those days you went in and you knew everybody by sight [in your suburb].'[12] The same classmate considered Pauline's life in the inner city to be unusual. 'It was a life that, you know, ordinary girls living in the suburbs, we had no concept of it at all . . . she was perhaps like a European girl with her exposure to other people . . .'[13]

Honora took in boarders while Herbert worked as manager of the Dennis Brothers fish shop in Hereford Street.[14]

Pauline's childhood was described in court as uneventful, but just before her fifth birthday she was diagnosed as having osteomyelitis in one leg. She spent her fifth birthday and nearly nine months in hospital, during which time she almost died. She had several operations which left obvious scars on her leg[15] and for two years after her release from hospital her leg continued to discharge and had to be dressed twice daily. Even in her teens, Pauline continued to experience pain in that leg and often took painkillers.[16]

After her release from hospital, Pauline attended a local primary school. For nearly two years at the beginning of her school years, she had to be in a class by herself because of the particular organisation of the school. Doctors had warned the Riepers that Pauline should not take part in games or physical activities which might further damage her leg. Therefore, she could not participate in many sports. Instead, she became interested in creative modelling using plasticine and wood, and became quite skilled at this. She was, however, able to go horse-riding and cycling.[17]

Pauline was eleven when her younger sister Rosemary was born. Rosemary lived at home until 1951 when she was two years old. At that time the Riepers placed her in Templeton Farm, an institution for the intellectually disabled, not far from the centre of Christchurch city. Templeton Farm was close enough for the family to visit regularly and for Rosemary to be brought home to Gloucester Street from time to time.[18] In giving evidence at the Supreme Court trial in support of his diagnosis of Pauline Parker, defence psychiatrist Dr Medlicott stated:

> '. . . her younger sister is I understand a Mongolian imbecile . . . The first baby . . . was a blue baby and died within 24 hours. I consider that background raises a query as to the stock from which she came.'[19]

This statement clearly gave the impression that he considered there was a hereditary factor in her 'madness'. A belief in genetic or hereditary causes for mental and physical illness was common at the time. Attitudes towards mental and physical difference were generally negative. People who did not fit a narrowly defined concept of normality were commonly regarded with pity, suspicion, or even hostility. This applied to intellectual, emotional and physical disability. Often people confused mental and physical disability so that physically disabled people were treated as if they were mentally ill or intellectually disabled as well. The *NZ Listener* reported in 1953 that:

'Not very long ago a child born deaf was automatically regarded as dumb also and sometimes treated as mentally defective.'[20]

Ralph Winterbourn, an educationalist, observed that people who were mentally ill or intellectually 'handicapped' faced even greater prejudice, and sometimes 'plain revulsion.'[21]

Intellectual disability and mental illness were sometimes interpreted as a punishment for something the parents had done.[22] Some people even thought that a whole family was 'tainted' because one of its members was mentally ill. Such families were sometimes 'cold-shouldered' by their neighbours.[23]

Ann Gath points out that terms like 'mongoloid defective' and 'mongol' were commonly used to describe people with Downs' Syndrome.[24] The term 'backward' was used to refer to people at Templeton Farm, where Pauline's sister was a resident.[25] The mentally ill were frequently called 'loonies' or 'lunatics' and jokes about mental hospitals were common.[26]

It is likely that opinions about Pauline Parker's 'stock' seemed sensible to many observers and may have been accepted as an indication of her alleged insanity.

The Rieper household was busy and active. As Honora took in boarders, there was usually a lot of domestic work to be done. There are many entries in the very full diaries Pauline Parker kept during 1953 and 1954 which describe how she helped her mother with the housework, apparently with some enjoyment. Given the location of the house, and the boarders, the household seemed to lack privacy. One contemporary described the house as 'ghastly' and commented further that 'it didn't look like a home to me . . . no decent rows to clear the air because there would always be other people around.'[27] At times, Pauline complained of lacking privacy and on a number of occasions recorded in her diary with some relief when she would be home alone.[28]

The number of boarders seems to have varied. Pauline recorded in March 1954 that the number of boarders had risen to four. As well as the lack of privacy, this disrupted the household for, three weeks later, Pauline noted that she and her mother had shifted the rooms around.

Honora's mother also visited the Riepers. Entries in Pauline's diaries for 1953 and 1954 indicate that Mrs Parker sometimes stayed with the Riepers, though it was not her permanent home.

The family sometimes went to the cinema or to a visiting show. During the summer, they had occasional picnics, or trips to the beach.[29] They also played cards together, and listened to the radio. Herbert had a vegetable garden at the back of their small city section. Wendy had an active social life which included playing sports.[30] Herbert and Honora visited friends and sometimes friends dropped in to see them.[31]

Pauline and Wendy attended the nearby East Belt Methodist Church regularly and Herbert and Honora sometimes attended services there. Through the Church, both Pauline and Wendy spent some holidays on a farm in North Canterbury. The owners of the farm provided holidays in the country for city children referred to them by the Methodist Church.[32] The Rieper family do not seem to have gone on holiday together in 1953 or 1954.[33]

Neither Herbert nor Honora appear to have been elected representatives to any public bodies, involved in community work, or to have held office in any clubs, organisations or associations.

The Parker/Rieper family were at the lower end of the Christchurch social scale. They had achieved home ownership but required two incomes to maintain their modest standard of living. Their circumstances contrasted sharply with those of the Hulme family, prominent members of the Christchurch upper classes.

The Hulme Family

Henry Rainsford Hulme was the son of James Rainsford Hulme and Alice Jane Smith, born in Southport, England on 9 August 1908. He was educated at Manchester Grammar School, at Caius

College, University of Cambridge, graduating as an MA, PhD, and ScD, and at Leipzig University. From 1931 to 1937 he was a Fellow of Gonville and Caius College. He lectured in mathematics at the University of Liverpool from 1936 to 1938.

Hulme was Chief Assistant at the Royal Observatory, Greenwich, from 1936 to 1938. During World War II he was part of Admiralty Research, becoming Director of Naval Operational Research in 1945. From 1945 to 1948 he was Scientific Adviser to the Air Ministry. In 1948 he was appointed the first full-time Rector of Canterbury University College and arrived in New Zealand in October 1948.[34] Clearly, his status far outweighed that of Herbert Rieper, manager of a local fish shop.

In 1937 Henry had married Hilda Marion Reavley, the daughter of Reverend J. Reavley, an Anglican Minister.[35] Soon after they arrived in New Zealand she became involved in the social and cultural life of upper class Christchurch. As the wife of the Rector, she played a prominent role in the life of the University. She was also on the Board of Christchurch Girls High School, which both Pauline Parker and Juliet Hulme attended. She became a member and, from 1952, one of the Vice-Presidents, of the Christchurch Marriage Guidance Council.

The Christchurch Marriage Guidance Council had been formed on 19 February 1948 and by 1954 had achieved a high profile in the community. Modelled on the British Marriage Guidance Council it was considered a daring and progressive organisation. The Council advertised its services through local newspapers and radio, as well as in pamphlets which were distributed widely. Hilda joined in 1949 and quickly took an active part in the activities of the Council. She was one of the organisers of a series of lectures intended to give advice to engaged couples. In 1950, she was nominated as the Council's representative on the Canterbury Council of Social Services. She also worked as a marriage counsellor, attending a course for social workers in Wellington in 1952. She remained active in the Council until her resignation in May 1954. Members then 'spoke eulogistically' of her work for the Council, 'particularly in the Counselling Service.'[36] Through her work she knew prominent members of the Christchurch social and religious establishment including Dean A.K. Warren, Anglican Bishop of Christchurch; Dr Mel Aitken, Dr M. Bevan-Brown and Dr Eleanor Mears, prominent local psychiatrists and doctors; and Rex Abernethy, the local magistrate who in July 1954 presided at the Magistrates' Court hearing into the murder of Honora Parker; as well as other clergy, educationalists and professional people. Dr Francis Bennett, who later gave evidence for the defence, was a member of the Council as well as one of its counsellors.[37]

Hilda Hulme's profile in the community was high. In 1951, she was a regular panel member of the Women's Session programme broadcast on 3YA, one of the local radio stations. The other main centres had similar programmes and exchanged recordings of these sessions. Topics such as religious instruction in schools, bringing up children, and whether school children should be compelled to wear uniforms were discussed by these panels. As part of a promotion for the series in 1951, Hilda was introduced to the public, along with other panel members, in a short article in the *NZ Listener*.[38]

The Hulmes had two children – Jonathon, who was born on 22 March 1944 in England, and Juliet, born on 28 October 1938 in Liverpool, England. Like Pauline Parker, she had been seriously ill as a child. She had also been separated from her parents for long periods. At the age of six years, Juliet had become dangerously ill with pneumonia and her schooling was interrupted for two years. At the age of eight she was sent to live with family friends in the Bahamas, where the warmer climate was better for her health. After a year she was sent to other family friends in Hastings, New Zealand.[39] Juliet was eventually re-united with her family two years later, in 1948, after Dr Hulme had become Rector. Within eighteen months Juliet was sent away again for health reasons, this time to a boarding school in the North Island. However, she was unhappy at the school and returned to Christchurch, starting at Christchurch Girls High School in 1952.[40]

The Hulmes considered Juliet to be highly intelligent and she was reported to have scored 170 on an intelligence test. They decided, in view of this, that she would get more mental stimulation at the local high school, where she would be part of a larger group of students than at a small private school.[41]

At the trial, both Juliet and Pauline were said to be extremely intelligent. Many people believed that intelligence was an inherited and fixed characteristic which could be measured.

Christchurch Sanatorium, where Juliet Hulme stayed in 1953. Photo: ATL.

Ideas that 'genius' was often accompanied by emotional instability were common[42] and the evidence presented at the trial reinforced these connections.

In 1953 Juliet developed tuberculosis and was sent to the Cashmere Sanatorium in Christchurch from mid May until early September. During this time both her parents were away in England – from 28 May to about 30 August 1953, almost the entire period of Juliet's hospitalisation.[43] This and other separations affected her deeply, and she felt some resentment and anger towards her parents, particularly her mother, as a result.[44] Meanwhile, Pauline and Honora Parker visited her while she was in the sanatorium.[45]

The Hulmes lived in the large two-storeyed homestead known as Ilam, in the affluent suburb of Upper Riccarton. Named after Ilam Hall, the English home of the Watts-Russell family who settled in the area in the 1850s, the site of this house had once been one of the main social centres of early Christchurch society.

The homestead in which the Hulmes lived had been built in 1914 after fires had destroyed the first two houses at Ilam. Its new owner Edgar Stead, a naturalist, developed a garden which became well-known for its azaleas and rhododendrons. In July 1950 the property was bought by the university and became the Rector's residence. It later became the University of Canterbury Staff Club. The Hulmes purchased a small house at Port Levy on Banks Peninsula which they used for holidays and on some weekends. This house had disappeared from Maori ownership after the death of the legal owner in 1943. The Maori Trustee (a Pakeha) had sold the house to a Pakeha business without consulting the surviving family who regarded the transaction as an injustice.[46]

The Hulmes entertained regularly at the Ilam residence. Prominent guests included members of the Christchurch social elite as well as visiting celebrities, such as English actor Anthony Quayle. Some of the guests were people the Hulmes had known in England, others were new connections made through the University and the Marriage Guidance Council. Because of their social position they also had access to the literary and artistic circles of Christchurch. Through her involvement with the Marriage Guidance Council Hilda Hulme met Walter Andrew Bowman Perry. A consulting engineer, Perry had been sent to New Zealand by a British company. When his marriage broke up he went to the Christchurch Marriage Guidance Council where Hilda Hulme was a counsellor. A close relationship developed between them and in December 1953, Perry moved into a flat at the Hulme house. It was widely believed later that Hilda and Walter already had a sexual relationship at this time, although Hilda denied this at the trial. We believe that by the time Walter Perry moved into the flat at Ilam their relationship had become sexual. Henry was aware of their relationship and seemed to accept it.[47]

Hilda was still prominent in the Marriage Guidance Council at this time, having been re-elected as a Vice-President of the Council in April 1953 and again in March 1954. The murder of Honora Parker and the revelations about the lives of the Hulmes stunned Council members. The Committee noted at the meeting following the killing that the vacancies for Vice-President and committee member caused by Hilda Hulme's resignation in May would not be filled in the meantime.[48]

Henry Hulme's career in New Zealand was not a success. At this time Canterbury University College, like Otago, Auckland and Victoria University Colleges, was part of the University of New Zealand, controlled by a University Senate made up of representatives from the College districts. Prior to 1948, a senior member of the academic staff had assumed administrative duties in addition to academic work. It was then decided to create full-time administrative positions at each of the Colleges. Accordingly, the University of New Zealand advertised four positions as Rector. Hulme was appointed the first full-time Rector at Canterbury University College.

The College was very pleased to have attracted a candidate whose qualifications seemed to be ideal for an institution eager to develop its schools of science and technology. They were quickly disillusioned. Within three months of his appointment in 1948 Hulme had voted against his own College Council regarding the site of a proposed School of Forestry.[49] This issue was an important one for academic politics because the Colleges were keen to establish faculties and schools which would be prestigious. Because of the small size of the country it was not economically viable to duplicate schools and facilities. Canterbury College was eager to have the School of Forestry and when Hulme voted against this on the University Senate his working relations with his colleagues at Canterbury were damaged. His relationship with the College deteriorated steadily as other issues arose until finally, in mid March 1954, he was asked by his colleagues to resign. He did so and spent the next few months applying for overseas positions. It was not until a few days before his official university farewell that he actually obtained another appointment.[50] His new job was at the Atomic Weapons Research Establishment in Aldermaston, England, where he became Chief of Nuclear Research in 1959.[51]

Hilda and Henry officially separated in 1954 and later divorced. In September, after the Supreme Court trial, Hilda changed her surname by deed poll to Perry.[52] Subsequently she married Walter Perry. Henry remarried in 1955.[53]

Both Hilda and Henry left New Zealand permanently in 1954. Henry left in early July as originally planned. Hilda, who had been required by subpoena to appear at the Supreme Court trial, remained in the country with Perry until after the trial, when they left together. Between July and September, she lived with Perry in the house at Port Levy. Henry's resignation meant that the family had to leave Ilam. Hilda applied to the university to stay on until after the trial but her request was declined. An auction at Ilam of the Hulmes' household effects in July attracted large numbers of people who were hoping to obtain souvenirs and to glimpse the grounds where Pauline Parker and Juliet Hulme had built 'temples' and buried 'dead ideas'.[54]

The Hulme family had fitted well into the upper classes of Christchurch society. They lived in a large residence, held positions of some status and had a prominent public profile. Some contemporaries found the Hulmes cold and arrogant, while others commented on Hilda's social charm and elegance and Henry's kindness. They maintained a large library, entertained frequently and mixed with prominent people. They were actively involved in the cultural and social life of the city.

There were clear differences between the physical and economic circumstances of the Hulme and Rieper households. The resources and privileges of the Hulmes, who were able to return to England on holiday for nearly three months in 1953, for example, were clearly greater than those of Honora and Herbert. The contrast between the modest inner-city Rieper house, with its boarders, its proximity to the Girls High School and its small vegetable garden, and the mansion at Ilam with many rooms, privacy, a housekeeper and extensive grounds made an impression on Pauline Parker. Pauline sneered at the ignorance of the people in her own family circle. She thought that Honora talked 'a lot of rot' and she was critical of the attitudes and conversations of visiting neighbours.[55]

Pauline was impressed by the Hulmes. She aspired to the 'cultured' English environment of the Hulme household and on one occasion recorded with delight that another passenger on a bus asked her how long she had been out from England.[56] On another occasion she was very pleased when 'a girl who sat at the same table as us in a milkbar', said 'how beautifully I spoke English, that I almost had an Oxford accent, what a refreshing change it was, and several other very pleasing things . . .'[57]

Hilda Hulme's liberal ideas on child-rearing and the freedom she allowed Juliet contrasted with the attitudes of Herbert and Honora, who held more conservative views.

Clearly, Pauline considered her home circumstances restrictive and she found her parents wanting.[58] Frequently after her visits to Ilam, Pauline would go into her room and keep to herself for some time.[59]

Despite their differences, both the Hulmes and the Riepers were families with secrets. These secrets concerned events and circumstances in both families which were unacceptable during the 1950s.

CHAPTER THREE

The Time

What were the 1950s like?

Alison: I was a teenager during the 1950s and recollect clearly the conservative and judgmental atmosphere of the times towards anybody who defied the status quo. Adults had grown up during the Depression of the thirties, had experienced World War II and had been affected by policies which promoted family life and domesticity. For me as a teenager this meant constant and prescriptive messages about how lucky we were to be living in a peaceful and affluent time and how important social order was. I was dissatisfied but found it difficult to imagine a focus for rebellion. There was no television so films were very important. The film Rebel Without a Cause *summed up for me exactly what I thought many of my friends and I were feeling – a strong dissatisfaction with what seemed a dreary and dull conformity but no clear idea about what could change or how this might happen. I think it is difficult for those people who grew up during later times to imagine the dreariness of the early fifties. Rock 'n' Roll was a burst of light for my generation – though I remember a deaconess banning it from bible class dances because she considered that it would unduly excite young people. Teddy-boys and girls, milk-bar cowboys/girls, and bodgies and widgies were our first youthful protest groups which challenged clothing styles and attitudes. None of this altered the power structures one bit.*

In 1949 the fourteen-year-old Labour Government had been voted out of office and replaced by a more conservative National Government. New Zealand was firmly linked to the United Kingdom and British Commonwealth and increasingly after the war to the United States. Peace-time conscription was introduced, the government sent a small force of troops to Korea in 1950, and signed the ANZUS defence pact with Australia and the United States in 1951. The imported Cold War ideology was used by the National Government as part of its campaign to crush the trade unions in the 1951 waterfront lockout. The government imposed strict censorship and suspended fundamental civil liberties.

Conservative values and ideas were presented and reinforced through the mass media which generally adopted a pro-United States, anti-communist perspective, reflecting the values of the government. The appointment of a communist as a senior lecturer in Mathematics at Otago University College prompted the editor of the *Otago Daily Times* to declare 'The people of Otago would not want a Communist to receive a salary of £1000-1250 a year.'[1]

The post-war years were also characterised by an increasing affluence. By the mid-1950s Pakeha New Zealanders had the second highest standard of living in the world. This had, in fact, been built upon the suppression, exploitation and domination of Maori from the beginnings of European settlement. Jane Kelsey has described the legal system which developed following the signing of the Treaty of Waitangi in 1840 and has documented the subsequent legislation which further institutionalised white supremacy.[2] The dominant culture, however, presented an image of New Zealand as a society which had no 'race problem'.

Pakeha proudly proclaimed to visitors from other countries that there was no 'colour bar' and that Maori were much better off than Blacks in the United States or in South Africa. One observer, while commenting that the colonisation of Maori by Pakeha was 'of the same order as that meted out to the Indians of North America and the Aborigines of Australia' nevertheless considered that 'We can be happy, however, that we have not the same causes for reproach as our nearest neighbour.'[3] The *NZ Listener* echoed this claim in an assimilationist and paternalistic manner in 1953:

> 'Relations between the two races in this country are so good compared with similar situations elsewhere that it may seem superfluous to mention the need for tolerance . . . The Maoris are in a situation which we have created for them. It is our duty to help them play their part until the day when there will not be two races in New Zealand, but only one.'[4]

A visiting American academic commented:

> 'The visitor is reminded time and again that the Maori enjoys complete equality with the European; that there is no colour bar and no racial prejudice or discrimination in New Zealand; that there are Maori doctors, mayors, bishops and cabinet ministers; and that the Maori is judged on his merits as an individual – if he behaves as a European, he is treated as one'.[5]

In reality Maori were oppressed and exploited. The fact that there were a few Maori in positions of power did not alter the situation. While there was no legalised system of separate development as in South Africa, an informal 'colour bar' existed and racist attitudes and behaviours were deeply established. During the 1950s the Maori population underwent significant changes. In 1945 three-quarters of the Maori population lived in rural areas. By the mid-1970s, three-quarters were living in urban areas, mainly in cheaper housing, with more than a fifth concentrated in Auckland.[6] As Maori came increasingly into contact with Pakeha more obvious incidents of discrimination occurred. Angela Ballara has documented the extent to which a 'colour bar' existed in New Zealand during this period.[7] Donna Awatere has discussed some of the effects of the shift by Maori to urban areas:

> 'The rural-urban shift of the fifties and sixties produced tension through a breakdown in cultural practices: a decline in social kin-based support, the workforce routine, white "superiority" in daily doses, white hatred in housing, jobs, education, health, justice.'[8]

Some contemporary observers highlighted the discrepancy between the widely-held beliefs and the facts concerning race. One headmaster confessed that he 'lamented' having to 'discourage my Maori pupils from taking the commercial course' because despite the pupils being good at the subjects it was a 'waste of time' because 'nobody wants to give them a try'.[9] Another writer reprovingly drew attention to the view of a government official who considered that:

> 'from a legal point of view, a good rule to go by is to assume that, unless proved to the contrary all Maoris are liars, stealers and adulterers, and when proved to the contrary, they are about as moral sexually as the average low-class Pakeha.'[10]

Pakeha racism was also directed at other races not of white, Anglo-Saxon origin. Chinese, Yugoslavs, Indians, Lebanese, Jews, for example, were all targets of the racist policies of the dominant culture.[11] Immigration policies excluded many people on the basis of race and ethnic origin. There were many instances of overtly hostile behaviour towards these groups. Indians, for example, were refused admission to certain seats in picture theatres.[12] Suggestions in the *New Zealand Woman's Weekly* in June 1950, that it would be a good idea if Pakehas deleted from their conversation terms such as 'Chink, Chow, Nigger, Dago, Wop and Wog' indicate that these words were commonly used.[13]

In the early 1950s the Communist newspaper, *People's Voice*, published a number of articles about racism in the early 1950s. In 1952 it suggested that a 'colour bar' was common practice in Auckland hotels. One article was published with an accompanying photograph of a sign reading 'NO NATIVES SERVED IN THIS BAR' above the door of the lounge bar on the King's Arms Hotel.[14] In 1954, it reported that the private bar of a 'five-star-plus' hotel in Christchurch refused to serve drinks not only to Maori but to any 'coloured people no matter what their position or education'. When questioned, the manager of the hotel explained that 'We are cleaning up the private bar for businessmen' and that Maori could get service in the public bar 'out the back'.[15] Other articles described instances of discrimination and attempted segregation in the workplace, refusals to provide accommodation to Maori, prohibition on speaking Maori in some schools and even the segregation of toilet facilities for Maori boys at a south Auckland district primary school.[16]

Mainstream media contained racist and patronising articles by Pakeha about Maori and people of colour. Some were blatantly insulting. One Pakeha doctor asserted authoritatively that there was a fundamental difference between Maori and European ways of thinking. 'The Maori has not the faculty of abstract thought . . .' he asserted.[17]

During the Parker-Hulme trial a number of newspapers highlighted evidence that Pauline Parker had become friendly with male students from Ceylon (now Sri Lanka) and that she had been alone with one of them on at least one occasion. The possible sexual implications of this and her association with 'non-whites' placed Pauline even further apart from 'normal' society – the white and racist dominant culture. This was used at the trial to portray her as immoral, criminal, and 'bad'.

The National Government generally promoted a conservative and rigid view of social issues. The state controlled and influenced the mass media. Radio networks were operated by the New Zealand Broadcasting Service – a government department. At the same time the main newspapers were dominated by conservative interests.

By the early 1950s a system of film and publication censorship was firmly established. Earlier, the Customs Department had begun to maintain lists of books which were considered indecent or seditious under the Indecent Publications Act. These confidential lists were then circulated to representatives of organisations such as the New Zealand Booksellers Association and the New Zealand Library Association so that members of these groups could be 'guided' when ordering and importing books.[18] By 1952 there were over 400 books on these lists.[19] Book importers colluded with this system, in effect censoring themselves to avoid legal action over books that might be considered indecent. Even though the lists had no legal standing this practice was still firmly entrenched during the early 1950s. Complaints from booksellers, librarians and others about the system of censorship forced the department to establish advisory committees in 1946 and 1953. Members of these committees were, however, simply representatives of the dominant culture – the 1953 committee consisted of a former headmistress who was the secretary for the Student Christian Movement and two university teachers.[20]

In 1955, the Customs Department alerted its officials to the possibility that a book which contained a chapter on the Parker-Hulme case might be imported. Officials were instructed to seize the book:

'As this gives the full story of the murder committed by the two girls mentioned above, delivery should be withheld and a copy sent to this office for examination.'[21]

The department may have wished to control how the respective family circumstances and the relationship between Juliet and Pauline was depicted.

The system of book censorship, however, did not operate in the same way for everyone. Certain groups were allowed to import books to which others were denied access. The lists of 'indecent literature' were classified into several categories.

One category of books could be imported on condition that they be sold only to 'professional men' and other 'experts.' Books in this category included works by Sigmund Freud and Krafft-Ebing. Another category allowed specialist groups, for example nudists, to import nudist magazines, at the same time preventing others from obtaining them. A third category contained books which were labelled as indecent without any exceptions – this included a number of books on birth control, for example, *A Common Treatise on Birth Control* by Margaret Graham, and Radclyffe Hall's classic lesbian novel *The Well of Loneliness* had been banned from import at least until 1936, though by 1950 it could be borrowed from some public libraries.[22]

There were two final categories – books that had been assessed by the department and could be freely imported, and books that had not been assessed and could be brought into the country with no guarantee that they might not be seized by police.[23]

Films were also subject to censorship. Every film intended for public screening had to be submitted to the office of the Chief Censor. Most films were imported, primarily from the United States and Britain. These were similar in theme,[24] most presenting and reinforcing a romantic heterosexual model of life. Audiences unwittingly watched lesbian or gay movie stars, like Rock Hudson, presenting an idealised version of heterosexual romantic love.

Radio broadcasting was also subject to censorship – this was carried out by officials and programme controllers within the New Zealand Broadcasting Service. The Service was noted for its reluctance to broadcast programmes which might be controversial or become the subject of complaints about 'bad taste'. One critic commented that:

> 'Subjects are rejected as "too risky just now", or "liable to embarrass the Minister" or "they might put the Government on the spot", or even "we'd be called Communists if we talked about that".'[25]

Serials and popular music also promoted and portrayed a narrow heterosexuality as the norm – indeed as the only possibility. Even within the narrowly defined scope of acceptable sexuality restrictions existed. Explicit references to sexual activity were censored. The mildly suggestive lyrics of Cole Porter's musical *Kiss Me, Kate!* were considered unacceptable and were on a list of banned songs maintained by the Broadcasting Service.[26] Depictions of heterosexual 'love', largely unreal, romantic and sanitised, were important themes particularly on the popular commercial stations.[27] Under these circumstances, lesbianism was certainly an unfit topic for public broadcast. (See also Chapter 10.)

After World War II, heterosexual family life was strongly promoted. Both men and women had experienced greater personal freedoms during the war and the dominant culture was anxious to re-establish social 'stability', and in particular to promote ‘the ideals of family life. This affected gender role expectations, especially for women, and great emphasis was placed on the role of the mother. All sex outside marriage was frowned upon, especially for women, despite practice to the contrary.

For those women who were in the paid work force, especially those who were married with children, there was a gap between what was socially desirable and what was a personal reality. After World War II women were pressured to give up their jobs in the paid work force to returning male soldiers. Some were co-erced and others, accepting the gender role defined for women, willingly gave up their jobs to return to the home. During the war many women had worked in jobs previously held only by men. In 1945 females comprised 25.2 per cent of the total labour force. However, by 1951 this percentage had dropped to 23.2 and did not return to the 1945 level until 1961.[28] New Zealand women experienced pressures similar to those experienced by women in other western countries after the war. (The documentary *Rosie the Riveter*, for example, shows the pressures that were brought to bear upon women in the United States to give up their paid jobs after World War II.)

In the 1950s female participation in the paid labour force was concentrated in a small range of occupations. Women tended to be over-represented in the lower ranks of the various occupations with few women occupying managerial or executive positions. In some occupations, when a woman married, she was forced to resign her position. For example, women who married while training to be teachers lost their studentships.[29]

Women workers were paid at wage rates lower than those for men.[30] A man's wage was said to include a 'social element'. This was the idea that the basic wage for a man should be sufficient for him to support himself, a wife and at least two children.[31] Female heads of households were expected to support their dependants on a smaller wage.

Within the education system the curriculum was gender-specific and reinforced traditional gender roles.[32] At the time many jobs were defined in gender-specific terms. For example, a 'hospital aide' was defined in the Hospital Employment Regulations of 1948 as 'a woman engaged in elementary nursing duties.'[33] Occupations such as teaching and nursing were seen as appropriate to the proper gender role of a woman. One recruitment advertisement for nurses said 'Yours is the only profession where there can be no competition between the sexes . . . a service which can only be borne on the shoulders of women.'[34]

Working mothers were held responsible for 'delinquent' children and women's magazines reflected images of devoted wives who 'held onto' their husbands by welcoming them home after a hard day's work outside the home, with attractive meals and home comforts.[35]

The family wage, state housing for families, the family benefit were all manifestations of family-oriented ideas. This defined an appropriate social identity for all individuals. Christina Simmons discusses American and British literature which promoted the companionate marriage, with its emphasis on individual romance and sexual fulfillment as the expected goals of marriage and family life.[36] She points out, however, that 'women had to walk a fine line between appropriate modesty and neurotic prudery'. Women's sexuality was, of course, 'acceptable only insofar as its energy was channelled into marriage and the service of men.'

Marriage was portrayed as the only desirable goal for women. Phoebe Meikle, writing under the pseudonym 'Leslie M. Hall' in 1958, pointed out that

'. . . A woman who does not marry is made in a hundred ways to feel a failure . . . marriage is the most generally accepted criterion of feminine success . . . it [is] an unshakeable New Zealand assumption that a woman who has not married is a woman who has not been asked in marriage.'[37]

Failure to marry was often seen as an inability to attract a partner. The *New Zealand Woman's Weekly* pointed out in 1951 that 'Psychologists say that, in view of the far wider and freer discussion of sex problems that is common today, the best way to avoid the unnatural single state is to encourage an interest in, and an understanding of, the physical and mental conditions of marriage at an early stage.'[38] Popular magazines gave 'helpful' advice to 'unsuccessful' women so that their chances would be improved. Women were encouraged to keep their skins 'bridal-perfect.' However, even women who obeyed the rules sometimes failed to find husbands. Mary Millar, a columnist for the *New Zealand Woman's Weekly*, worried that 'girls who have maintained a very strict standard of conduct have still got left on the shelf.'[39] Of course, these ideas of the family were based on European and Christian views and ignored Maori whanau, hapu and iwi structures. It was a narrow model of a married Pakeha heterosexual couple and their children.

Deviations from this model were by definition, 'abnormal', 'bad', 'immoral', or sometimes, 'unfortunate'. Those who transgressed were punished. Children whose parents had divorced, were described as coming from 'broken homes'[40] or even as living in 'half homes'. Divorced women were regarded as 'loose', or 'immoral'.[41] A common attitude to unmarried mothers was that they were 'inferior beings who had sinned and fallen by the wayside and must be punished for their moral wrongdoing.'[42] A large proportion of these women were teenagers (about twenty-two percent of all unmarried mothers, in 1955), while only about four percent of married mothers were under twenty years. Some saw unmarried mothers as being encouraged in their 'immorality' by the state, which provided limited assistance for women in this position under the Social Security Act 1938.[43]

Organisations such as the League of Mothers (founded in 1926) and the Marriage Guidance Council (established in 1948-49 throughout New Zealand) helped promote these ideas. The League of Mothers claimed a membership of 10,459 in 1954, spread over 138 branches throughout the country. It was open to all women and one of its main aims was to '[uphold] the sanctity of marriage.'[44] The Marriage Guidance Council of Christchurch adopted the general principles established by the National Marriage Guidance Council in London. These saw 'the family unit' as the basis of society and that the right foundation for such a unit was 'permanent monogamous marriage'. It was firm that sexual intercourse 'should not take place outside of marriage'. The Council saw it as a public duty 'to do everything possible to prevent the tragedy of the broken home, and the train of evils which it initiates . . . Everything possible should be done to promote fertile unions', it declared. Therefore, while it considered that contraception could serve a purpose in assisting 'married couples' to space their children, it was a:

'danger when misused to enable selfish and irresponsible people to escape the duties and disciplines of marriage and parenthood.'[45]

Given the policies of the Council, it is ironic that Hilda, a marriage guidance counsellor and wife of the University Rector was involved in a relationship with another man, a previous client of the counselling service. Her close involvement with the Council was subsequently very damaging to its reputation and the repercussions of the case were said to have set its work back fifteen years.[46] A history of the Council went further and claimed that the movement 'was on the crest of a wave when it was swamped'[47] by the Parker-Hulme case. It said that '. . . 35 years after the debacle suspicion still prickles . . . at least once a year, someone raises the Parker case . . .'[48] By 1960 when the Council decided to preview all intending marriage guidance counsellors, it took a 'deliberate decision not to take divorced people on as a matter of public image.'[49] This was a direct result of the Parker-Hulme case, which exposed Hilda Hulme's situation. Public image was still a concern in 1987 when a former member of the Christchurch Marriage Guidance Council attempted to distance the Council from the case by assuring us that Hilda Hulme had been only peripherally involved with it.[50] She had in fact been Vice-President as well as a counsellor.

Neither the Parker/Rieper nor Hulme families conformed to the desired model. Herbert had deserted his first family. He and Honora had never legally married and therefore, their children were, according to the ideas of this society, technically 'illegitmate'. Given the pressures on women to conform, it is not surprising that a number of people commenting on the case expressed the opinion that 'the wrong mother got it.'[51] Hilda was seen as immoral and as a negligent mother. People implied that her neglect of Juliet was one of the causes of the murder. Honora, in contrast was perceived as the good mother, the one who had tried to break up the undesirable relationship.

However, many others were in situations similar to that of the

Riepers and the Hulmes. The numbers of divorces were increasing and it was slowly becoming more acceptable to abandon a marriage.[52] In so far as 'illegitimacy' was concerned, researcher W. Glass concluded in 1959 that the rate for Europeans had remained at a constant level of about forty-five per thousand births for the eighty years from the mid-1870s to the mid-1950s.[53] Some women also had abortions (which was a criminal offence). For those who were unmarried, conditions were very dangerous. Glass estimated that over the ten-year period between 1944 and 1953, of the forty-five deaths for unmarried mothers eighteen, or forty per cent, were due to septic abortions, compared with twenty-seven out of 483, or about five per cent, for married mothers.

In spite of these realities social prescriptions were rigid. Flaunting of non-conformity attracted social punishments. Those who did not conform survived by discretion, secrecy and duplicity.

However, the 1950s did contain some of the seeds of the resistances and social upheavals of the 1960s. There were people who opposed the dominant ideas and there was resistance and protest in many areas.[54] Peace activists attempted to promote discussion of the Cold War alliances, while socialists and left-aligned thinkers worked through groups and organisations for social changes on class issues. Equal pay activists continued fighting the rigid gender codes, while lesbians and gay men met together. Maori activists continued to object to land confiscations and daily race discrimination, and people with disabilities tried to raise disability issues in the media. Many young people, including the so-called 'juvenile delinquents', broke the sexuality codes.

It was an awareness of the potential for youthful resistance to authority which deeply worried adults during the 1950s, although many adults confused aspects of the developing youth culture, for example the new Rock 'n' Roll music and the motorcycle gangs, with youth crime. At the same time, there was a growing campaign against the importation of 'indecent' literature and American comics which were criticised for depicting violence and sex.

In July 1954, a month after Honora Parker's murder, when reports of 'immorality' among teenagers in the Hutt Valley, Wellington appeared in newspapers, the government set up an inquiry into the matter. A committee of six, two women and four men, chaired by Wellington lawyer, Oswald Mazengarb, was quickly established. The Mazengarb Committee received submissions from over 200 individuals and organisations and held hearings throughout the country. These were closed to the public and the press was restricted to simply reporting the committee's trips to various cities to hear evidence.

The committee was composed of a Justice of the Peace, the Headmaster of Christchurch Boys High School, the Director of the Child Hygiene Division of the Department of Health, the President of the Catholic Women's League, a minister of religion, and the President of the New Zealand Junior Chamber of Commerce.

The committee was concerned with what it thought was a rising wave of 'sexual delinquency', including homosexuality. It cited the Christchurch murder, noting that 'these girls were abnormally homosexual in behaviour'[55] and also claimed that 'senior pupils of an intermediate school were concerned in depravity, both heterosexual and homosexual.'[56] The committee searched for causes of these apparent trends. It placed much of the blame on working mothers and on 'precocious girls' who it claimed 'corrupted the boys'.[57] Listing other factors as well, the committee deplored the high wages paid to adolescents, the loss of religious faith, and the number of 'objectionable publications' available in the country. Committee members also considered that the disruption of two world wars had led to an increased use of contraceptives, a liberalisation of the divorce laws, an increase in pre-marital sex and the spread of new psychological ideas.

It reported its findings to parliament on 20 September 1954. Prime Minister Sidney Holland, whose electorate included the Hutt Valley, and his government, which was shortly to face an election, supported the report unanimously and 300,000 copies of it were distributed – one to every home receiving the family benefit. While the findings of the committee were treated with scepticism and even ridicule by many people, including some government officials, the government nevertheless hastily implemented some of its recommendations. After 1954 the Indecent Publications Act required publishers and distributors of any printed material to be registered, the Child Welfare Amendment Act was broadened so that girls under the age of sixteen could be defined as delinquents if they had sexual relations with any male, and the Police Offences Act made it an offence to give contraceptives, or information about contraceptives, to anyone under the age of sixteen.

By the late 1950s New Zealand, following British, Australian and American trends, showed a growing official preoccupation with 'juvenile delinquency' and the body of literature on the subject increased. The media increasingly reported incidents of 'youth hooliganism'.[58] One response to juvenile crime was the 'creation of the Juvenile Crime Prevention Section of the Police, in 1957, modelled on earlier British examples'.[59] We think that the main impetus behind the interest in and responses to juvenile crime was the desire on the part of those in power to maintain a particular social order, possibly as a response to the upheavals produced by the war years, the 'baby boom' generation and the growth of a youth culture in the western world. No matter what the actual extent of juvenile crime, the issue revealed that some young people at least did not conform to the prescribed mould. We would define this culture as a resistance to the existing social order, whether or not the individuals at the time consciously saw themselves in that way.

Although Hilda Hulme, Juliet Hulme and Pauline Parker were all represented at the trial and through the media as females who deviated from the accepted norms of respectability, they were not uniquely deviant. Many women did divorce and have extramarital relationships, as Hilda had. Many girls did sneak out to meet boys as Pauline did, and many girls also had lesbian relationships. Many women lived in long-standing unmarried heterosexual relationships as Honora Parker had.[60] Despite the prescriptive norms of the dominant ideas, many girls and women resisted them in varying ways and to different degrees.

CHAPTER FOUR

The Relationships

The Riepers and the Hulmes were very different. Under any other circumstances it is unlikely that they would have met. However, because the Hulmes had decided to send Juliet to Christchurch Girls High School, she and Pauline met when they were both placed in the same class, the top stream of the third form. This was the initial point of contact between the two households.

Subsequently, a complex set of relationships developed. There was the relationship between Pauline and Juliet, the relationships between the members of each household, and that between the households as circumstances changed.

At Christchurch Girls High School both girls did well. They were considered to be intelligent and imaginative. School records show that their marks were average in their class. They were noticed by teachers and other students at the school because from early 1952 they became very close, sitting together and walking in the school grounds, hand in hand.[1] At that time, showing this amount of affection publicly was seen as unusual.

By the end of 1952 their relationship was firmly established. Pauline wrote at the start of her 1953 diary that during the previous year they had sneaked out at night together on three occasions, once cycling to a nearby beach to swim.

In her diaries for 1953 and 1954, Pauline recorded in some detail the activities which she and Juliet enjoyed together – horse-riding, walking round the Ilam grounds (including midnight excursions and adventures), play acting and dressing up, plasticine modelling, reading, playing records and dancing, singing together, playing cards and board games, going to the pictures, going to plays or concerts and talking endlessly together, including telephone conversations which sometimes lasted for several hours.

They also spent a lot of time writing. Between them they produced a significant output. At the time of the murder they were reported to have written six novels, as well as plays, poetry, and an opera.[2]

The girls experimented with language, reading their poems

and stories to each other, changing words around, and inventing their own code for their favourite pop singers, film stars and for people they knew. They referred to Mario Lanza as 'HE' and James Mason as 'HIM', and the Ceylonese students they knew as 'THEM'. They used the term 'the Saints' for film stars and pop singers, and changed their favourites from time to time like many teenage girls.

Pauline was sometimes invited to spend holidays with the Hulme family at their beach cottage. Her diary for 1953 contains an entry for Good Friday 3 April, when she was with the Hulmes at Port Levy for Easter. This entry became a central item during the trial when defence psychiatrists attached a great deal of importance to it as an indicator of insanity.

> 'Today Juliet and I found the key to the 4th world. We realize now that we have had it in our possession for about 6 months but we only realized it on the day of the death of Christ. We saw a gateway through the clouds. We sat on the edge of the path and looked down the hill out over the bay. The island looked beautiful. The sea was blue. Everything was full of peace and bliss. We then realized we had the key. We now know that we are not genii as we thought. We have an extra part of our brain which can appreciate the 4th world. Only about 10 people have it. When we die we will go to the 4th world, but meanwhile on two days every year we may use the ray and look in to that beautiful world which we are lucky enough to be allowed to know of, on this Day of Finding the Key to the Way through the Clouds.'[3]

The entry can be read in many different ways – it could refer to a religious experience, it could be experimental writing, it could be over-romantic prose describing a beautiful setting, or it could refer to an emotional-physical encounter between the two girls. There are also Maori interpretations which consider the spiritual aspects of the entry. (See Chapter 9.)

Not long after this experience Juliet developed tuberculosis and was in the sanitorium from 21 May until 9 September 1953, when she was allowed to return home. Pauline wrote on this date, 'It was wonderful returning with Juliet . . . it was as if she had never been away . . . I believe I could fall in love with Juliet.'[4]

The girls continued to develop a close physical relationship. Pauline wrote about long baths which she and Juliet took together at Ilam. Sometimes they were able to sleep together as well, though by April 1954 they were worried about being

Port Levy, in about 1940. Photo: Thelma Kent Collection, ATL.

discovered by adults. This did not deter them and in mid June 1954 Pauline wrote:

'We enacted how each Saint would make love in bed, only doing the first seven as it was 7.30am by then. We felt exhausted and very satisfied . . . [the next night] we came to bed quite early and spent the night very hectically. We went to sleep after getting almost through. We had a simply marvellous time and we definitely are mad but very pleasingly so.'[5]

The following day Pauline wrote:

'. . . we spent a hectic night going through the Saints. It was wonderful! Heavenly! Beautiful! and Ours! We felt satisfied indeed. We have now learned the peace of the thing called Bliss, the joy of the thing called Sin.'[6]

On the sixteenth she said:

'We came to bed late and spent a very hectic night. It was wonderful. We only did 10 Saints altogether but we did them thoroughly. I prefer doing longer ones. We enjoyed ourselves greatly and intend to do so again . . .'[7]

On the seventeenth, however, they:

> '. . . confessed that we were disappointed in the Saints so we had an absolute clean-up and threw out 8 of them. We discussed the ones left fully and felt very happy over them. We did not misbehave last night.'[8]

The two girls were constantly together and clearly had intense feelings about one another. After a 'disagreement' with a boy in October 1953, Pauline wrote '. . . not that I mind at all, it is so nice to think that Juliet and I could continue our friendship unmolested with no outside interests.'[9]

Did Juliet and Pauline have a lesbian relationship? In our view they did though there are difficulties involved in using the term 'lesbian' for women and girls of the past who may not have defined themselves in this way. What is meant by the term 'lesbian'? There has been considerable feminist debate regarding the use of this term. Adrienne Rich, in her article 'Compulsory Heterosexuality and Lesbian Existence'[10] sees all female-to-female experience as existing within a 'lesbian continuum', which she defines as all 'woman-identified-experience', not simply sexual experience. She argues that all women exist on this lesbian continuum and move 'in and out' of it through a variety of female experiences ('suckling a mother's breast' to dying at ninety 'touched and handled by women'), whether or not we identify as lesbian. There are problems with this all-inclusive approach. However, as Jacquelyn N. Zita in a critique of Rich's article points out, Rich's lesbian continuum does rid the word lesbian of a 'clinical fixation . . . by defining it in political terms.'[11] In this sense, lesbianism may be understood as resistance to male domination through various societies in various ways. However, many lesbian-feminist theorists prefer a less inclusive definition than Rich's. Ann Ferguson, for example, suggests that a lesbian is '. . . a woman who has sexual and erotic-emotional ties primarily with women or who sees herself as centrally involved with a community of self-identified lesbians whose sexual and erotic-emotional ties are primarily with women; and who is herself a self-identified lesbian.'[12]

Other lesbians consider this definition to be narrow and restrictive – it excludes a great many women both past and present and risks becoming prescriptive. It does not take account of the process or stages by which a woman may identify as lesbian.

(At which moment can she name herself/can we name her as a lesbian? What kind of lapses from the ideal can she be permitted?) This definition could be applied only to women living in late twentieth-century Western societies. Clearly women living in other and earlier societies do not/did not understand or call themselves lesbian in this modern way.

There are many ways in which lesbians have understood themselves, depending upon the society in which they lived, the prevalent attitudes towards women and lesbianism and their access to information about other lesbians. Some New Zealand lesbians from the 1950s said that prior to meeting other lesbians, they had thought that 'I was the only one on earth like it.'[13] One woman simply wondered 'why I couldn't get interested in men' and eventually went to a doctor about it. He referred her to the Outpatients' Clinic at Sunnyside Hospital, Christchurch, where in 1958 she received a form of aversion therapy.[14] Other lesbians of the fifties thought of themselves as men who had been trapped in women's bodies.[15]

Adult lesbians of the time commonly experienced difficulty interpreting and defining their lesbianism. It is unclear how Juliet and Pauline thought about themselves. When questioned directly by the defence psychiatrist about whether they had a sexual relationship, Juliet seemed surprised and said 'But how could we? We are both women.'[16] However, Pauline writes that she and Juliet:

> 'had the intriguing conversation about what her parents would think if they concluded that she had changed into a male. It would have explained a great many things extraordinary to them.'[17]

Two weeks later, Pauline writes that:

> 'We did not sleep together as we were afraid Dr Hulme might come in.'[18]

This indicates that however they viewed themselves, they were aware that sleeping together was not approved of. Honora Parker had taken Pauline to Dr Francis Bennett, a local doctor, because of her concern about the girls' relationship and had discussed the matter with Henry Hulme as well. The school was also worried about the relationship between the two girls. It is unclear what discussions were held with Pauline and Juliet at that time and whether explicit reference was made to a lesbian relationship between them.

The girls saw one another daily when they could. Juliet seldom came to Pauline's home – although she did do so on some occasions. In part, this was due to Juliet's ill-health. However, Pauline preferred to spend time at Ilam with Juliet, rather than crowd into Gloucester Street with her. There were also more compelling reasons. Pauline's relationship with her mother was difficult and she did not want to spend time at home. When giving evidence at the Supreme Court trial, Hilda Hulme stated:

'She told Juliet and myself many times that she was very unhappy at home: she felt her mother did not understand her and did not love her. She felt happier at Ilam among our family than she had ever felt before. Sometimes after a related quarrel with her mother she would be in great distress. Juliet would then be upset, often to the point of weeping, and that is one of the reasons why Pauline was invited to come to Ilam.'[19]

Hilda also stated at the trial that 'Pauline gave me to understand quite clearly that her mother often subjected her to severe corporal punishment.'[20]

Pauline's diaries record a number of instances when her mother 'nagged' or 'threatened' her and one occasion when she slapped Pauline over the face several times. This does not seem to be 'severe corporal punishment' and she does not always explain what the 'threats' were. It is possible that Pauline may have exaggerated reports of quarrels with her mother in order to be able to stay at Ilam with Juliet. However, we think it is clear that the relationship between Honora and Pauline was very difficult.

Pauline's attraction to the liberal and upper middle-class household of her friend, compared with the more ordinary Rieper home, was very obvious. The Hulmes enjoyed an affluent standard of living – Pauline mentions with excitement that 'we are getting a radiogram worth sixty pounds', when referring to a new purchase which Henry was making for the Hulme household. She also mentions picking grapes from the vines in the Ilam grounds and drinking 'burgundy' from the supply of wines kept by the Hulmes. Wine drinking was uncommon in New Zealand during the early fifties, except among the upper middle-classes or some European settlers. There was also a housekeeper at Ilam.[21]

Pauline was made to feel welcome at the Hulmes' during her frequent visits. She had been very impressed by the glamorous Hilda Hulme at least since March 1953. On 15 March 1953 she recorded that 'Mrs Hulme was very grateful for the cigarettes and kissed me twice. . . .' During Easter 1953, Pauline wrote:

> 'The days I spent at Port Levy were the most HEAVENLY ones I have ever experienced . . . Mrs Hulme did my hair. She calls me her foster daughter.'[22] And on 26 April, she recorded: 'Mrs Hulme said she wished I was her daughter. I too . . .'

A year later, on 1 May 1954, Pauline reported that '[Mrs Hulme] made a lovely remark. She said Won't it be wonderful when we are all back in England. Do you think you will like England Gina. I was delighted . . .'

Pauline and Juliet referred to each other by a number of different names. Deborah was Juliet's current name, which had, according to Pauline, been suggested by Hilda Hulme as an alternative for Antoinette, a previous choice.[23] Pauline called herself Gina. We think it is common that teenage girls experiment with names and identities in this way.

Hilda Hulme may have been thoughtless in her remarks to Pauline, encouraging her to believe that she might be able to go overseas with some members of the Hulme family. At the trial, Hilda denied that she had made any such statements to Pauline.[24]

Pauline also admired Henry Hulme, referring to him as 'Poor Father' when she learnt that he and Hilda were to divorce, indicating the extent to which she considered herself to be a part of the Hulme family. She wrote with enthusiasm on 3 June 1954 that 'there was a wonderful photo of a portrait of Dr Hulme in the paper, so wonderful that I have cut it out and pinned it on cardboard on my wall . . .'

Pauline's attitude to Perry is difficult to assess. According to her diary she seems to have had little contact with him.

Juliet rarely visited Pauline's family. However, while she was in the sanatorium, Honora visited her three times with Pauline. During this period Hilda and Henry were in England. Prior to their departure, it had been suggested that Juliet stay with the Riepers during her parents' absence. However, because of her illness, she spent the time in the sanatorium. When the Hulmes returned on about 30 August, Hilda gave Pauline several presents and also gave Honora a powder compact.[25]

Apart from this, there was little contact between Honora and Herbert on the one hand, and Henry and Hilda on the other. In late 1953 though, Henry Hulme did visit by arrangement to discuss the relationship between the two girls with Herbert and Honora, and Pauline was sometimes dropped back at her home by Henry, following her visits to Ilam.

Juliet's relationship with her mother seems to have been ambivalent. She confided later to a prison official that the many separations from her parents, and in particular from her mother, had upset her deeply.[26] A former classmate commented that she thought Juliet was '. . . very neglected . . . I could picture them at home with lots of intellectual and stylish talk and absolutely none of the comforts and softness that children need.'[27] In this context, for Juliet, her relationship with Pauline was very important.

However, this close relationship did not mean that they were isolated from other people, although both were later described by the defence psychiatrists as 'living in a world of their own.'[28]

Juliet's relationship with her brother, Jonathon, was alleged by Hilda to be difficult. According to Hilda, Juliet had been most upset when Jonathon was born and had never really developed a warm relationship with her younger brother. Although he sometimes played with Juliet and Pauline at Ilam, it seems that Juliet did not spend a lot of time with him, preferring her own activities, especially those with Pauline. She was of course seriously ill and had spent a lot of time away from her family. We think this must have affected the way she related to Jonathon and perhaps inhibited the development of a close attachment between the two. In any case, he was six years younger than she was.

The Rieper household gave little opportunity for privacy, or for living in a world of one's own. Although Pauline found this irritating at times, in general she seems to have accepted a situation in which she was required to relate to a number of strangers within her own home. There are numerous references to the boarders in the diaries, many of them concerned with what new boarders would be like, or detailing interactions with them. The boarders lived as part of the Rieper family, eating and sometimes socialising with them.[29]

Conditions at the Hulme household were very much more comfortable. Although there were many visitors including students and university staff, the spacious home and surroundings allowed for more privacy. Despite her poor health, Juliet took

part in the activities of her home. Hilda and Henry do not seem
to have excluded her from dinner parties, even when celebrities
like Lady Rutherford came to dinner. She was also very interested
in socialising with some of the students who came to Ilam; in
particular, the group of students from Sri Lanka.

These students feature prominently in Pauline's diaries, as
being of great interest to Juliet as well as to her. Pauline secretly
met some of them and was also interested in one of the boarders.
She had a brief sexual relationship with this boarder, but was
caught by her father. The boarder was asked to leave the house,
but Pauline continued seeing him. After a while she broke off the
relationship.

Medlicott notes that 'the most striking thing about the sexual
behaviour was the apparent lack of real erotic involvement on
her part.'[30] He further reports that when he asked Pauline about
sexual intercourse with this young man, she explained that 'It
wasn't for me. I wasn't interested.'[31]

While her relationship with Juliet was most important, Pauline
maintained contact with many other people. Various friends are
mentioned in her diaries.[32] Although the girls had a special and
close friendship at school, they did have contact with other
classmates. One former classmate recalls that during the fourth
form year in 1953, they had invited her and another girl to join
them for a midnight adventure. She reported that 'they came to
two of us and said come and ride horses in the middle of the night
with us because you are like us and I thought oh yes that would be
lovely . . . we were going to have cloaks and ride in the night . . .
but neither of us did.'[33] This classmate recalled that it would have
been impossible for her to have got out at night to join the pair.
Another former classmate remembered them as:

> '. . . just so much more mature than the rest of us, Juliet in particular and
> Pauline was too. I think they might have been quite a bit older . . . either
> one or both was a year older, I think Juliet had TB so she had missed a
> year.'[34]

One of the former classmates felt that Pauline and Juliet had:

> '. . . set themselves apart . . . they made themselves special by being
> different so they didn't converse very much in the class, they didn't
> horse around, they were making themselves important by being
> different . . . I don't remember them ever starring in anything or doing

amazingly well in exams . . . anything sort of solid or conventional. Anything conventional would be unacceptable to them, they would have to set the standards and run the race and be absolutely original.'³⁵

The other remembered Pauline as:

'. . . being so stroppy that she wouldn't give tuppence halfpenny to anybody, especially teachers, very proud and not the sort of person who would speak up in class because she couldn't give a stuff . . . Juliet was also very proud and haughty but extremely bright, so I mean certainly able to speak up in class because that was the thing to do, so she would give a certain amount, she could play the game of being bright, passing exams and things like that.'³⁶

Both former classmates had clear recollections of what the girls were like physically. Medlicott had described them as follows:

'Pauline is a dark, rather sulky looking but not unattractive girl of stocky build . . . while Juliet is a tall, willowy, frail attractive blonde with large blue eyes.'³⁷

The classmates saw them quite differently. One said of Pauline that she was:

'. . . like wild, she was like a gypsy or something. I remember her frowning a lot in this really dramatic way. She was more attractive than Juliet . . . she sort of had a wild gypsy look about her with dark flashing eyes . . . knock you dead at 10 paces . . .'³⁸

This classmate recalled Juliet as '. . . striking, like a thorough-bred horse.'³⁹

The other classmate commented that 'Pauline was very beautiful, dead white skin and a long oval face, black curly hair . . . she was a mature beauty in the fifth form, very aggressive and a withdrawn smouldering sort of person . . . I would say [she] was more of a woman [than Juliet] although she was quite mannish in her sort of aggressive stances, she didn't want to be a female in whatever the traditions were.'⁴⁰ Of Juliet, she said, 'Juliet . . . trumpeted a lot with her red, runny nose. Very unattractive girl.'⁴¹

One of the defence lawyers saw Pauline as '. . . dull and uninteresting . . . not a lot going for the poor soul . . . desperately sad.'⁴² This view and Medlicott's are not the way their peers saw them. One classmate pointed out that they were certainly a 'match for one another.'⁴³ They made an impression on at least these classmates, one of whom said that the particular class was 'a very bright one', with high achieving girls in it from all over

Christchurch. She said that many girls in the class wrote poetry and had intellectual interests, so that Pauline and Juliet were not unusual in this respect.

In a more conventional sense Juliet was remembered by a former teacher as having participated in a French play, and Pauline was remembered by one classmate as having scored 100 per cent in Latin tests from time to time when she made the effort.[44]

While Juliet was in the sanatorium, girls from the class visited her – this was mentioned in Pauline's 1953 diary, and one of the classmates recollected the occasion, and that they had taken Juliet a cyclamen.[45]

At the time of the murder both girls had left Christchurch Girls High School – a fact which one former teacher stressed, as though to distance the school from any association with Juliet and Pauline.[46] Juliet had left because of her continued illness and her proposed departure from New Zealand on 3 July. Pauline had left for reasons which are less clear. Suggestions were made that she had fallen behind in her school work. The school record shows no indication of this.[47]

Pauline wrote in her diary on 14 March that 'Mother came out and said that I was not going back to school as she did not see why she should keep a horrid child like me . . .'[48] She claimed that 'The absolutely ironical part of it all is that I want to leave school terrifically but my pride would not let me ask.'[49]

Some days later Pauline recorded that:

'Mrs Hulme has put her foot in it. She has tried to talk me into going back to school. Apparently Stew [Miss Stewart, the headmistress] rang her as she was worried about my leaving. This is all very flattering but nevertheless a bloody nuisance.'[50]

A former teacher thought that Miss Stewart may have contacted Hilda Hulme as she was on the School Board. Pauline wrote on 10 April that her mother 'went to see Miss [Stewart] before tea'. It appears that the school was concerned that a bright student was leaving in her School Certificate year. However, the decision does not seem to have been seriously reconsidered and Pauline started a commercial course at Digby's Commercial School on 21 April.[51] Prior to this she had applied for jobs 'with the Airways' but was unsuccessful.

Although Pauline's contact with boys and 'sneaking out at night'[52] was one of the factors which created disharmony between her and Honora, it was her relationship with Juliet which came to be the main area of contention. In the beginning, both the Rieper and Hulme parents had welcomed the friendship between Pauline and Juliet.[53] By late 1953, the Riepers in particular had become very concerned about Pauline. According to one of the teachers, the school had contacted both the Riepers and the Hulmes sometime in 1953 regarding the 'unhealthy' relationship between the two girls and to say that the school 'didn't like their association'. The teacher said that Hilda Hulme replied that 'she wasn't prepared to interfere in her daughter's friendships . . .'[54]

In late 1953 at Honora's request, Henry Hulme called at the Rieper house to discuss with Herbert and Honora what could be done to 'break down' the relationship between Pauline and Juliet.[55] As a result, Honora, apparently concerned that Pauline was losing weight (though at seven stone she appears to have been average), took Pauline to Dr Bennett in December 1953. Bennett quizzed Pauline about her relationship with Juliet but she would not cooperate with him and told him nothing. Bennett informed Honora after this consultation that in his opinion the relationship was homosexual. He thought that Pauline would grow out of this.[56]

In April 1954, Herbert and Honora contacted Henry Hulme again about the relationship, and were pleased to learn of his plan to take Juliet with him when he left New Zealand on 3 July.[57] Despite this, Henry consulted Dr Bennett on 8 May 1954 about the relationship between Juliet and Pauline.

The decision that Juliet leave New Zealand, while apparently a solution to the problem as the parents saw it, precipitated a crisis for Pauline and Juliet.

The crisis occurred following a period of intense change and upheaval for Pauline. In the space of just a few months she had left school and started training at a secretarial college which she seemed to have generally found tedious; she was now facing separation not only from Juliet, but from the entire Hulme family and their idyllic home at Ilam, with which she had come to identify strongly. In addition, the Hulme family was breaking up, they were leaving Ilam to go their separate ways. The household was about to disintegrate. Henry's forced resignation meant that the family also had to leave Ilam, a university residence. It is clear from the diary that Pauline was shocked and upset by the idea that the Hulmes were divorcing. The entry for 23 April is very revealing, whether it is based on a real event or not, of how she perceived the situation. The following entry was read out in court, and parts of it disputed by Hilda Hulme. Pauline wrote:

'Friday 23 April 1954 . . . I played Tosca and wrote before ringing Deborah. Then she told me the stupendous news. Last night she woke at 2 o'clock and for some reason went into her Mother's room. It was empty so she went downstairs to look for her. Deborah could not find her so she crept as stealthily as she could into Mr Perry's flat and stole upstairs. She heard voices from inside his bedroom and she stayed outside for a little while, then she opened the door and switched the light on in one movement. Mr Perry and Mrs Hulme were in bed drinking tea. Deborah felt an hysterical tendency to giggle. She said "Hello" in a very [illegible] voice. She was shaking with emotion and shock although she had known what she would find. They goggled at her for a minute and her Mother said "I suppose you want an explanation." Yes, Deborah replied, I do. Well you see, we are in love, Mother explained. Deborah was wonderful. But I know THAT she exclaimed, her voice seemed to belong to someone else. Her Mother explained that Dr Hulme knew all about it and that they intended to live as a threesome. Anyway, Deborah went as far as telling about our desire to go to America in [illegible], six months, though she could not explain the reason of course. Mr Perry gave her 100 pounds to get permits. Everyone is being frightfully decent about everything and I feel wildly happy and rather queer . . . I am going out to Ilam tomorrow as we have so much to talk over.'[58]

The relationship between Hilda and Walter added another dimension to the complex situation at Ilam.

On the following day, 24 April, Pauline reported that:

'Deborah was still in bed when I arrived and did not get up until some time afterwards . . . Then Dr Hulme came upstairs and asked us to come into the lounge to have a talk with him. He said we must tell him everything about our going to America so we told him as much as that we wanted [illegible] for acting characters to act each part. He was both hope-giving and depressing. We talked for a long time and then Deborah and I were near tears by the time it was over. The outcome was somewhat vague. What is to be the future now. We may all be going to South Africa and Italy and dozens of other places or not at all. We none of us know where we are and a good deal depends on chance. Dr and Mrs Hulme are going to divorce. The shock is too great to have penetrated in my mind yet. It is so incredible. Poor Father. Mrs Hulme

was sweet and Dr Hulme absolutely kind and understanding . . .
Deborah and I spent the day soaring between hell and heaven . . . Such
a huge amount has happened that we do not know where we are. Dr
Hulme is the noblest and most wonderful person I have ever known of.
But one thing Deborah and I are sticking [to] through everything (We
sink or swim together).'[59]

It was two days after this entry, that 'removing Mother' was
mentioned for the first time in Pauline's diary. In February 1954
she had written about her mother:

'I also overheard her making insulting remarks about Mrs Hulme while
I was ringing this afternoon. I was livid. I am very glad because Hulmes
sympathise with me and it is nice to feel that adults realise what Mother
is. Dr Hulme is going to do something about it I think. Why could not
Mother die. Dozens of people are dying all the time, thousands, so why
not Mother and Father too. Life is very hard.'[60]

However, the main references to what she initially called
'removing mother', which later became 'the moider', occurred in
Pauline's diary from the 28-30 April 1954, with a gap until 20 June
1954, when over the last three days before the actual killing she
planned the crime. On 28 April Pauline wrote:

'Mother went out this afternoon so Deborah and I bathed for some time.
However I felt thoroughly depressed afterwards and even quite
seriously considered committing suicide. Life seemed so much not
worth the living, the death such an easy way out. Anger against Mother
boiled up inside me as it is she who is one of the main obstacles in my
path. Suddenly a means of ridding myself of this obstacle occurred to
me. If she were to die –.'

The next day, 29 April, she wrote:

'I did not tell Deborah of my plans for removing Mother. I have made
no [illegible] yet as the last fate I wish to meet is one in a Borstal. I am
trying to think of some way. I do not [illegible] to go to too much trouble
but I want it to appear either a natural or accidental death.'

On the 30 April, she reported 'I did not write this evening but
sat up and talked to Mother. I told Deborah of my intentions and
she is rather worried but does not disagree violently.' There were
no further references to murder until June.

Pauline wrote on 18 June: 'We planned our various moiders
and talked seriously as well.'

Then on 19 June she wrote:

'. . . our main idea for the day was to moider Mother. This notion is not a new one, but this time it is a definite plan which we intend to carry out. We have worked it out carefully and are both thrilled by the idea. Naturally we feel a trifle nervous, but the pleasure of anticipation is great. I shall not write the plan down here as I shall write it up when we carry it out (I hope). . .'

On 20 June she wrote:

'. . .I tidied the room and messed about a little. Afterwards we discussed our plans for moidering Mother and made them a little clearer. Peculiarly enough, I have no (qualms of) conscience (or is it peculiar, we are so mad.)'

The next day, on 21 June, she reported that:

'Deborah rang and we decided to use a rock in a stocking rather than a sandbag. We discussed the moider fully. I feel very keyed up as though I were planning a surprise party. Mother has fallen in with everything beautifully and the happy event is to take place tomorrow afternoon. So next time I write in this diary Mother will be dead. How odd yet how pleasing . . .'

The final entry on the following day, headed 'The Day of the Happy Event', 22 June, was written early in the morning. Pauline wrote, 'I am writing a little of this up on the morning before the death. I felt very excited and the night-before-Christmas-ish last night . . .'

The Rieper and Hulme families were interlocked by the relationship between Pauline and Juliet. Within each family there were many lies and many secrets – recent and longstanding – and the strain of this must have caused stresses, however subtle, not only for Pauline and Juliet, but for the adults involved in all these deceptions. Juliet and Pauline were not the only ones who were involved in relationships unsanctioned by the wider society.

The murder ruptured all of the relationships. Pauline and Juliet precipitated immediate change into what was already a disintegrating situation. They had wanted never to be separated, and in one sense the murder meant that Parker and Hulme became permanently linked. However, the reality was that they were permanently separated by the authorities and their relationship ended. Their relationships with other people changed irrevocably, as did the relationships between the members of both households.

CHAPTER FIVE

The Diaries

Pauline Parker's diaries were a central exhibit at the trial. They have been described as 'one of the strangest and most terrible exhibits in criminal history'.[1] They were produced as evidence at the trial for a number of reasons. The prosecution used them to show that the murder was clearly premeditated. The defence used them to demonstrate that Pauline and Juliet were insane. Many extracts were read aloud during the trial and these were sensationalised by the media. It was unusual to have such a detailed account, actually written by the accused, available as evidence.

There are two diaries – one for the whole of 1953, and one for 1954 up until 22 June, the day of the murder. The 1953 diary begins with a brief synopsis of important times during 1952 and includes a number of poems. The original diaries were transcribed for the defence and the prosecution. In transcript, the 1953 diary contains 120 pages, with entries completed for nearly every day. The partially completed 1954 diary contains fifty-two pages, again with almost daily entries.

As we were unable to locate the original diaries we have used quotations as they appear in the official transcripts. However, these contain a number of omissions (marked in the transcript) and errors – for example, the word 'Christmas-sy' instead of 'Christmas-ish' and 'ike' instead of 'idea'. We were able to identify these as errors by comparing the transcripts with newspaper photographs of pages from the original diary and by reading the Supreme Court trial transcripts, which record the discussion and correction during the trial of the misspelt word, 'idea'.

The contents of the diaries are a record of events and circumstances as Pauline Parker saw and interpreted them. While external events were more easily verified, events within the Rieper and Hulme households were more difficult, or impossible to confirm. Since the diary was a personal record, it is unlikely that it was intended to deceive others, even though it is possible that Pauline may have misinterpreted events or recorded inaccurately.

Juliet Hulme may also have kept a diary. Comments in

Pauline's diaries strongly suggest this. However, after the murder the police were unable to find any diary. There were rumours that her diary had been destroyed prior to her arrest, but these were never substantiated.[2]

Pauline's diaries show her as mature for her age and very literate – the spelling, grammar, and sentence construction are good and there are few errors. The choice of topics reflects the usual interests of an adolescent – school homework, books read and pictures seen, outings, popular songs on the radio Hit Parade, and so on.

Because of the murder entries, and because of the context in which they were read, the diaries became sensational texts even though most of their content is concerned with mundane activities. During the trial many entries were read out of context and given sensational interpretations. For example, an entry for 10 January 1953 which reads 'never before have I hit so many creatures so hard for so little reason' was interpreted as evidence of Parker's brutality. The entry refers to an incident during a summer holiday visit to a farm, when she was helping muster sheep. The phrase can be interpreted in a number of ways, including that Pauline was shocked by the unnecessary suffering of the sheep. Also the line itself is suggestive of the rhythm used in a famous speech by Winston Churchill. It is possible that Pauline had studied or heard this speech and was experimenting with form. She uses similar constructions elsewhere in her diary. She was very interested in creative writing, and from March 1953 she began including synopses of her stories in the diary. The use of actual phrases, or their form, taken from elsewhere occurs frequently and there is a good deal of language play. She also employed a number of expressions such as 'frightfully', 'ghastly', 'pleasingly' which show a marked English influence, perhaps from her mother or possibly from the Hulmes.

The defence psychiatrist considered Pauline insane and her diary entries were selected and interpreted from this perspective. However, different selections of entries give very different views of her. For example, the following entries show Pauline as a girl closely involved in the life at home with the boarders.

'. . . Mother says she is going to have Training College boarders . . .' (31 January 1953)

'. . . Harry arrived today. He seems quite nice and is about 35. He is very polite so far . . .' (9 February 1953)

'. . . I do hope Ross turns out to be nice. I have been looking forward to his coming so much that I will probably be disappointed . . .' (10 February 1953)

'. . . Mother was not well so I got up and prepared Harry's breakfast and had my own . . .' (13 February 1953)

'. . . Ron, the new boarder arrived. He is quite nice and about 25 . . .' (18 February 1953)

'. . . Ross was up late this morning. Out for dinner and by the time I got home so I have not seen him all day.' (20 February 1953)

'. . . This evening after tea we decided to go to the beach. Mother and Nana did the dishes. Ron came with us. Ross was out to tea so naturally he did not come. We went to Brighton. Ron, Wendy and I went for a swim. Mother bought some chocolate and biscuits which we had in the car on the way home . . . A Man called to buy Ross's motor-bike.' (22 February 1953)

'. . . Today many people came about board. We may be getting a Frenchman. I hope very much that we are . . .'(4 March 1953)

'. . . John helped me with my home work for about an hour. He says Damn a lot. I did a lot of homework . . .' (9 March 1953)

'. . . Ross and John were home for dinner, to which Juliet came . . .' (11 March 1953)

'During the morning a boy came to see Mother about board . . . he arranged to come for two months and he arrived to stay this evening. He is tall and slim with glasses and fair hair. He seems to regard me as the maid-help aged 10.' (12 January 1954)

Another selection of entries shows that Pauline did a great deal of housework – obviously necessary in a boarding house. She recorded many entries on this topic:

'This morning I got up at seven o'clock and did some washing before Nana came down for breakfast. I worked hard all morning and did some baking.' (5 January 1953)

'Mother kicked up a fuss about the way I always insist on doing the dishes and not letting anyone help. She says it worries her to think I'm working too hard.' (10 February 1953)

'I rose at about 9 this morning and spent until 2 working very hard helping Mother.' (1 January 1954)

'I rose at about 9 this morning, and worked hard about the house which was not unpleasant as it sounds as I truly enjoy housework.' (2 January 1954)

'I did a great deal of housework today as Mother and everyone else seemed to be dashing off to see the Queen all the time.' (19 January 1954)

'This morning Mother gave me the most fearsome lecture because I started to wash the kitchen floor in my house coat.' (25 January 1954)

'I rose at 5.30 this morning and did all the housework before 8 o'clock, including taking Wendy her breakfast in bed.' (11 April 1954)

'. . . Father came and told me that Mother was not well so I got up and prepared the breakfast. I did all the housework and had a row with Wendy this morning.' (13 April 1954)

The above entries are a small selection only from a considerable number which deal with the topic of housework. Even the examples given here present a very different picture of Pauline from that given in the courtroom – she seems willing to help and eager to please. Any number of strands could be selected from the diaries in this manner to show different sides of her personality – undoubtedly the case with anybody's diary.

Why did Pauline keep a diary? In her article 'The Diary as a Transitional Object in Female Adolescent Development', Deborah Anne Sosin notes that '. . . the teenage diary becomes a safe, private, all-accepting partner – a transitional object – which facilitates the passage into adulthood'[3] She says that this concept of the transitional object was first developed by D.W. Winnicott in 1953, and he 'used the term to describe those objects and activities which serve as "substitutes" for the mother or mothering functions.'[4]

Sosin comments that the adolescent diary has also been called a 'soothing psychic structure' equivalent to a teddy-bear or a loved blanket for a toddler; adolescents, rather than using toys, may use diaries'.

Sosin made a study of seven women aged eighteen to twenty-three who had kept a diary between the ages of twelve to eighteen, and her findings suggest that 'the diary is an adjunct to, not a substitute for, real object relationships'[5] '. . . [it] is an object the diarists sought when they felt besieged by confusing or intense emotions'[6] and cites P. Blos, who suggested in 1962 that 'living through experiences and emotions by putting them down in writing closes the door – at least partially and temporarily – to acting out.'[7]

One of Sosin's informants commented:

'I probably would be dead if I hadn't written things down because when I saw myself getting into trouble, writing it down really made me realize, "Whoa! You've really got to stop!" It was like a safety valve. I think I would have turned violent, and I had a mouth like a sewer.'[8]

Another subject said that she would often write directly in her diary after she had 'a fight with my mother. I would go to my room, burst into tears, and then begin to analyse it in my diary'.[9] A third informant explained that:

'When a girl starts writing a diary, she's discovering her own self and that discovery leads to the realization that, whether she knows it or not, she IS separating from her family for the first time. The minute you start writing things down, you've separated yourself! Because you're suddenly keeping something – something tangible – from your parents.'[10]

Yet another informant said that when she argued with her mother, she could 'tell myself things like, "Well, she's just going through menopause", or "She's trying to be sympathetic, but she doesn't understand my feelings." And then in the diary I would talk about how I felt about it. It was kind of like being my own mother in a way.'[11]

Sosin concludes that her pilot study suggests that 'the diary mirrors, soothes, helps inhibit frightening impulses, and helps integrate inner and outer realities. These functional aspects of the diary become internalized into the evolving psychic structure. . .'[12]

In Pauline's case, the 'frightening impulses' were not 'inhibited', and the 'accepting partner' of the diary did not 'close the door' to the 'acting out' of emotion. She did commit the murder of her mother which she had planned in the diary: it was acted out in reality. What seems incongruous, is the fact that she planned a murder in writing, leaving the diary unattended in the same house as her intended victim. During the trial Herbert was questioned whether other people might have tried to read the diary. He responded that no one would have done this since they thought it dishonourable to do so. In fact, she had experienced other people reading her diary without her permission. On 14 January 1953, while staying at a farm on holiday, Pauline reports that '[two men] put a note in my diary to say that they found it very interesting. I got a terrible fright when I read it.'[13]

A few days later, she had a similar experience at the farm. In her own home, although her immediate family may not have read her diary, there was still a risk that any of the boarders might do so. It is difficult to understand why she took the risk of writing down her plans. The question may be raised as to whether she hoped to be discovered and prevented from carrying out the plan. However, even after the murder she wrote an incriminating diary note at the police station. This was later used in evidence at the trial. At this stage it seems as though the diary process functioned either as a sounding board or as a way of letting others know about her ideas and feelings. We believe that the process was both these things at different times. Although Pauline uses the term 'moider' instead of 'murder' in her diary, she also uses the unequivocal word 'death'. This suggests to us that at times she may have been play acting and distancing herself, while at other times she was aware of what she was planning to do. She may not have fully appreciated what her plans would mean in reality.

The inclusion of the murder entries meant that diaries which originally functioned as personal records for Pauline entered the public domain. They became a central feature of the trial and of subsequent accounts of the case. The entries selected from them for the trial and for these accounts portray Pauline in a very limited manner, and give the impression that the diaries were filled with violence and murderous fantasies. This was certainly not the case. We have found the diaries complex in places (the entries discussing the Hulmes' proposed divorce), and dull and mundane in other parts, especially where Pauline lists outings, baths, housework etc. The diaries are probably quite typical of a teenage girl of the time. The murder entries were not a major part of the diaries.

CHAPTER SIX

The Trial

The Magistrates' Court hearing had been held from 14 July 1954 and had determined that there was a case to be answered in a higher court. The Supreme Court hearing was duly scheduled. We studied transcripts of the Supreme Court trial and interviewed some of the people directly involved at the time. We have selected for discussion aspects of the trial which in our view are of particular interest.

The Supreme Court trial began in Christchurch on Monday, 23 August 1954 and lasted until Saturday, 28 August 1954. The defence counsel for Parker and Hulme entered a plea of not guilty to the charge of murder, by reason of insanity.

Both local and foreign media interest in the case was immense. Not only were the circumstances of the case of great interest, but the particular defence presented for Juliet Hulme and Pauline Parker was unusual, in that *folie à deux* or joint insanity was to be argued. Reporters and photographers from foreign newspapers were sent to Christchurch to cover the case, while local newspapers carried full accounts of the proceedings. Each day, hundreds of spectators queued to obtain seats in the small courtroom. *NZ Truth* reported 'Whenever the girls entered or left the dock spectators in the gallery stood and craned their necks for a better view.'[1]

The prosecution was led by Allan Brown, an experienced criminal lawyer. Brown had joined a local legal firm in January 1920, becoming a partner in 1924. He had recently (February 1954) been appointed as the Crown Prosecutor in Christchurch, after working for many years with the previous Prosecutor. He had appeared in a number of notable trials, but the Parker-Hulme case was his first murder trial after his new appointment.[2]

Assisting Brown was Peter Thomas Mahon. Mahon, born and educated in Christchurch, had joined the firm where Brown was a partner in 1941. After service in the army during World War II, he returned to work in association with Brown and the previous Crown Prosecutor. He succeeded Brown as Crown Prosecutor in June 1957, when Brown resigned.[3] Mahon later had a long and distinguished career, becoming well-known as chairman of the

Left: *Crown Prosecutor, Allan Brown.* (Christchurch Star) Top: *Counsel for Hulme, T.A. Gresson.* Bottom: *Dr A.L. Haslam, Counsel for Parker.* (N.Z. Truth)

Commission of Inquiry which investigated the crash of an Air New Zealand passenger plane into Mt Erebus, Antarctica.

Hilda and Henry Hulme engaged Terence Arbuthnot Gresson to defend Juliet. Gresson was from a well-known South Island legal family, and had met Henry Hulme at Cambridge University. The two re-established contact after Hulme's arrival in New Zealand. On occasions, Gresson had been a guest of the Hulmes at Ilam. Highly regarded, Gresson became, in 1956, one of the youngest judges appointed in New Zealand.[4] He was found dead, an apparent suicide, of carbon monoxide poisoning in the garage of his Auckland home in 1966 while a senior judge in the Auckland Supreme Court.[5]

Brian McLelland assisted Gresson. Like Mahon, McLelland was born and educated in Christchurch, and had attended Canterbury College. Following war service he began practising in Christchurch, working for Gresson's firm, and later becoming a Queen's Counsel.

Pauline was defended by Alec Haslam, the Rieper family lawyer. A former Rhodes Scholar, he had his own law practice in Christchurch.[6] He was assisted by J.A. Wicks, who later became a judge.

The judge, Francis Boyd Adams, came from a family of well-known Dunedin lawyers. He had been appointed a judge of the Supreme Court in 1950.[7]

Proceedings began with the empanelling of an all-male jury. At that time, jury service was compulsory only for men (with some exceptions), while women had to apply for inclusion on the jury lists. The National Council of Women, which consisted of a wide range of women's organisations, campaigned for changes in the law so that women would serve on the same basis as men. As part of a boycott campaign they urged women not to put their names forward but to agitate for legal change instead. As a result, few women were available for selection and the local police who drew up the lists of prospective jurors typically nominated men.[8] Three jurors asked for exemption. The defence challenged nine jurors, while the prosecution challenged five. Once formed, the jury were kept together for the duration of the trial, staying at a nearby private hotel, supervised by two constables.

On the first day of the trial eleven reporters attended, including representatives of a number of foreign newspapers, and this level of interest was maintained throughout the trial.[9]

The Crown Prosecutor opened the prosecution case late in the morning of the first day of the trial. The adversarial nature of the New Zealand justice system meant that the debate between the defence and prosecution could be reduced to a simple dichotomy – in this case were the girls 'mad' or were they 'bad'? The girls' defence was that they were not guilty by reason of insanity. But, in the course of an hour-long address, Crown Prosecutor Brown contended that:

> '. . . this plainly was a callously planned and premeditated murder, committed by two highly intelligent and perfectly sane but precocious and dirty-minded girls.'[10]

The Crown alleged that Juliet and Pauline had planned to murder Honora Parker, had lured her to Victoria Park and then beaten her to death with a half brick in a stocking. The motive suggested by the Crown was that since Honora Parker had refused Pauline permission to leave New Zealand with Juliet, the girls regarded her as an obstacle in their path and murdered her so that they could remain together.

Most of the first two days of the trial were taken up with the case for the prosecution. Police and medical witnesses described the murder scene, and the condition of Honora Parker's body.

The manager of the Victoria Park tearooms, Agnes Ritchie, described the events immediately preceding the murder and the action she took afterwards. Most of her evidence was not disputed by the defence lawyers. Then Gresson questioned William Ramage, a constable and the official police photographer, suggesting that, given the condition of the body and its location away from any rocks, Parker and Hulme had chosen a very unsuitable place to stage an accident. However, Ramage also stated that the murder site was a very secluded spot. Gresson then questioned Kenneth Ritchie, caretaker of the park, who agreed that as soon as he saw Honora's body he knew that she could not have died simply as the result of an accident. Ritchie replied to Gresson's questions regarding Juliet's demeanour that she seemed 'excited' but not 'hysterical' when he saw her, shortly after the murder. Other than these questions by Gresson, there was no other cross questioning by either defence counsel at this point.

Brown also called as prosecution witnesses, Hilda Hulme, who appeared on subpoena, Herbert Rieper, and Walter Perry. These witnesses gave details of the respective family backgrounds of Parker and Hulme, including the development of their relationship, as well as the circumstances preceding the murder. Gresson cross-examined each of these witnesses, while Haslam questioned only Hilda Hulme and Herbert Rieper. Again, most of the evidence of these witnesses was not disputed and the questioning by the defence lawyers mainly drew out aspects of the respective personalities of Parker and Hulme, their relationship with each other, their home backgrounds and their illnesses.

Henry Hulme was not present for either the Magistrates' Court hearing, or the Supreme Court trial, having left the country as originally planned in early July, taking with him Juliet's brother Jonathon. The question may be asked as to why Henry Hulme did not give evidence either at the Magistrates' Court hearing in July or at the Supreme Court trial, given that he had been directly involved immediately after the murder. He had collected Pauline and Juliet from the tearooms just before the police arrived and had taken them, still in their blood-stained clothing, back to Ilam. Yet while Hilda was subpoenaed to appear, Henry was not. In our view, Henry was protected and conveniently allowed to remove himself from the scandalous situation. He abandoned his daughter and Hilda and took up his new job at Aldermaston. He was reported as saying 'The world will just have to think of me as an unnatural father.'[11] We believe it is unlikely that Hilda Hulme would have remained in the country for the trial had she not been subpoenaed by Allan Brown. We think that her separation from Henry and the fact that she was living with Walter Perry ensured that she was not allowed to leave the country. Her adultery meant that she forfeited her superior social status as the wife of Henry Hulme. As a result, unlike Henry, she was not exempted from the embarrassment of a court appearance. In any case, neither she nor Henry acted as good advocates for Juliet.

The defence case began in the afternoon of the second day of the trial. Defence strategy was restricted by the fact that both Pauline and Juliet, interviewed separately, had made full confessions to the murder of Honora Parker. Initially, both girls had given false statements to the police, with Pauline saying she had acted alone and Juliet denying any participation in the killing. The Hulmes and Herbert Rieper had permitted the girls to be questioned without a lawyer present, and Walter Perry, with both Hilda and Henry's consent, had advised Juliet that she should tell the truth.[12] The full confessions which the girls made, and the incriminating Parker diaries (even though they were accepted as evidence against Pauline alone), left few legal options. Neither family had engaged lawyers until after the confessions had been signed. Therefore, the only possible defence for both Parker and Hulme was that of insanity.

There were a number of problems associated with such a defence. The first concerned the rules applying to any defence of insanity. The New Zealand legal system followed the British example in cases where a defence of insanity was used. Section 43 of the Crimes Act defined the law relating to an insanity defence. This was based on the 'McNaghten rule', established in 1843. David McNaghten, a Scottish farmer who was convinced that Robert Peel, the British Prime Minister at the time, was persecuting him, killed Peel's secretary, believing that the victim was Peel. He was tried and found not guilty by reason of insanity. Subsequently the McNaghten rule was established, using this case as a precedent. The rule required that, for defendants to be found not guilty on the grounds of insanity, the defence had to show that the defendants did not know what they were doing, or, if they were aware, that they did not know it was wrong. More formally stated:

'At the time of the committing of the act, the party accused was labouring under such a defect of reason, from disease of the mind, as not to know the nature and quality of the act he was doing; or, if he did know it, that he did not know that he was doing what was wrong.'[13]

Therefore, the defence had to show that, because of mental disease, Parker and Hulme did not know 'the nature and quality' of their act of murdering Honora; or, if they did, that they did not know that the murder of Honora was 'wrong'.

Thus, a clear distinction was made between a legal definition of insanity, and a medical or psychiatric definition. This also highlighted another fundamental difficulty – the philosophical incompatability of the law and psychiatry. William Winslade and Judith Ross, in their 1983 discussion of the insanity plea, note:

'The law tells us that if we commit illegal acts, we must be punished. But the law assumes that we have freely chosen to perform these acts. Psychiatry does not make any such assumption about free will or choice.'[14]

The second major problem for the defence was that although the New Zealand legal system assumed all accused persons to be innocent until proved guilty, it also assumed them to be sane. The prosecution was required to prove the guilt of the accused person, but with a plea of insanity the burden of proof was on the defence to show that the defendant was insane. Therefore, Gresson and Haslam had to show that Parker and Hulme, who were being tried jointly, were both insane.[15]

Even though Parker and Hulme were represented separately, the respective defence lawyers had adopted a joint defence because the incriminating statements and evidence implicated both girls. With insanity as the only possible not guilty defence, the defence had to prove that both Juliet and Pauline were insane – and that they were insane at the same time.

It was in this context that the diagnosis of the major witness for the defence, Reginald Warren Medlicott, was fortuitous. He said that Parker and Hulme were suffering from 'paranoia' in a setting of *folie à deux*, which he claimed was a form of communicated and joint insanity where two sane people supposedly become insane in each other's company. He considered that there were similarities between the Parker-Hulme case and the case of Leopold and Loeb, two American youths who had jointly murdered a young boy in the 1920s. The defence, then, had a way out.

Gresson, acting for Juliet, began the defence case. In his opening address he stated:

> '. . . the Crown had seen fit to refer to the accused as ordinary, dirty-minded little girls, but the evidence for the defence would be that they were nothing of the kind, but were mentally sick and were more to be pitied than blamed. Their homosexuality was a symptom of their disease of the mind.'[16]

He then called Reginald Medlicott to give evidence. Medlicott, in his early thirties, was already a prominent psychiatrist. For the previous seven years, he had been superintendent of Ashburn Hall, a private psychiatric hospital near Dunedin. He was also a member of the Royal Australian College of Physicians, visiting psychiatric physician to Dunedin Hospital, lecturer in psychiatry at Otago University Medical School, and had held a Rockefeller Fellowship through which he had spent a year in the psychiatric department of a university hospital in Cleveland, Ohio. He had never before appeared in court to give psychiatric evidence.

Medlicott was commissioned by Gresson to give a psychiatric diagnosis of his client Juliet. Because of the joint defence strategy, this also involved an evaluation of Pauline. Medlicott interviewed Juliet and Pauline separately on the 27 and 28 June 1954, for two and a half and one and a half hours respectively, and on the 11 and 12 July for approximately two to three hours in total. At this stage both girls were in Paparua prison together. After the Magistrate's Court hearing on 14 July they were separated when Pauline was sent to Mount Eden prison in Auckland. On her return in mid-August, Medlicott interviewed them separately on 23 August, the evening before the Supreme Court trial. He also interviewed Herbert Rieper, Hilda Hulme, Francis Bennett, Pauline's sister Wendy and Pauline's grandmother Amy Parker.

He read Pauline's diaries, some of the fictional writings of both Juliet and Pauline, as well as some correspondence between them.
Medlicott presented his diagnosis:

'As a result of my investigation into the matter I consider they suffer from paranoia of an exalted type and that it is in the setting of a *folie à deux*. Paranoia is a form of systematized delusional insanity. It can be of various types, the usual type is the persecution type. In this instance I consider the paranoia from which these girls suffer is of the exalted type. *Folie à deux* . . . is used to describe communicated insanity. In arriving at my diagnosis I have had to consider the girls' family background and health. I have had to examine the history of their association here. As far as their general background is concerned, my evidence is that both were sensitive, self contained, imaginative, selfish and showed inability to tolerate criticism.'

He considered that their respective illnesses and consequent separation from their parents as young children may have had deleterious effects on them. In relation to Pauline and her osteomyelitis, he said:

'From what she said the illness was talked about . . . as to whether she would live or not and I think it is reasonable to assume that at least some children who have been through such experiences and have very frequently heard their parents referring to having nearly lost them – they develop a sense of being unusual and of having defied death.'

He stated that their relationship was a homosexual one, and claimed that:

'Before developing mature capacity to love a person of the opposite sex the adolescent frequently goes through a stage of forming passions for a member of its own sex – what everybody must term as adolescent pashes . . . There is evidence from the diaries that the relationship between the accused rapidly became a homosexual one. There was no proof at any time that it was a physical relationship . . . Homosexuality and paranoia are very frequently related.'

Later, under cross-examination by Brown, Medlicott conceded that the evidence from the diaries was 'strongly suggestive' of a physical aspect to their relationship.
Medlicott stated that he was firmly convinced that Juliet and Pauline were both insane:

'Their mood was the most striking abnormality. There was persistent exaltation and during my interviews they would sometimes swing into fury. Their mood was grossly incongruous. They exalted over their crime and showed no reasonable emotional appreciation of their situation . . . Each girl would have sudden spells of intenseness. They would, you might say, click into gear, talk so rapidly for a time as to be almost incoherent. They showed a conceit which was quite out of the world of normality . . . On the second visit of the second weekend that I saw them, they really could not be bothered giving up a walk in the sun to talk to me. There was also a very gross reversal of morals or of moral sex . . . they admired those things which were evil and condemned those things which the community considers good. It was obvious that the normal personalities [sic] defences against evil had almost completely gone. It became obvious when I started to discuss borderline religious and philosophic topics with them that they were harbouring weird delusional ideas . . . they said they had their own paradise, their own god and religion and their own morality.'

Medlicott attached particular importance to the diary entry written in April 1953, which he described as the 'Port Levy revelation'. Quoting from this entry, Medlicott commented:

'Parker there refers to a 4th world that she and Hulme have found the key to. She also refers to the extra part of their brain which permits them to appreciate the 4th world. It appears that only ten people have this . . . This 4th world has now become paradise to the girls and it is something they have discussed with me. Their notion seems to be that in some peculiar way they are outstanding geniuses with their own special paradise.'

Medlicott related to the Court in some detail conversations with Juliet and Pauline on these subjects.

Referring to a poem written by Pauline entitled 'The Ones I Worship', Medlicott said that 'the statements in this poem are quite fantastic'. Quoting diary entries for early March 1954, he drew attention to Juliet and Pauline building 'some form of Temple of Minerva' in the garden at Ilam. In his first interview with Juliet Hulme, he related, she had said that they had their own religion, that 'their god was not a Christian one, and that the main difference was that all people in their religion were not equal'.

Medlicott's contention was that the girls' madness was in inverse proportion to the time they spent together, and that this could be seen, for example, in the increase in bloodshed and violence in the fictional writings that Pauline did at these times. He quoted extensively from the 1953 and 1954 diaries to support this contention:

'From the medical viewpoint, the period May and June 1954 . . . the whole thing rises to quite fantastic crescendos . . . As the diary goes on evil becomes more and more important and one gets the feeling they ultimately become helplessly under its sway.'

Medlicott said he had no doubts about their insanity, although he stated that they had tried to prove themselves insane to him during the interviews:

'When I first saw the two girls I knew that they were trying to prove themselves insane . . . After however a very short time with them I myself was convinced that they were definitely insane. The two were so alike, not simply in what they told me, but in their mood and reaction.'

Medlicott also stated that '. . . they still thought until Juliet finally confessed that Parker would be declared insane and that the Hulmes would be able to take responsibility for her and take her with them out of the country.'

He did not explain when Juliet and Pauline could have discussed this, since they had no contact with each other after Pauline was arrested and before Juliet had signed a confession. It is more likely that they were simply trying to mislead Medlicott and impede his diagnosis. Nevertheless he concluded:

'In my opinion Parker and Hulme were insane at the time they attacked Mrs Rieper . . . If I were asked today if I considered Parker and Hulme certifiably insane I would answer yes. I myself would have not the slightest hesitation in certifying them.'

Brown's cross-examination of Medlicott began with his eliciting an acknowledgement from Medlicott of his lesser experience in medico-legal matters compared to that of the prosecution psychiatric witnesses who were yet to give evidence. The detailed cross-examination which followed challenged each of the main contentions made by Medlicott, and his interpretations of many diary entries. Brown's questioning was directed towards showing that Parker and Hulme knew that murdering Honora was wrong, and that they knew what they were doing when they killed her. To this end, the evidence showing that they had planned the murder was highlighted by Brown. He also spent a considerable amount of the cross-examination on Pauline's heterosexual experiences and clandestine behaviour in order to demonstrate her criminality, in contrast to her supposed insanity.

The next witness was Francis Oswald Bennett, a registered medical practitioner from Christchurch whose family had settled in Canterbury in the 1860s. He began private practice in Christchurch in 1934. In 1935 he became an honorary part-time staff member of Christchurch Hospital, later becoming an anaesthetist and an assistant physician (both honorary appointments). Like Medlicott, he was a Fellow of the Royal Australian College of Physicians.[17] He had known the Hulmes for a number of years and had worked with Hilda in the Christchurch Marriage Guidance Council.[18]

Called by Haslam for Pauline's defence, Bennett was a general practitioner, not a psychiatrist, although he had experience with 'psychiatric cases' in private and hospital practice as well as in the army during World War II. He had examined Pauline in Honora's presence in December 1953 and had been consulted by Henry Hulme also. He was consulted again by Henry on 8 May 1954 regarding the relationship between Juliet and Pauline, which Hulme considered 'unhealthy'. He next saw Pauline at the police station on 24 June. He also saw Juliet on that date, interviewing them separately, each for approximately three-quarters of an hour. He saw each of them again one more time – Juliet on the 6 August 1954, and Pauline on the 14 August 1954, after they had been separated. He also interviewed Herbert and Wendy Rieper and read Pauline's diaries and other writing. He stated:

'I have formed the conclusion that their recent activities can be explained only on the basis of mutual insanity . . . The general pattern of their behaviour is so grossly abnormal that they are automatically removed from the category of the sane. Regarding the nature of insanity I agree with Dr Medlicott that they are suffering from paranoia. In this condition . . . the patient suffers from delusions, one or more, but apart from these they are apparently, I stress apparently, capable of clear and logical reasoning . . . All other considerations take second place as the patient is driven on by the relentless compulsion of a delusion. If in this process the patient has to make a choice between observing the moral values of the community or abandoning the delusion they reject the moral values. They have to. They follow the delusion wherever it leads. They therefore become amoral, anti-social, and in any community dangerous. The particular delusion of these two is their delusion that they are specially gifted, that they are mentally brilliant, that they are superior to the general run of mankind . . . They formed a society of their own in which every act thought deed was approved and admitted by the other. They lived in a world of elation and ecstasy.'

Bennett, like Medlicott, quoted extensively from the diaries. However, he considered that these extracts did not give the picture that a complete reading of the diaries would:

'. . . of how they spend all the time they possibly could at Ilam endlessly discussing the saints and the plots of their books, bathing and bedding together; photographing each other in fancy borrowed dresses and in the nude; talking all night; dressing up; getting up at night, going out on the lawn and acting; ignoring other people; making a little cemetery in the grounds that they later extended into what they called the temple of Raphael Pan where they buried a dead mouse and put up a cross over it, and later put up a number of other crosses to represent the burial of dead ideas which they had once had and since discarded. They had no friends of their own age; they never went to dances with one exception in the case of one; they never read the newspapers; Pauline records how she hated school; she hated Digby's College; she said the girls at her place of work were fools. She went to the swimming sports and wrote a novel all through the events.'

An even more damning indictment in Bennett's view was that 'During the Queen's visit they made no attempt to see the Queen or the decorations.' Further, he related how Juliet had commented on the bible:

'. . . [S]he also expressed the view that the bible was bunkum. That is her actual word . . . They claim that Pauline had broken the ten [commandments] and Juliet had broken only 9.'

To illustrate his view that they had 'contempt for the moral code', Bennett quoted a diary entry describing how Juliet and Pauline had cheated when playing a board game with Juliet's brother. He then concluded:

'To us sane I hope, it was a murder that was bestial and treacherous and filthy. It is outside all the kindly limits of sanity. It is a thousand miles away from sanity. They are still not sane and in my opinion they never will be sane . . . In my opinion they are both *folie à deux* homosexual paranoics of the elated type.'

Brown's cross-questioning of Bennett followed a similar pattern to his cross-examination of Medlicott, including comparing Bennett's experience to that of the Crown medical witnesses. Before Bennett stood down as witness, Justice Adams asked him whether he considered that Parker and Hulme knew the nature and quality of their action in murdering Honora:

'Then may your view on these points be summarised in these words that in your opinion they knew the act was contrary to the ordinary moral standards of the community but nevertheless it was not contrary to their own moral standards?'

Bennett replied, 'Yes. You have completely summarised it.' This response was damaging for Pauline and Juliet's defence as it completely undermined the insanity argument.

Before the prosecution presented the case in rebuttal, Mr Justice Adams called the defence and prosecution into his rooms and informed them that in his opinion the defence case had not been established satisfactorily. He said that he was considering instructing the jury that no defence had been presented and that the prosecution had no case to answer. He told them that in his opinion the evidence that had been given was not sufficient to raise even a possibility of insanity. The two assistants, Mahon for the prosecution and Brian McLelland for the defence, searched the Law Library for precedents. They found only one legal precedent of two insane persons combining to commit a crime. Mahon told the judge on behalf of the Crown that he could not support the idea that the defence would be ruled insufficient by the judge. Mahon had a strong sense of justice and fair play and considered it unthinkable that the defence case should be dismissed at that stage. Although he was the prosecution assistant, he cooperated with defence counsel to ensure that the case continued. Adams, then, allowed the trial to continue.[19]

On the Friday morning, the Crown presented its case in rebuttal. This consisted of the evidence of three psychiatrists, each of whom had interviewed Parker and Hulme and had read their fictional works as well as Pauline's diaries.

The first Crown medical witness was Kenneth Robin Stallworthy, Senior Medical Adviser of Avondale Mental Hospital, Auckland. Stallworthy had fifteen years' experience working in psychiatric hospitals in New Zealand and in England. He held Bachelor degrees in Medicine and Surgery and a Diploma of Psychological Medicine (England).

Stallworthy interviewed Pauline on six different occasions and Juliet on four occasions over a period from 26 July to 19 August 1954. His firm opinion was that Parker and Hulme were sane:

'Generally, the factors that made me think the accused knew what they were doing were: the evidence in the diary that there had been written down what they intended to do; the evidence that they were able to give an accurate account of what did happen; and their own separate and repeated and clear accounts of what did take place. Under those circumstances it was impossible to arrive at any conclusion but that they well knew the nature and quality of their act.'

He considered that Parker and Hulme did not exhibit the same type of behaviour as others who had been termed paranoic and firmly disagreed with the contention of the defence that homosexuality and paranoia were closely related:

'I do not know of any actively practising homosexual who has developed paranoia. The kind of homosexuality that is related to paranoia is the kind which the individual because of his background and upbringing is unable to accept within himself . . . It is repressed homosexuality that is related to paranoia and I think in this case there was nothing repressed about the homosexuality.'

He considered that their relationship was homosexual and physical, but that it was a 'stage' which many adolescents go through and 'grow out of' and that in their case the homosexual aspect of their relationship had been 'over-stressed'.

Stallworthy did not agree with the emphasis the defence placed on the so-called 'Port Levy revelation', pointing out that:

'I have some experience of adolescents' diaries. I would say that adolescence is commonly a very conceited age and that very often in the diaries of adolescents there are to be found recorded the most conceited opinions without the adolescent concerned having any firm and fixed belief in what had been written.'

In fact, he thought that both girls had some justification to be conceited, finding them articulate and capable of answering difficult questions with some shrewdness. He did not consider that they were 'extraordinarily exalted', at the same time, finding their lack of overt remorse for the murder not unusual:

'. . . I have seen murderers in whom no question of insanity was ever raised who showed the same apparent coldness and callousness in regard to the situation as has been commented upon in this case.'

He also thought that their ideas about god and religion, their lying, their shoplifting as well as their clandestine activities were not in themselves evidence of insanity.

Gresson's cross-examination of Stallworthy raised the question that medical opinion, even between respected and competent psychiatrists, could differ and that paranoia could be extremely difficult to diagnose. He pointed out that Stallworthy had not interviewed Parker and Hulme until over a month after the murder. Stallworthy replied that he did not think that this had limited his diagnosis in this case.

The final two witnesses were James Edwin Savill, medical officer at Sunnyside Hospital, Christchurch, and James Dewar Hunter, superintendent of Sunnyside Hospital. Savill held Bachelor of Medicine and Surgery degrees as well as a Diploma of Psychological Medicine (London). After working in general practice, in 1937 he began work in mental institutions in England. He came to Sunnyside Hospital in 1946 after eight years as a medical officer in the prisons service in England and Wales. Hunter had qualifications similar to those of Stallworthy and Savill, and had been employed by the Department of Mental Hygiene in New Zealand for the previous twenty-nine years, excluding two years spent as a medical officer in Scotland.

Savill had interviewed Pauline and Juliet separately on 24 June and on 12 and 26 July. On 26 July, and 13 and 20 August, he interviewed them again (still separately), this time accompanied by Hunter.

Hunter interviewed them separately on 29 June, and on 14 and 26 July. He also interviewed Juliet on 2 August, after Pauline had been sent to Mount Eden.

Neither considered that Parker and Hulme were insane. Haslam questioned Hunter, noting that medical opinion could differ on such matters.

This completed the evidence, leaving only the final arguments of defence and prosecution, and the Judge's summing up. Justice Adams then decided to continue the trial on the following day, which was a Saturday. This was not usual, but it appears that he did not want the case dragging on into the next week. An important Ranfurly Shield rugby match was being played in Christchurch on that afternoon. This led some observers to speculate whether the jury may have made their decision hastily so that they could attend the match.[20] We think this is unlikely since the case for the defence had been legally weak.

The prosecution and defence gave their final addresses, followed by Justice Adams summing up. He pointed out to the

Jury that both medical witnesses for the defence had agreed the girls knew that what they did had been wrong in the eyes of the law. He instructed them that in accordance with the law:

'You really have no option but to hold the accused guilty of murder on the ground that the defence of insanity of the required nature and degree has not been proved.'

The Jury had little alternative but to find Parker and Hulme guilty. At 12.10 pm the jury retired to rooms beside the Court to consider the verdict. They returned to the courtroom at 2.53 pm and announced a verdict of guilty.

According to a report in the *People's Voice*, a member of the jury said that the jury believed that Parker and Hulme were insane but had found them guilty anyway, because:

'they would not serve long in prison, whereas if they brought in an insanity verdict the girls would be locked up for life in a mental hospital.'[21]

However, it was also rumoured that most of the jury were certain that Parker and Hulme were sane and should be punished.[22]

Some newspaper reports stated that Pauline and Juliet seemed unconcerned about the verdict and that they preserved the 'same calm and a demeanour of almost indifference which had been characteristic of them throughout the trial.'[23]

Justice Adams then formally raised the matter of the ages of the girls, as under the Capital Punishment Act 1950 this was significant. The defence counsel submitted that there had already been evidence of their ages. However, Justice Adams put the question to the jury to decide. The foreman said that the jury were all satisfied that the pair were under the age of eighteen. The judge then formally stated:

'You both being held to be under the age of eighteen, the sentence of the Court is detention during Her Majesty's pleasure. That sentence is passed on each of you.'

In 1950 a National government had reintroduced the death penalty for murder, after it had been abolished by a Labour government in 1941. Section 5 of the Capital Punishment Act 1950 specified that offenders under the age of eighteen years were not to be hanged, but detained 'during Her Majesty's pleasure'. This meant that they would be detained at the discretion of the Minister of Justice who could decide when they might be released. However, the licence for release could contain any conditions that the Minister of Justice wished to place on it and could at any time be revoked or varied. If the Minister revoked a licence, then the person to whom the licence related was to return 'to such place as the Minister of Justice may direct'. Failure to do so would result in arrest.

Hulme and Parker were the first persons to be found guilty and sentenced under this part of the Act.

After being sentenced they were taken immediately to the covered prison van which had been backed right up to the door leading to the Court cells. This had been done throughout the six-day trial to prevent the gathered crowds from seeing the prisoners. They were both kept in Paparua Prison until Juliet was transferred to Mount Eden Prison, less than a week later.

In the following weeks it was rumoured that the lawyers for Juliet Hulme had considered an appeal against the sentence. It appeared, however, that the Hulmes did not wish to pursue this any further.[24] Herbert Rieper could not have afforded an appeal even if he had wanted one. It took him some years to pay the legal fees even though these were reduced when the lawyers realised the difficulties he had paying for the defence.[25]

Following the trial, the people associated with the case received large amounts of mail, some from other countries. Much of it was bizarre. McLelland, for example, received a woman's complete black outfit, including an evening gown, and an abusive note addressed to Hilda Hulme.[26] There were also letters which were either antagonistic to Juliet and Pauline or offered to rehabilitate them.

We think that it was easier for observers to objectify Juliet and Pauline because they were not called to give evidence at the trial. A local Christchurch psychiatrist, M. Bevan-Brown, commented later that '[t]he girls who were the central figures seemed to be treated as robots or dummies.'[27] Therefore it was easier for commentators to describe them as evil, callous, and monstrous. They were not called because the defence lawyers thought that they would have antagonised the jury and prejudiced their own case. Although a legal strategy, this silence illustrated the boundaries of debate so that it was largely the voices of the

The Judge, Mr Justice Adams. (Christchurch Star)

representatives of the dominant culture, for example, psychiatrists and lawyers, which were the ones heard and recorded. Although the defence lost the case and narrowly avoided having their case dismissed by the judge, Medlicott's views, echoed by Bennett, were repeated through the years (see Chapter 8).

This trial was one of the most sensational that has occurred in New Zealand. At that time when murders were comparatively few, murder trials received considerable publicity. From 1920 to 1966, 105 people were convicted of murder in New Zealand.[28] Only nine of these were women. However, this trial, not only because of the gender of Juliet and Pauline but their circumstances and ages as well, generated more publicity than was usual even in the 1950s. The trial reports in the media were avidly followed by many people in New Zealand and in other countries (see Chapter 8).

CHAPTER SEVEN

The Punishment

We have based this chapter largely on the Department of Justice prison inmate files for Juliet Hulme and Pauline Parker. We requested these under the Official Information Act 1982 and were given access to the files on condition that we took notes but did not photocopy departmental documents, other than the judge's summing up and the coroner's report; that we did not directly quote or reference specific reports by institutional or specialist personnel; that our final text was not to include the names of any departmental staff or other prison inmates; and that any material drawn from the inmate files would be seen and approved by departmental staff in draft form prior to any publication or presentation.

It was clear to us from our reading of the files that the conviction of Juliet Hulme and Pauline Parker on 28 August 1954, had posed what Samuel Thompson Barnett the Secretary for Justice described as 'the most complex and difficult custodial problem the penal administration has yet faced.'[1]

First, the Department had to decide where to imprison the girls. The second problem was what to do with them during their imprisonment.

The Department, with the agreement of Thomas Clifton Webb the Minister of Justice, decided that Parker and Hulme should be in separate institutions. There was concern about them being in the same institution. The Department acted as if the legally rejected *folie à deux* defence argument had some substance, though the girls received no psychiatric treatment. We are sure that the Department also wanted to ensure that their lesbian relationship did not continue. There was no question about it: the girls were to be separated immediately and to be kept apart, certainly while they were in custody. In fact, the Department went further and arranged for Juliet to leave the country before Pauline was released so that there was no chance that the two would meet.

However, there were only three prison facilities which catered for women. Paparua, outside Christchurch, was unsuitable as it had neither the staff nor the facilities for high-security prisoners.

Arohata, near Wellington, was a borstal for minimum security
female prisoners. At the time of Pauline and Juliet's conviction a
new high security block was still under construction. Auckland
Prison, or Mount Eden as it was commonly known, was a
maximum security prison holding both male and female
prisoners.

The Department was reluctant to put either Juliet or Pauline in
Mount Eden. However, it could not use Paparua on a long-term
basis and it could not place both of them in Arohata at the same
time. The Secretary for Justice concluded that 'Hulme is the more
dominant personality and the leader of the two. She is likely to
present the greater custodial problem.'[2] He recommended that
Juliet be placed in the more secure Mount Eden, providing
medical tests showed that her tubercular condition was inactive.
Medical tests subsequently confirmed that there was no present
risk. Pauline, meanwhile, was to remain in Paparua until building
was completed at Arohata. The Secretary for Justice stated
'Obviously they should be treated equally and my present mind is
that they should each have an experience of Mount Eden.' The
Minister of Justice harshly expressing similar sentiments in
public, vowed that both girls were to have 'a taste of Mount Eden.'[3]
This provoked some protest and the Howard League for Penal
Reform condemned the Minister's statements.[4] Ian Hamilton,
writing in October 1954, questioned the value of punishment as a
deterrent:

> 'A deterrent? The magistrates are always using the word. By subjecting
> these two girls to the hell of boredom and uncreativeness in the Mount,
> we're going to stop other adolescents forming abortive love
> relationships that end in murder. Boy meets girl has always been suspect
> outside the picture theatres. From now on, if girl meets girl she'll have
> to be careful.'[5]

On the Friday following the verdict, Juliet was taken by an Air
Force plane to Whenuapai, Auckland, where she was met by
Superintendent Haywood and taken to Mount Eden prison.

Mount Eden had been built in the 1880s with prison labour and
was intended to be an exact replica of Pentridge Gaol, England.
The *NZ Truth* described the prison as 'a disheartening symbol of
the past with its massive walls, its castellations, watch towers and
ugly colonial gothic architecture'.[6] It also described the

conditions that Juliet Hulme would have experienced during her first months in Mount Eden. The paper said that she was put in a stone-walled cell, approximately two and a half metres long by two metres wide with walls four metres high and a small barred window at the top, too high to see out. It described the contents of the cell as an iron bedstead, a straw mattress, six blankets, a pillow, a stool and a small cabinet. The floor was concrete with one small mat and no heating or central plumbing.[7]

Donald MacKenzie, the first prison psychologist employed by the Department of Justice, was at Mount Eden during the 1950s. In 1954 the average daily male prison population in Mount Eden was about 150 long-term and 130 short-term prisoners.[8] The average daily female population for that year was twenty-eight.[9] MacKenzie points out that there were approximately one hundred prison staff – ninety men and ten women – whose tasks at that time were mainly custodial.[10] He says that the staff monitored three of the four wings of the prison from a central point known as the 'Dome', and describes the smell from this point as acrid: 'urine, sweat, carbolic soap, and other smells mingled and produced a stomach-turning stench as the poor ventilation and humidity percolated the output from over three hundred prisoners. Showers were restricted to one per week.'[11]

MacKenzie says that there were three toilets in the enclosed exercise pen and that the middle one had a painted notice reading 'VD only'.[12] He says that self-esteem among the women prisoners was low, and that:

'the low self-image was accentuated by primitive provisions for menstrual hygiene – sanitary towels were not provided and women had to make do with rags which after use had to be washed and used again.'

He reports that in these degrading conditions some women resorted to wrist-slashing, swallowing pins, spoons and glass, or personal neglect as protests against their conditions.[13]

Juliet would have been aware of and may even have heard the five hangings which took place at the prison while she was there. MacKenzie says that the hangings generally took place in the evenings at seven pm. The wire-mesh-covered yard containing the scaffold was covered with tarpaulins for the event so that spectators on nearby rooftops or planes could not see. 'Flapping tarpaulin was thus a normal accompaniment to the macabre scene below.'[14] Men held in the punishment block took their daily exercise round the base of the scaffold, or 'Meccano Set' as one official dubbed it.[15] From the east wing of the prison, the outline of the scaffold was visible to all prisoners who could also hear the footsteps of the condemned prisoner and the accompanying officials on the walk to the execution. The 'loud metallic clang of the gallows' trapdoors ringing out through the wings as they struck the scaffold supports' was a signal to the whole inmate population that the condemned man 'was at that moment twitching in his death throes'.[16]

Pauline remained in Paparua until the new security section at Arohata was completed and she became one of its first inmates. The surroundings and conditions were more pleasant and modern than those in Mount Eden. The security wing, where she was imprisoned, was closed off from the remainder of the institution. As it was intended for 'difficult' prisoners, it had its own exercise yard which was completely screened. This yard ran down one side and one end of the building and was fully enclosed by heavy hurricane wire netting. Pauline's cell at Arohata was a wooden sound-proof room, about two by three metres with 'a normal-sized window' covered by strong meshed wire. A grating in the ceiling covered the light bulbs, and the wooden bedstead, table and stool were all fixed to the wall.[17]

Arohata was intended for women and girls from throughout the country sentenced for borstal training, and 'other young offenders of a type who are not yet widely experienced in crime, and who with individual treatment, might be expected to reform'.[18] The Department of Justice, in general, found women prisoners a problem. Whereas the Department considered Pauline and Juliet the most difficult *custodial* problem, it regarded the inmates of Arohata as the most difficult *penal* problem in New Zealand. This was because the Department considered the women 'moral problems'.[19]

Having decided where to place Pauline and Juliet, the next difficulty facing the Department was what Juliet and Pauline should do in prison. They were not typical female prisoners. At that time there were approximately thirty women in each institution. Among the prisoners in Mount Eden were three other women serving sentences for murder – all considerably older than Juliet. In Arohata, the prisoners tended to be young. Most of the prisoners were 'ship girls' – women arrested on suspicion of being aboard ships for sexual purposes. Many were Maori and almost all were older than Pauline. Most had little secondary education.[20] Work for women in both institutions usually consisted of gardening, sewing and garment-making for the prison service and mental hospital service, or laundry work.[21]

To the public, the Department insisted that Juliet and Pauline were to be treated in the same way as any other long-term prisoners:

> 'They will wear the ordinary prison clothes, eat the ordinary prison food, do the ordinary prison tasks set long-sentence women prisoners and be subject to the ordinary prison discipline.'[22]

However, despite the official pronouncements, Juliet and Pauline were not treated just like any other long-term prisoners and the Department, from the Minister of Justice to the local prison staff, took a special interest in them. The Secretary for Justice, Sam Barnett, took a direct and personal interest in them.[23] Responsible for remodelling the New Zealand penal system during the 1950s, Barnett adopted a 'hands-on' approach to prisons – possible in the smaller prison system of the time. However, it was still unusual for the Secretary to concern himself with an individual prisoner's correspondence and visitors, as he did with Parker and Hulme. Regular reports about their progress were sent directly to him.

Superintendent Haywood at Mount Eden, also, gave special attention to Juliet Hulme. He and his wife are reported to have taken Juliet to their home for weekends.[24] MacKenzie pointed out that:

> 'Those who came from "good" or "middle-class" families were the rare exception, and in subtle ways they were deferred to. Their cases violated the accepted theories that good behaviour stems from a "good" upbringing and bad behaviour from an unfortunate background. They were therefore likely to receive more official attention, less of the usual run-around and more deference because of social status, education or wealth.'[25]

Referring to Juliet Hulme he commented 'One of these, a young female murderer, received very special attention by departmental order.'[26]

While their ages and gender were significant factors,

undoubtedly the social prominence of Juliet Hulme's family meant that both she and Pauline were given special treatment during their imprisonment. The Department was also very conscious of the widespread public interest in Parker and Hulme and certainly wanted to demonstrate that it had successfully rehabilitated them. The Department at that time was attempting to place more emphasis on reform rather than punishment, in line with more liberal views about the purpose of prisons.[27]

Prison staff who dealt with Pauline and Juliet on a daily basis closely monitored each of them. Weekly reports about Juliet and Pauline were sent to the Secretary for Justice from both Mount Eden and Arohata. These eventually became three-monthly, and later, half-yearly reports. A close interest was taken in their education, with information about their progress being sent to the Secretary. Both were allowed to study and write. By December 1954, Pauline had enrolled for correspondence courses in English, French, Latin, Mathematics, Drawing and Design, and later Maori. Juliet studied English, Mathematics, and Italian. Both girls passed School Certificate and University Entrance and by the time of her release Pauline had partially completed a university degree. Outside tutors, including university professors, were permitted to personally coach the girls from time to time. The university professors were colleagues and friends of the Hulme family – for example, Professor Maidment of Auckland University College.

For the first three months of their imprisonment, both were kept segregated from other prisoners. It was claimed that Pauline had unsuccessfully attempted to smuggle a letter to Juliet.[28] Pauline was reported as 'trying desperately to find out what has happened to Hulme'.[29] During this period the Department took a strict attitude towards Parker and Hulme. One person we interviewed complained that Juliet's requests for simple articles such as knitting wool and a radio had been denied during this period.[30]

It seems to us that the Department wanted to both punish and to rehabilitate Juliet and Pauline. It took a strongly paternalistic and protective attitude towards them from the beginning, which involved not only isolating them but also screening and monitoring all letters and visitors. This was apparently done to protect them from negative outside influences – as interpreted by the Department. At the beginning, the Secretary for Justice himself monitored all requests to either write to, or visit, the prisoners. One newspaper noted that:

> 'Each week from all over New Zealand and Australia and even from abroad, scores of people, principally religious cranks, plain stickybeaks, and sometimes the sexually abnormal, write to the girls. The prison authorities read all the letters and return them to the senders.'[31]

Many requests to visit the girls were received by the Department. Most were refused. For example, evangelists from the Moral Re-Armament organisation were barred from either visiting Parker or Hulme, or from sending them religious magazines. Each girl, though, had regular visits from a number of approved visitors. Approval to write or visit was generally given to people who had had some personal contact with Juliet and Pauline, such as family friends or teachers. In some instances, approval had to be obtained for each visit. Approval for the visit had to be first obtained from the Secretary for Justice who would advise whether the application was successful. Permission obtained, the applicant then arranged a date and time with the prison Superintendent. In 1955 one approved correspondent (claiming to be a friend of the Hulme family) complained to the Secretary that Juliet was not replying to her letters. The Department had held back a letter to Juliet in which this same correspondent made veiled threats as to the consequences if Juliet did not reply. The Department asked Juliet herself to write to this person discontinuing the correspondence, which she did. While Pauline and Juliet had reasonable freedom to write letters to family and friends, they were never allowed to correspond with or to meet each other.[32]

At first, Juliet and Pauline had no personal contact with their families except by letter. Herbert Rieper first visited Pauline about one year after the sentencing. He found this visit depressing and his reluctance to see her is understandable given the circumstances. Later, when she was transferred to Paparua prison in Christchurch she had more contact with her family.[33] This was not the case after her release.

The Hulmes did not visit Juliet at all during her imprisonment. Hilda Hulme left the country with Walter Perry soon after the Supreme Court trial, telling journalists who interviewed her in

Sydney that Juliet was mad and that nothing could be done for her. Henry was already in England by then. Neither Henry or Hilda returned to New Zealand during Juliet's imprisonment and their correspondence with her was infrequent.[34]

Despite the original plan that Pauline and Juliet would both serve part of their sentences in Mount Eden, this was never done. The Department decided that this would be disruptive for both of them. Instead, Juliet remained in Mount Eden and Pauline in Arohata until 1958 when, in preparation for their release, the Department moved Pauline to Paparua Prison and Juliet to Arohata. Both came to be regarded as model and co-operative prisoners.[35]

Through 1958 and 1959, prison and Departmental officials were concerned about adequately preparing the girls for life outside prison. They feared that the pair, particularly Juliet, because of her experience in Mount Eden, were in danger of becoming institutionalised. The parole board which considered the question of their release decided that five years imprisonment during their adolescence, and being separated from one another was enough punishment and that they should be rehabilitated into society. The Minister, then, decided to release Juliet and Pauline on recommendations from the Secretary and his department. This decision drew some criticism. Some saw it as humane while others protested at Juliet and Pauline's release, with one correspondent wondering 'what value does Executive Council place on the sanctity of human life.'[36]

Juliet was released first, in November 1959. She was provided with an escort employed by the Department to help her make arrangements to leave the country, and to assume a new identity. She left within a few days of her release and joined her mother, who was by then married to Walter Perry. After Juliet had left the country, Pauline was released in late November 1959. The Department helped her to assume a new identity and found her accommodation and employment. She was released on probation, which meant that she was required to report to Justice Department officials on a regular basis and to comply with any directives given her by the Department. If she failed to meet Department requirements, she could have been recalled to prison to resume her sentence in custody. She remained on probation until 1965 when she was finally discharged. Immediately afterwards she left the country.

These arrangements for the release of Juliet and Pauline contrasted sharply with usual procedures. The Department took great pains to preserve their privacy and to protect them from the media, continuing the paternalistic interest shown from the beginning.[37]

Pauline and Juliet may have been fortunate in that they were found guilty and sent into the prison system, rather than into the mental health system. Writer Janet Frame describes the use of electro-convulsive therapy at this time and also discusses the fact that she herself narrowly avoided receiving a pre-frontal lobotomy.[38] In *Good and Mad Women*, historian Jill Matthews describes the lives of a number of long-term women mental patients in Australia and suggests that release was difficult once women had entered the psychiatric system.[39] Parker and Hulme would have been regarded as patients suffering from a mental disease and given medical treatment which would certainly have included treatment of their lesbianism. The Department of Justice, however, did not concern itself directly with their lesbianism, except in separating them, and prohibiting sexual contact between prisoners in custody, as was generally the case. Assessments of Parker and Hulme by departmental psychologists concentrated mostly on their general progress and rehabilitation. During Parker's probation period some concern was expressed by officials about her lesbian associates.[40] This seems to have been based on the fear that an intense lesbian relationship would lead to criminal activities. It seems to us that Department officials saw a connection between lesbianism and criminality.

The treatment received by Juliet and Pauline in prison was unprecedented. Each was treated differently from other prisoners because of who Juliet was, the circumstances of the murder, and the huge interest in the case from people in New Zealand and in other countries. We think it is ironic that because Pauline Parker murdered her mother she received five years of secondary and tertiary education from the state, including private tuition from university professors. She was able to leave prison and continue with her university studies, eventually obtaining her degree. We believe that Pauline was treated differently from other prisoners because she was associated with Juliet. As a girl from an ordinary background, she would not have received special treatment from the Department. Her connection to the high status Hulme family and the circumstances of the murder ensured that she received privileged treatment. It may seem that Juliet, because she served nearly all her sentence in Mount Eden, was more harshly treated. As stated, the Department had wanted to alternate the girls but decided against doing this.[41]

Parker and Hulme served time in a prison system during a period of reform. Therefore, the emphasis seemed to have been on rehabilitation rather than on harsh punishment. Both Pauline and Juliet were encouraged to continue their education in prison and were protected from publicity, sensation seekers and intrusion. They were finally released into new lives after serving only five years of a sentence which could have been far longer under a different administration.

CHAPTER EIGHT

The Stories

There are numerous accounts about the Parker-Hulme case. We found newspaper and magazine reports, entries in popular crime anthologies, medical analyses and fictional accounts.

The case is described in *Famous Criminal Cases* (Furneaux, 1955), *Famous Australasian Crimes* (Gurr and Cox, 1957), *The World's Worst Murderers* (Franklin, 1965), *Queens of Crime* (Sparrow, 1973), *The Hallmark of Horror* (Gribble, 1973), as well as such other anthologies of famous crimes as *Encyclopaedia of Murder* (Wilson and Pitman, 1961), *The Murderers' Who's Who* (Gaute and Odell, 1979) and *Look for the Woman* (Nash, 1984). There is also a thinly disguised fictional account – the novel *Obsession* (Gurr and Cox, 1958). A 1967 Australian play, *Minor Murder* by Denham and Orr, was loosely based on the Parker-Hulme case and featured two teenage girls who kill the mother of one of them.

Detective sergeant Archie Tate published an account of the case in the *Australian Police Journal* (Tate, 1955), while one of the defence psychiatrists, Dr Reginald Medlicott, published several articles – 'Paranoia of the Exalted Type in a Setting of *Folie à Deux*: A Study of Two Adolescent Homicides' published first in the *British Journal of Medical Psychology* (Medlicott, 1955) and later reprinted in *Deviant Behaviour: New Zealand Studies* (Medlicott, 1979); 'Some Reflections on the Parker-Hulme, Leopold-Loeb cases with special reference to the concept of omnipotence' (Medlicott, 1961), where attempts were made to draw parallels between the two cases; and 'An examination of the necessity for a concept of evil: some aspects of evil as a form of perversion', published in the *British Journal of Medical Psychology* (Medlicott, 1970) where he compares Parker and Hulme to cases like that of Albert Fish, who mutilated and murdered children, and to Ian Brady and Myra Hindley, the Manchester Moors killers. Medlicott continued to refer to the Parker-Hulme case in much of his writing and at staff training sessions for many years.

The case is also mentioned in a local history (Ogilvie, 1978) and a New Zealand encyclopaedia (McLintock, 1966) and there are other accounts and descriptions in a variety of publications.

Most of the accounts we reviewed were inaccurate and made

little attempt to place the case in a context other than that of portraying Pauline and Juliet as 'mad' or 'bad.' While this framework was defined in large part by the adversarial system of justice, the media could have presented a wider perspective on the events. Instead, the media typically sensationalised the case, depicting Pauline and Juliet as monsters or curiosities, adding to the already large volume of published material of derogatory and stereotyped accounts of lesbians.

We found it interesting that the murder victim herself received little media attention at the time or subsequently. No photographs of her appeared in the press. Very little detail was given about her life, her interests or what sort of person she was. She was represented simply as a 'mother'.

Newspaper and magazine stories

We knew that the media coverage of the case had been extensive. Initially we obtained clippings from New Zealand newspapers and then sent for clippings from Australian and British newspaper archives. We collected the main magazine articles but did not succeed in finding details of radio coverage although we had confirmation from people we interviewed that the case was covered on radio.[1] There was no television operating in New Zealand at that time.

We take as given that the mass media is not objective and that it not only presents information but represents the values of the dominant culture.[2] The owners and editors of the main New Zealand media during the 1950s presumed that their audience either was, or ought to be, white, heterosexual, anti-Communist, and firm supporters of fixed gender roles and the nuclear family. In our view, the Parker-Hulme case became a cautionary tale for this audience. It was selected by·the media as newsworthy, given top priority as front page news, written about extensively at the time and has been resurrected regularly throughout the years. We think the stories contained clear warnings to readers about the possible consequences of lesbian relationships and of 'permissive' family life. In the Parker-Hulme case these messages were communicated by the way in which the stories about it were presented – words were sometimes put in the mouths of subjects of news items, certain features were highlighted while others were ignored, events were distorted and misrepresented, some material was blatantly invented, highly emotive adjectives were used, and selected aspects of the case were juxtaposed with others to emphasise certain ideas.

The main local daily newspapers carried full and extensive reports of the trial and, in particular, of the medical evidence. Overseas newspapers also highlighted the case. A local newspaper commented on the media coverage in the British press:

'Not for many years has news from New Zealand received such prominence as the British Press is giving to the Christchurch teen-age murder trial. Each day of the trial most newspapers have published at least half a column, generally on the front page, and in some papers this space has been greatly exceeded. Two tabloids have been giving an extensive display to the case in inside pages.'[3]

Agitation for censorship of 'pulp comics' and other similar publications had reached a peak in 1954 in both Australia and New Zealand and in this climate several observers deplored the way in which newspapers reported the trial proceedings. In New Zealand the conservative Catholic weekly *Zealandia* asked 'Just how far can the detailed reporting of a particularly sordid murder trial be justified in the interests of public information.'[4] In Australia, Premier J. Cahill criticised Sydney newspapers for reporting the details of the case and cautioned that the press should 'not allow itself to be laid open to charges that it is presenting matters that adversely affected the morals of the community.'[5] Some conservatives of the time obviously believed that complete silence and ignorance about sexuality and non-conformity to accepted gender roles was the best method of ensuring a compliant population.

In New Zealand the mass circulation weekly *NZ Truth*, which claimed a total readership of 350,000 in August 1954, gave especially detailed reports of the trial, publishing photographs of the Victoria Park murder site, the house at Port Levy where Hilda Hulme stayed with Walter Perry during the trial as well as other people involved with the case. The exposé of the private lives of the upper middle-class Hulmes was a focus of this newspaper and it published details about Hilda Hulme changing her name by deed poll to Hilda Perry. Regarded by many as an unsavoury publication because of its reports of scandals, divorce cases, rape, incest and other trials, it was extremely popular and functioned in part as an easily obtainable source of information about sex and sexuality. It flourished by exploiting the gap between prescriptions and reality – by publishing full details of the realities of people's lives at the same time as it promoted the ideologies of the time.

Certain elements of the case were selected by the media and given prominence – the ages and gender of Parker and Hulme, their personalities and relationship, and the details of the killing. Headlines read – 'GIRL MURDERERS' (*The Press*, 30 August 1954), 'TEENAGED GIRLS' (*Christchurch Star-Sun*, 16 July 1954), 'GYM-TUNIC MURDERESSES' (*Daily Sketch*, 3 September 1954) and even 'LITTLE GIRLS' (*Evening Standard*, 23 August 1954). Many reports referred to them as 'schoolgirls' – actually incorrect, since at the time of the killing Juliet and Pauline had left school.

One paper published a childhood photograph of Juliet with the caption 'THE FACE OF A GIRL ACCUSED OF MURDER.' (*Daily Sketch*, 28 August 1954) Only on closer inspection could a reader learn that the photograph had been taken some years previously and showed Juliet as a much younger girl.

The method of killing and the fact that it had been planned were also emphasised. Words such as 'SLAYING' (*Christchurch Star-Sun*, 16 July 1954), 'PLOTTED', 'CALLOUSLY PLANNED' (*Sydney Morning Herald*, 29 August 1954), were headlined and evidence was presented to readers in distorted ways. For example, Honora's injuries were reported in such a way that readers were led to believe that she had been hit more than forty times. One newspaper reported that the plan to kill had miscarried and 'repeated blows had to be struck. Mrs Parker had 69 injuries to her head and hands.' (*Daily Herald*, 24 August 1954.) In fact, the coroner's report had clearly stated that Honora's body showed 'forty-five discernible injuries' with perhaps one blow causing several injuries.

One headline read 'I KILLED MY MOTHER WITH A BRICK' (*Evening Standard*, 16 July 1954) – a distortion of part of Pauline's confession, by the amalgamation of several separate statements.

Because women and children are more frequently the victims rather than the perpetrators of violence, this case overturned expectations. Juliet and Pauline were objectified as special and monstrous girls who had become killers.

The fact that Juliet and Pauline appeared to show no remorse and even said that they had been 'terribly happy' since the murder was simplistically quoted in many accounts of the trial. With a sense of relief, one paper later declared 'GIRL IS NOW SORRY FOR MURDER' in a report about Juliet's progress in prison. In the same article, though, in small print it noted that Pauline was 'reported to be sullen, morose, and unrepentant.' (*Sun*, 10 December 1954).

Their relationship was presented as 'WILD INFATUATION' (*The Press*, 27 August 1954), 'DISASTROUS ASSOCIATION' (*The Press*, 30 August 1954) and 'STRANGE HAPPENINGS ON MOONLIT LAWNS.'(*NZ Truth*, 22 September 1954) These subtitles guided readers to a particular perspective.

Their lesbian relationship was presented as integral to the case – they had committed the murder because they didn't want to be separated (lesbians are selfish and ruthless when thwarted because they are evil monsters): or they had committed it because they were insane (and lesbianism is a symptom of insanity). That 'sexual perverts' could become 'killers' seemed a logical development to those who believed that sexual 'perversion' led to worse things.

Comparatively little attention was given to the circumstances of the Hulme and Rieper households, with the major emphasis being on the state of mind of Parker and Hulme and on their activities prior to the killing. Their relationship was discussed within a framework which allowed only the possibilities that they were either 'mad' or 'bad'.

The media connected lesbianism with 'insanity'. Subheadings such as 'HOMOSEXUALITY AND INSANITY' (*The Press*, 28 August 1954) gave unequivocal messages. Headlines such as 'TWO GIRLS WILL NEVER BE SANE, CLAIMS DOCTOR AT TRIAL'(*Dominion*, 27 August 1954), 'INCURABLY INSANE' (*The Press*, 28 August 1954), 'HIDEOUSNESS AND UGLINESS' (*The Press*, 27 August 1954), and 'BOTH WERE SANE'(*Dominion*, 28 August 1954) overlaid reports of the trial and emphasised the 'mad' or 'bad' dichotomy already established there. The Crown Prosecutor's declaration that they were 'dirty-minded girls' was widely quoted.

Most papers also published entries – or simply phrases from entries – from Pauline's diary, usually the lines relating to the killing. Many newspapers published photographs of the diary entry for the day of the killing. At the same time, phrases which appeared to be in the words of Pauline or Juliet – or which were distortions of phrases actually said by them – were also published. One caption underneath a photograph of Pauline read: 'GIRL WHO CUT HER PARENTS' (*Daily Herald*, 24 August 1954). The paper was actually referring to evidence given by Herbert Rieper that Pauline had 'cut' him and Honora out of her affection. Sometimes careful use of punctuation could convey the impression that a phrase was a direct quote, for example – 'Girl "Said She Helped Batter Friend's Mother" ' (*Evening News*, 16 July 1954).

One newspaper produced a very garbled version of part of the evidence:

' . . . a psychiatrist, said the girls had invested their "fourth world" paradise – located at Port Levy a nearby holiday resort, with saints based on film stars.' (*Star*, 26 August 1954)

The sentencing of Juliet and Pauline was certainly not the end of interest in the Parker-Hulme case. Commentary on the case continued. In October 1954 an account appeared in a local periodical, *Here and Now*, liberal social commentator Ian Hamilton took a sympathetic view towards Parker and Hulme:

'I don't know if these girls really did discover the fourth dimension . . . But at least they've shown us the limits of our three-dimensional existence when it comes to dealing with people who have been deprived of love. Anyone who has lived with a Maori family, anyone who has seen the effect of real sympathy on children or adults, can tell you that it would be easy to cure these two girls of the desire for murder.'[6]

But, while rejecting Medlicott's diagnosis, Hamilton too was firmly convinced that they were insane. His explanation of the source of their 'insanity' was more straightforward. 'And [their] attitude? You get out of my way, Or Else.'[7] He also saw causes for their 'madness' in their home backgrounds and implied that they were neglected. While attempting to place the events in context, Hamilton nevertheless also drew an association between lesbianism and insanity.

The case became part of the juvenile delinquency debates which were occurring not only in New Zealand but in England, the United States and Australia in the post-war world. An article on juvenile delinquency in *Time* magazine in December 1954 questioned whether Juliet and Pauline and other so-called juvenile delinquents were 'REBELS OR PSYCHOPATHS?'[8] Quoting the psychologist Robert Lindner, the article stated:

> 'The youth of the world today is touched with madness, literally sick with an aberrant condition of mind formerly confined to a few distressed souls but now epidemic over the earth.'[9]

From 1954 to 1959 many articles appeared speculating on the girls's progress while they were in prison. In 1958 and 1959 there were occasional reports that Hulme and Parker were soon to be released, keeping the case before the public.

A British article in 1964 reinforced the 'bad' explanation, describing their action as a 'sin' and Honora Parker as the 'victim of a sexual obsession'. Edgar Lustgarten in his account of the murder for the *London Evening Standard* described their 'devotion' to each other as 'frightening in its homosexual intensity'. In a bizarre attempt to imagine their thoughts, he wrote:

> 'Who might try to separate us? That was the explosive question always at the back of their agile, depraved, suspicious, guilty minds. Their suspicions did not, in the long run, prove unfounded'.[10]

Over time new images of the case were developed in New Zealand at least, enhancing the earlier stories. The case was presented as one of a series of articles for 'holiday reading' in 1969 when a Sunday newspaper headlined their story with 'TEEN PASSION FLARES – MOTHER HAS TO DIE' (*Dominion Sunday Times*, 16 March 1969). Accompanying the story was a sketch of Pauline and Juliet looking into each other's eyes supposedly satisfied, with their victim lying dead in the background. In 1982 another paper wrote 'PAIR ACCUSED OF PARK MURDER' (*The Star*, 29 December 1982). In an article discussing a supposed Christchurch 'crime wave' in 1986, the case was introduced as the 'repulsive 1954 Hulme-Parker murder'. The report stated that 'The girls lived in a strange fantasy world and believed they were superior beings' (*NZ Times*, 18 May 1986). A 1987 report simply stated that Parker and Hulme took Honora to the Port Hills and 'battered her to death so they could continue their lesbian love affair undisturbed' (*Dominion Sunday Times*, 31 May 1987) And in

1989 *The Press* featured an article titled 'SEPARATION THREAT TRIGGER FOR A BRICK ATTACK' (*The Press*, 17 June 1989). It included a photograph said to be a 'reconstruction of the murder scene', complete with dummy corpse and brick lying on the path. The article asserted that the murder was 'the culmination of a bizarre relationship which developed between the two girls' and reproduced evidence from the trial including the *folie à deux* argument and the claim that 'homosexuality is frequently related to paranoia'.

The media accounts generally constructed particular views of the case, ones which continue to inform popular opinion about lesbianism and its supposed consequences. The association of lesbianism with murder continued. In this sense the case continues to function as a cautionary tale.

Popular crime stories

Within the extensive popular crime literature the case has received some attention. A number of popular works present the details of the case with varying degrees of accuracy. As with the print media, the authors of these accounts construct a social reality for their readers which assumes a particular, shared, world view. Parker and Hulme are pictured either as 'mad' or as 'bad' and the facts of the case are presented from within one or other of these models. While Parker and Hulme were still in prison the first of these publications appeared.

Rupert Furneaux in his book of 1955 *Famous Criminal Cases* writes that 'We have to go back to Chicago in the early nineteen-twenties to find a murder case as shocking.' He takes the view that Parker and Hulme were 'bad':

> 'To Pauline Parker and Juliet Hulme the rights of others were of no importance. Complete egotists, they were insane only in the sense that their ideas were those of animals rather than human beings . . . Their law was the law of the jungle and like wild animals they must be caged until they have shown themselves to be capable of living together with other human beings.'[11]

He describes them as girls who 'lived in a world of their own', based on the defence evidence at the trial and evidence from other medical and psychiatric witnesses. His account included the discussions concerning their homosexuality.

Gurr and Cox in *Famous Australasian Crimes* introduce Pauline
and Juliet as the 'Murdering Girls' and describe their friendship
as 'deep and dark', 'terrible' and 'abnormal'.[12] Pauline is
objectified as 'dumpy' with 'cunning brown eyes' and Juliet as
'staring coolly from her slanted eyes at one person after another
in court'. This undoubtedly suggested negative associations to
readers.

For further dramatic emphasis, Gurr and Cox include pictures
of the site where Honora Parker was murdered, with streams of
blood clearly visible, a photograph of the diary entry for the day
Honora was killed, and a school photograph of Pauline Parker,
taken in 1953. Using extravagant language they construct images
of madness and deviance:

> 'The story they told was one of the strangest ever read in a court of law;
> it became a phantasmagoria; the twisted shapes of a disordered
> imagination seemed to swirl visibly in the heavy air of the courtroom.'[13]

Borrowing from Medlicott's analysis, they claim that the diary
entries relating to the planning of the murder rose to 'a febrile
crescendo'. In noting that Juliet had tuberculosis they ignorantly
state that this is a disease 'found often in cases of sexual
divergence.' Not surprisingly, for Gurr and Cox the case
remained a mystery. They state that:

> 'The normal mind shrinks from the implications of this tragic story. In
> many other crimes lessons of some sort or other are to be found. Here
> there is little but horror, sadness and bafflement.'[14]

However, they are in no doubt that Parker and Hulme had
'vicious and depraved tendencies' and that 'their coming
together, as if by the magnetism of some strange force in the
hinterland of their minds, was a fatal conjunction of
abnormality.'[15]

The original article by Gurr and Cox was reprinted in a
collection of murder stories with the title *Killer Couples* in 1989 by
Richard Glyn Jones.[16] The subtitle read 'Terrifying true stories of
the world's deadliest duos.' Juliet and Pauline were placed
alongside mass murderers, including Ian Brady and Myra
Hindley who together tortured and murdered several children,
before burying the bodies on the Manchester moors.

In 1958 Gurr fictionalised these ideas in a novel based on the case.[17] Titled *Obsession*, it describes the events in a thinly disguised manner. It attempts to copy the novel *Compulsion*, which was a fictionalised account of the Leopold-Loeb case. *Obsession*, published in England, was available in New Zealand and was read by many people.

After Parker and Hulme were released from prison, accounts continued to be published. Charles Franklin, writing in 1965, considered Parker and Hulme to be among *The World's Worst Murderers* along with 'Jack the Ripper' and various mass murderers. His account reflects the defence presented by Medlicott and he compares them to Leopold and Loeb, grouping them together in a chapter titled 'The Young Intellectuals'. He repeats the discussions concerning the relationship between Juliet and Pauline including the erroneous idea that 'homosexuality is frequently related to paranoia'.[18]

A particularly lurid account was given in 1973 by Leonard Gribble in another pop crime collection, *The Hallmark of Horror*. He states that Pauline and Juliet's relationship was 'capable of breeding terror' and was 'unnatural and unhealthy.'[19] According to Gribble, Juliet and Pauline 'with youthful eyes wide . . . decided to become joint murderesses'.[20] He extends this portrayal of madness and evil to include others involved in the case – Honora and Herbert are portrayed as a 'curious couple' while Henry Hulme is pictured as a person who made 'unexpected decisions', in a reference to his decision to leave New Zealand – hardly unexpected given the circumstances surrounding his position at Canterbury University College.

Gerald Sparrow, also writing in 1973, calls them 'Satan's children', who lived in 'a sex dream world' and who were among the 'great women criminals' with minds that were 'twisted and terrible'.[21] He adds that 'It is well known that unnatural relationships often go hand-in-hand with moral delinquency.'[22] Further revealing his ignorance of lesbians and of the case, he defines their friendship using a stereotyped model of lesbian relationships:

'The girls lived together as a married couple but the usual pattern of the dominant one and the submissive one was not completely clear.'[23]

Sparrow also subscribes to the view that physical and mental illness are related and inherited:

'A young relative of Pauline was a mongolian imbecile and her eldest sister had been born with a blood defect that entailed transfusion for her to survive. In these cases the inherited defect was apparent. Had it in fact invaded Pauline and taken a much more secret and malignant form?'[24]

His account of the planning of the murder is bizarre:

'They held regular "murder sessions" at night and this was merely the most important item on a business agenda. Blackmail and sex were other subjects frequently discussed. They had decided that the man-made world was contemptible and a fraud. They rejected all the moral standards of their family and adopted evil and its pursuit as a natural and much more enjoyable way of life. In the Middle Ages they would have been described as "possessed".'[25]

Sparrow then comments: 'I cannot help feeling some pity for these two horrifying girls who submitted to an evil spell that led to their doom.'[26]

The productions of popular crime writers have more permanence than the ephemeral contemporary news stories and magazines. Collections of crime anthologies and encyclopoedias of murder are to be found in libraries and bookshops. This ensures that the crime writers' versions of reality, captured in a durable form, will persist and will be accessible over time. Such books continue to contribute towards the construction of sensational and inaccurate versions of the Parker-Hulme case.

Medical stories

The role of the medical and psychiatric institutions in supporting and maintaining the gender order has been exposed and discussed by many writers.[27] These institutions have played a crucial role in the construction of femininity, and in controlling the minds and bodies of women. Jill Matthews has pointed out that:

'Psychiatry is an institution very strongly implicated in the maintenance of the gender order in so far as it is concerned with "curing" deviation and restoring normality.'[28]

Implicit in this has been the definition and enforcement of norms regarding sexuality. The medical and psychiatric views of

Parker and Hulme presented at the trial may be better understood when placed in this context. Also, when placed in the context of an adversarial justice system which implied a framework in which two opposing sides debated the issues, a dichotomy was already set up. There seemed to be only two possibilities – 'mad' or 'bad.'

The mass media had included simplified versions of the medical and psychiatric evidence presented at the trial. Subsequently, the only in-depth medical or psychiatric discussions of the case are two articles written by defence psychiatrist Reginald Medlicott and published respectively in 1955 and 1961. His 1970 article discusses the case in less detail. There is also an essay by Christchurch psychologist, M. Bevan-Brown, which was written in 1955 but not published until 1961.

Medlicott referred to the case again in an address to the 1985 N.Z. Sexology Conference. This address was subsequently published as an article in the *NZ Sexologist* with the title 'Concepts of Normality and of Moral Values'.[29]

Medlicott's first article entitled 'Paranoia of the Exalted Type in a Setting of *Folie à Deux*: A Study of two Adolescent Homicides' was published in 1955 in the prestigious *British Journal of Medical Psychology*, reaching a wide audience of health professionals including those in New Zealand. This article was published again, unchanged, in 1979 in a collection entitled *Deviant Behaviour: New Zealand Studies*.[30] This was done despite the fact that Medlicott's diagnosis had been rejected, not only in the legal sense, but also in medical terms, at the Supreme Court trial. Psychiatrists for the prosecution had clearly refuted the concept of *folie à deux* and had explicitly denied that there was any connection between paranioa and homosexuality. At the trial, only Francis Bennett supported Medlicott's diagnosis. Nevertheless, Medlicott submitted his discredited ideas to the *British Journal of Medical Psychology* one year after the trial, and then reproduced them in 1979 – without any further comment.

The article begins by presenting the family backgrounds of Parker and Hulme, describing how they met, how their relationship developed and the events leading to the killing of Honora Parker. Then it describes their 'psychiatric condition' at the time Medlicott interviewed them and concludes with a discussion of the diagnosis of *folie à deux*. This includes descriptions of 'similar' cases as well as a brief consideration of homosexuality. Medlicott includes a definition of paranoia which he says is based upon that given by Kraepelin. He states that:

> 'Paranoia . . . [is] a fixed type of disease due exclusively to internal causes and characterised by persistent systematised delusion, the preservation of clear and orderly thinking and absence of hallucinations. [It may be divided] into two groups, egocentric in which the delusions centre around the patient's personality and eccentric when the delusions relate to subjects external to the individual. The egocentric paranoias have been subdivided into persecuted, querulous, exalted, religious, amorous, hypochondriacal types.'[31]

The diagnosis of Parker and Hulme is based on this definition. He says that they were suffering from 'paranoia of the exalted type in the setting of a simultaneous *folie à deux*.'[32] Medlicott explains that he has applied the further qualification of *folie à deux*, or 'communicated insanity', to Parker and Hulme because he considers them to have been equally involved in the planning and execution of the murder. He states that 'there is no evidence of either of these two girls imposing their ideas on the other, and there seems no doubt that they developed their psychoses simultaneously.'[33] He then asserts that 'these girls unfortunately went into adolescence already strongly narcissistic and each acted on the other as a resonator increasing the pitch of their narcissism.'[34]

Medlicott bases his diagnosis on limited interviews with both Juliet and Pauline while they were in prison waiting for their trial, and on readings of Pauline's diaries and other writings. His diagnosis may be criticised on a number of levels. By his own account his diagnosis was based on a Freudian approach – he looked for the causes of the murder in the personalities and psyches of Juliet and Pauline, trying to identify early childhood experiences which could explain the events of 1954.[35] There is no room here to give a critical analysis of the Freudian school – there has been considerable feminist criticism of these ideas in recent years.[36] In any case, his diagnosis is suspect even within its own frame of reference. At points the diagnosis is internally inconsistent, there are errors of interpretation and of fact, and some of the assumptions are questionable.

Medlicott considered that Pauline and Juliet were 'paranoid.' One of the supposed characteristics of 'paranoia' according to the definition he used is an 'absence of hallucinations'. Yet, he also claimed that 'both the girls could consciously hallucinate almost at will, hearing music and voices and seeing fleeting scenes.'[37] Medlicott states that when the two girls were first interviewed, he knew 'that they were trying to prove themselves insane, with the idea that in a mental hospital they could "recover" and be at liberty quite soon.'[38] He determined that they really were insane, he says, 'when they entered into religio-philosophical discussions.' However, he does not consider that their descriptions of hallucinations may have been an invention designed to assist a diagnosis of insanity. This is in spite of the fact that his acceptance of the hallucinations as a symptom of paranoia does not concur with his own definition of their supposed illness.

In the article Medlicott also links homosexuality and paranoia, asserting that:

> 'Repressed homosexuality has a special role in persecutory paranoia, but there is some reason to believe that homosexuality might be prominent in other types of paranoia . . . Burr (1935) states that he cannot recall a case of paranoia in which he really knew the conduct of the patient and did not discover that he[sic] was homosexual.'[39]

He considers the homosexual relationship between Parker and Hulme as a further proof of their paranoia. This view is indicative of the sickness model of homosexuality promoted by the medical and psychiatric institutions and is an expression of a political viewpoint which prescribes heterosexuality as a norm. In any case, prosecution medical witnesses rejected any connection between paranioa and homosexuality. And even if there were homosexuals who were also 'paranoid', this could easily be explained in terms of the negative social conditions under which lesbians and gay men were forced to live at that time.

The article also contains a number of factual errors. He asserts that before Honora was dead 'forty-five blows had been struck'. Obviously Honora received a 'great many blows', on Pauline's own admission, but not as many as forty-five, a figure used in the article as an indication of the girls' brutality, giving an impression of them as frenzied killers.

Also, Pauline's diary for 19 June 1954, three days before the killing, was quoted incorrectly. 'We practically finished our books today and our main Ike for the day was to moider Mother.'[40] The word 'Ike' was an error made during the transcription of the 1954 diary. The word Pauline actually wrote was 'idea'. This error was discussed in court and the correct word noted at the time. The perpetuation of this error by Medlicott in his article is inexcusable. It further constructs images of insanity and strangeness. (Note: The word 'moider' is correctly quoted.)

Medlicott presents Juliet and Pauline as isolated individuals:

> 'Having their own company they were able to isolate themselves more and more from the usual outside interests of adolescent girls and the socialising experiences of group relationships'.[41]

While it is true that Juliet and Pauline spent a great deal of time together, both of them had considerable contact with other people. (See Chapter 4.)

Many of Medlicott's other interpretations may be challenged. For example, he dismissed their writings as 'untalented', 'grandiose' and 'morbidly aggressive', even though he had no particular training in assessing literature. These are obviously areas where other interpretations could be made, but Medlicott gives no recognition that other opinions might regard the poems as talented. He includes the text of 'The Ones that I Worship,' a poem written by Pauline, because he considered it proof of her so-called 'extraordinarily exalted' state:

> There are living among two dutiful daughters,
> Of a man who possesses two beautiful daughters,
> The most glorious beings in creation
> They'd be the pride and joy of any nation.
> You cannot know nor yet try to guess
> The sweet soothingness of their caress
> The outstanding genius of this pair,
> Is understood by few, they are so rare.
> Compared with these two every man is a fool
> The world is most honoured that they should deign to rule
> And above us these Goddesses reign on high.
> I worship the power of these lovely two
> With that adoring love known to so few
> 'Tis indeed a miracle, one must feel
> That two such lovely creatures are real,
> Both sets of eyes, though different far, hold many mysteries strange,
> Impassively they watch the race of man decay and change
> Hatred burning bright in the brown eyes with enemies for fuel,

Icy scorn glitters in the grey eyes, contemptuous and cruel
Why are men such fools they will not realize
The wisdom that is hidden behind those strange eyes,
And these wonderful people are you and I.[42]

As with all poetry this piece can be interpreted in a variety of ways. Further, Pauline wrote the poem when she was fifteen years old, in 1953. It could be criticised as immature and over-emotional in parts, but it does contain some interesting lines, with a lively use of language and some sense of rhythm. To dismiss the poem as untalented, along with all of Pauline and Juliet's other writings as well, is a wide generalisation based on a limited knowledge of creative work. It is interesting to speculate how Medlicott would have regarded the youthful writings of the Bronte sisters, for example, much of which is fanciful and violent.

Juliet and Pauline's plans to travel overseas and publish their writings are put forward in Medlicott's article as further evidence of their 'neglect of reality'[43] and yet Medlicott describes how the girls took practical steps towards achieving their goal. For example, he says that 'Pauline was visiting shipping companies, and between then and the murder they collected money by various means including stealing.'[44]

He also complains that their 'books were mostly unfinished and untyped' as evidence of a 'more than usual' neglect of reality, although he admits that 'ambitious plans are not unusual in adolescents'. As feminist scholars have discussed,[45] many women and girls have written poetry and novels which have not been published because of oppressive publishing controls and dismissive male critics. Some of these women dreamt of publishing their work, dreams which could also be labelled as unrealistic, given their circumstances. Few of these women would have 'typed' or perhaps even 'finished' their work – and yet it would be unthinkable to use this as a symptom of 'madness' and so label them as mentally ill. Medlicott seems to be using details common to many women as evidence of mental illness.

Further, he describes the plan to kill Honora as 'extraordinar-ily naive'. However, Pauline and Juliet had considered the plan carefully and while it did not work out as expected this did not mean that it was 'naive'. Pauline had visited Victoria Park only a few months earlier and knew the area. She would have known that there were secluded parts, as well as clusters of rocks in some places of the Park. Therefore, the idea that they could disguise Honora's death as an accidental fall was not unreasonable.

Medlicott states that 'their murder' was a 'direct result of pervasive personality changes', so disallowing any real consideration of their backgrounds and environment. He states for example, that 'Pauline's mother was not a persecutor' and that 'Pauline's illicit behaviour over the year or more before the murder could not be attributed to a lack of discipline or neglect on the part of her parents.'[46]

This dismisses any real possibility of placing the case within a context of family and circumstance. The relationship between Pauline and her mother is not explored in any depth and Medlicott dismisses any ideas that there may have been conflict in the home. He points out that:

> 'The father said [Honora] was a lovable woman, and that they had never seriously quarrelled during the many years they had lived together. There seemed no doubt that she was intensely interested in her children . . . It is apparent from Pauline's diaries that her mother assumed the major responsibility in disciplining her. This discipline had been reasonable, had never been severe, and corporal punishment according to her father was never resorted to.'[47]

By placing the entire reason for the murder within Pauline and Juliet themselves, Medlicott depicts them as special and unique individuals. His article adds to the 'monsterisation' and 'eccentrification' of Parker and Hulme which had begun at the trial.

Pauline's diaries reveal that there had been conflict between her and her mother over a long period and that Pauline found the relationship difficult. Juliet's relationship with her mother was also difficult.[48] Medlicott does state that after a long separation from her mother at eight years of age:

> 'On being reunited with her mother she was for a start dramatically over-dependent and it was very difficult to fit her into the family group . . . at eleven years of age at the time of her menarche . . . she was sent to a private boarding school. After a time she was unhappy there and returned home.'[49]

Yet he fails to explore the implications of his own statement or to consider the conflicts between Juliet and Hilda which may have arisen from the many long separations. In what way was it difficult to 'fit Juliet into the family group', for example, and was this resolved in the long term? Medlicott also maintains that Pauline's diaries clearly showed that their 'abnormality' was proportional to the time spent in one another's company – a dubious conclusion which can be challenged from a more general reading of the diaries.

An important object of Medlicott's diagnosis in the article is to show that Juliet and Pauline had rejected 'moral values', set themselves above the law and had 'totally embraced the superman philosophy'. He makes much of their comments that Christianity was a 'stupid religion' and that they had formed their own religion. He also quotes from Pauline's diary where she described how she and Juliet had found the key to the 'Fourth World'. This idea was mentioned at only one point in the diary, but was raised again by Medlicott during his interviews with the girls. He includes their replies in his article as evidence of their delusions, but once again seems convinced that the girls were telling him the truth in spite of his earlier statement about their attempt to portray themselves as insane.

Finally, Medlicott supports his diagnosis by using six examples described as being 'close analogies' to the Parker-Hulme case. These cases include philosopher Friedrich Nietzsche, whom Medlicott dismisses as a 'frail, unhappy man'. Medlicott gives a brief resume of Nietzsche's views of 'the superman'. He then discusses writer Max Stirner and his interpretation of Stirner's rejection of moral ideas. Medlicott claims that Pauline and Juliet's ideas were 'similar to' those of Nietzsche and 'consistent with' those of Stirner. He then compares the two girls with a character from a novel – Raskolnikov, in Dostoevsky's *Crime and Punishment*, and claims that the description of Raskolnikov's behaviour 'corresponds vividly' with that of Pauline and Juliet after the murder. Medlicott goes on to compare the Parker murder to the 1924 case of Leopold and Loeb – sons of Chicago millionaires, who had murdered a young boy. Their case received wide publicity at the time. They were defended by the famous criminal lawyer, Clarence Darrow, who saved them from a death sentence with a defence of insanity. Medlicott considered that the two cases paralleled each other – in spite of crucial dissimilarities such as the gender, age and circumstances of Leopold and Loeb, as well as their selection of the victim (a young boy scarcely known to them) and the facts of the killing (they attempted to obtain ransom money from the boy's family). He also includes Aleister Crowley as a 'close analogy' to Pauline and Juliet, as well as the Nazi S.S. Organization, which he claims was 'of a paranoiac nature'. He asserts that:

> 'the frequently senseless and sickening brutality carried out by members of the SS without any sense of pity, shame or remorse, and in a mood that was often frankly exultant, was very similar to the way these girls approached their crime and responded to it afterwards . . . In the case of the SS, sanction by the group became the main ego support, while in the girls' case sanction one of the other provided this . . . With the SS there was a progressive destruction of the taboo against killing . . . Death was deprived of its real meaning and cheapened by the process . . . Both the girls came to treat death very cheaply as something of no particular concern.'[50]

This comparison was an extraordinary attempt to draw parallels and substituted a simplistic and ahistorical perspective for any real consideration of the vast differences between the two situations. These analogies are quite out of place in a so-called 'scientific' medical article. There is little evidence to substantiate any of the claims. The inclusion of a fictional character as evidence proves nothing while the analogy to the Nazi S.S. is sensational and inaccurate. Pauline and Juliet did not kill numbers of people unknown to them, nor is there any evidence that they 'came to treat death cheaply'. At the time the article was re-published, in 1979, Medlicott was well aware that neither Parker nor Hulme had re-offended and that they had not exhibited any on-going murderous propensities. The judgment of the editors in republishing this article is questionable.

In 1961, Dr Medlicott published another article, entitled 'Some Reflections on the Parker-Hulme, Leopold-Loeb Cases with Special Reference to the Concept of Omnipotence' in the *New Zealand Law Journal*. This contained some of the material from the previous article and presented a more lengthy comparison 'because of the extraordinary similarity of the two cases.'[51]

Medlicott considered that the two pairs were alike in the following respects – they grew up under the influence of world wars, had 'satisfactory' home backgrounds, and were highly imaginative, wilful, and self-centred; both pairs had few lasting relationships, were 'immature' emotionally and were homosexual; both pairs experimented with crime before the murders, 'embraced the superman philosophy', showed 'gross exaltation' after the killings and felt that no one cared for them. He also considered that the planning of the two killings showed gross defects and was 'not in keeping with genius'.[52]

The significance of many of these similarities in relation to the respective murders is questionable – for example, that they had grown up under the influence of world wars, or that they were intelligent, or that they were homosexual. The same factors in common could be assembled for large numbers of people and have no relevance to murder whatsoever.

In fact, there were significant differences between the two cases. First, Leopold and Loeb came from similar social, economic and cultural backgrounds and had known each other since they were young children. They were both Jewish, and their victim was chosen at random from a group of Jewish children. There was no immediate or overt threat to the continuation of their relationship at the time they decided to kill someone. Juliet and Pauline were from different social and economic backgrounds and their victim was a close family member, killed for specific reasons.

In 1970, Medlicott published his article 'An examination of the necessity for a concept of evil: some aspects of evil as a form of perversion' in the *British Journal of Medical Psychology*. In this article he complains that his colleagues have avoided:

'. . . facing the existence of evil as a concept and facing the fact that individuals can actively pursue evil as a way of life.'[53]

He defines good and evil as existing within a 'polarity or dichotomy' and says that:

'. . . the impulse to good is life-orientated, the impulse to evil appears to be invariably death-orientated, with suicide or murder as the ultimate goal.'[54]

He then claims that evil is 'a form of perversion' with 'salient features' such as 'driveness' and 'exaltation' and as in his earlier article gives as examples the philosopher Nietzsche, the fictional Raskolnikov and Parker and Hulme. He says that 'pre-genital aggressiveness' is shown and that:

'. . . bisexuality and fantasies of omnipotence run through the majority of instances cited . . . No case achieved anything approaching mature heterosexuality . . . Homosexual elements of either overt or covert nature could be found in most instances.'[55]

Citing Aleister Crowley and his semi-religious groups, Parker and Hulme, Leopold and Loeb and Brady and Hindley as examples he claims that these 'partnerships' boosted 'alien tendencies' and featured 'the element of conspiracy'. He follows on to give what he calls 'Fictional, Historical and Clinical Examples of Evil as a Perversion' treating all these cases equally. The fictional characters, including Mr Hyde, Rhoda from *The Bad Seed* and the Marquis de Sade's creations are discussed as if real persons. Among the 'historical examples' he includes the Roman Emperors and says they:

'. . . run the gamut of infantile sexual perversions . . . few achieved stable heterosexual alliances or responsible parenthood.'[56]

Medlicott now turns to the 'clinical cases' and says that his:

'. . . first major concern with the concept of evil arose out of [his] examination of two teenage girls, Parker and Hulme, and [his] reading at the same time all available material about the two Chicago boys, Leopold and Loeb, who were extraordinarily similar to Parker and Hulme.'[57]

He then refers readers to his two previous papers on the topic as discussed above. Now follow Parker and Hulme described as

'. . . two intelligent adolescent girls, both imaginative, self-absorbed and self-willed, who when they came together formed a two-person society of their own with a rich fantasy world with characters who became increasingly evil. The two girls themselves became increasingly conceited and arrogant setting themselves above almost everyone else in the world with their own superman philosophy. Moral values were reversed and they embraced evil as good. In an increasingly exalted state after experimenting in crime, they set about matricide with joyous abandon and afterwards continued to exalt in their crime.[58]

He concludes his discussion by saying that:

'The two girls have ultimately redeemed themselves and are now leading reasonably constructive lives. Like Raskolnikov they illustrate that adoption of evil is not necessarily irreversible.[59]

It is unclear what he is trying to establish here. He goes on to compare Parker and Hulme to Albert Fish who:

'. . . lived out for many years an intensely sadomasochistic existence with the mutilation and murder of children and eating their flesh.'[60]

He says that Fish was undoubtedly psychotic, but that he 'could be described as both mad and bad', which seems confusing. The next examples are Ian Brady and Myra Hindley. Medlicott says that 'Brady became more and more . . . elated as the pair succeeded in their murders' and he suspects that although they had heterosexual relationships there is 'a strong homosexual element'.[61]

Medlicott concludes this article with a further discussion of evil and criticises 'liberal humanism' for preaching that 'evil is to be found not in man but in social and political institutions'. He insists that:

'Whether or not the word "evil" is banned permanently from psychiatric usage there remains a need to distinguish the pursuit of destructiveness for its own sake.'[62]

This article appears to be an attempt to discuss 'evil' as a form of insanity. It would seem that Parker and Hulme, like Albert Fish, should now be considered as both mad and bad.

During our interview with him in 1987, Medlicott discussed the notion of evil as he believed this related to Pauline and Juliet and showed us a longer work he was writing on the subject. His death meant that this work may not be published. As part of the discussion he described a dream he had about Juliet, where he thought that an evil scorpion-type creature which crawled out of a wall symbolised her. Even nearly thirty-five years later he was still preoccupied with ideas of evil about the two girls.

In his article in the *NZ Sexologist* based on his addresss to the 1985 N.Z. Sexology Conference, Medlicott claims that he reconsidered his original diagnosis of Parker and Hulme, and admits that he 'misdiagnosed' them. But he now simply substitutes one label for another, and terms them 'adolescent megalomaniacs'.[63] This article in fact makes it clear that his perceptions of Parker and Hulme did not change markedly from the time of the trial up until the publication of his last article. He shows no interest in exploring the context of the case, but instead uses a good deal of the article on a discussion of 'moral values' and the destructiveness of the 'Dionysian experience' which he claims 'partake[s] of the same primitive regression' as was apparent in 'the two girl murderers, Parker and Hulme'.[64] Medlicott also used the Parker-Hulme case to illustrate his theories of mental illness during staff training sessions at Ashburn Hall for some time after 1954.[65]

The other medical writer, Christchurch psychiatrist M. Bevan-Brown, rejected the analysis presented by both the defence and the prosecution at the Parker-Hulme trial. In his article 'Mental Health and Personality Disorder', published in 1961, he says that the killing of Honora was a consequence of 'inadequate nurture'. Bevan-Brown claims that Pauline and Juliet suffered from a mental disorder which he labels 'Pathological Character Trait'.[66] Bevan-Brown tries to understand all of the persons involved in the case and as depoliticised individuals, and asks readers to consider what he calls 'this urgent matter of mental hygiene and infant nurture' so that such events could not happen again.[67] He further says that:

> '. . . It is not desirable that the whole matter should be regarded as inexplicable and a horrible episode which it is better to forget.'[68]

Like Medlicott, Bevan-Brown considers the girls' homosexuality an abnormality. 'Homosexuality in late adolescence is always a sign of emotional immaturity.'[69] But this view still individualises their experience and undermines the social and political significance of lesbianism. His essay represents what Celia Kitzinger (1987) calls a psychologised liberal humanistic approach. Kitzinger points out that this approach does not allow the lesbian 'to define herself in terms of her role, her sociopolitical location, her representation of herself as a challenge to the patriarchy.'[70]

Both the conservative and liberal psychiatric views of Parker and Hulme labelled them 'abnormal' and 'deviant', and in different ways drew connections between lesbianism and murder. These articles made the details of the case accessible to a wide 'professional' audience. Little attempt was made to place the events in a context broader than the individual personalities of Parker and Hulme.

In our view there is little distinction between the writings of journalists, 'pop' crime writers, and medical 'experts'. Each type of writing added to the development of the cautionary tale.

CHAPTER NINE

Why was Honora Parker Killed?

The central question at the trial was not whether Juliet and Pauline had killed Honora. It was why. The defence claimed that they were 'mad'. The prosecution insisted they were 'bad'. These alternatives were presented within the context of the New Zealand adversarial system of justice, which established a framework where there could be only two possibilities.

We found it difficult, at first, to understand exactly what went on at Victoria Park – how Juliet and Pauline were able to break down their inhibitions against violence and killing and actually kill Honora Parker. Many children experience rage at parents and have elaborate fantasies about killing them. For most children, such ideas remain fantasies. We turned to the literature about women who have killed and found some useful starting points, particularly in the work of Ann Jones and Carol Smart. Then we considered some psychological, sociological and criminological studies of children who have killed. We found these useful, but were conscious of the problematic nature of knowledge constructed in these disciplines. We also approached Maori scholars and asked them to read and comment on some of the diary entries, particularly those relating to Port Levy and the '4th World'.

All of these approaches suggested ways in which the murder may be understood and go beyond the simplistic 'mad' or 'bad' dichotomy.

Women who kill

Women in western societies are typically seen as passive, and as the victims rather than as the perpetrators of violence. In the Parker-Hulme case, this pattern was disrupted. In cases of this kind, the women or child offenders have frequently been portrayed, especially by the media, either as 'evil' or 'insane'. In western societies women who kill are typically considered deviant and as intrinsically different from men who kill. American lesbian philosopher, Jeffner Allen, commented on this, concluding, 'A woman, by definition, is not violent, and if violent, a female is not a woman.'[1]

Such essentialist views maintain that behavioural differences between men and women are inborn, and that 'masculinity' and 'femininity' are a natural outcome of being male or female. It is argued that there is a purer, finer, female nature. This makes it impossible to evaluate or to understand the violent female offender without considering her to be either 'monstrously unwomanly' or 'insane'. From this position, the violent male offender is deviant because he offends against particular laws and restraints, but his violence is not in and of itself unnatural, whereas the violent female offender offends not only against particular laws but against her 'proper' place in society, and against the perceived 'true nature of womanhood'.

Early male criminologists certainly took this view of criminal women. Caesar Lombroso and William Ferrero in their study *The Female Offender*, published in 1895, put forward a theory of the born criminal woman.[2] They maintained that the true woman was incapable of criminality and asserted that the criminal woman – especially the violent female offender – was excessively masculine. They measured the craniums of criminal women, studied their pictures, looked at every aspect of their physical appearance, including the number of moles and tattoos the women might have, and asserted that women who killed showed unusual muscular strength. They concluded that:

'In general the moral physiognomy of the born female criminal approximates strongly to that of the male . . . the female criminal . . . is excessively erotic, weak in maternal feeling . . . and dominates weaker beings sometimes by suggestion, and others by muscular force; while her love of violent exercise, her vices, and even her dress, increase her resemblance to the sterner sex. Added to these virile characteristics are often the worst qualities of woman: namely, an excessive desire for revenge, cunning, cruelty, love of dress, and untruthfulness, forming a combination of evil tendencies which often results in a type of extraordinary wickedness.'[3]

They included in their study, as if they were evidence for their theories, a number of quotations from classical literature which incidentally revealed centuries of prejudice against women. For example:

'No possible punishments can deter women from heaping up crime upon crime. Their perversity of mind is more fertile in new crimes than the imagination of a judge in new punishments.' (Corrado Celto, 15th century)

'Feminine criminality is more cynical, more depraved, and more terrible than the criminality of the male.' (Rykere)[4]

When a liberal tradition of criminology developed in the 1920s it emphasised socialisation rather than biological factors as the source of criminal deviance. W.I. Thomas, a liberal writing at that time, argued for the importance of the environment over biology. Nonetheless, in many ways he still saw biology as destiny. For liberals the female offender had deviated from her true role because environmental factors had interfered. Where this had occurred, individual treatment to assist her to conform to societal expectations was his solution.

Carol Smart, a feminist criminologist, comments on Thomas, 'He perceived a certain reality in the relationships of men, women and children and assumed that it was the "natural" order of things.'[5] She says that he:

'. . . managed to reduce all social problems to individual ones and to reduce the social structure to individual situations. Analyses of the class structure, the position of women in society and concepts of power and control all become unnecessary in Thomas's work on female criminality.'[6]

Later, she concludes that:

'His ideological stance encourages the repression of any moves towards a lessening of social constraints on women, emphasising as it does the conservative, non-criminal nature of the traditional female role.'[7]

Another liberal was Otto Pollak, whose ideas were also developed in the 1920s and became popular again in the 1960s.[8] Carol Smart points out that Pollak's ideas, like those of Thomas, were based on biological determinism coupled with an interpretation of social factors. His ideas were highly speculative and much of what he claimed was not substantiated. He claimed that because women can disguise their lack of sexual response all women learn that they can deceive and manipulate men and that this was not confined to criminal women. Further, she says Pollak claimed that most crimes committed by women remain undetected, that the victims of female offenders (usually their children or spouse) do not report the offence, and that female offenders are treated more leniently than men when they are detected. Smart points out that Pollak went so far as to claim that women are more likely to kill than men and that this was because women might seek revenge because of the unequal social situation of men and women. He attempted to 'prove' this by comparing the percentages of male and female prison inmates convicted for murder. Smart points out that that Pollak's vengeance analysis was very similar to Lombroso and Ferrero's contention that women, when 'roused', are more dangerous than men.

Gerald Sparrow, writing in 1970, is typical of a number of pop-criminologists on the subject of women who kill. He asserts that:

'Women being different from men in their mentality, thought-processs, intuition, emotional reactions and in their whole approach to life and death, when they murder, do the deed in a way that a man often would not contemplate. Their crime does not bear the mark of Cain, it is stamped with that characteristic subtlety and horror that has distinguished the rare evil women of all times.'[9]

This view assumes that although it is not acceptable when men kill (after all, they bear the mark of Cain), their crime is less shocking than killings (stamped with 'horror') done by special, 'evil' women. His view encapsulates the idea that women who kill are monsters, driven by their sexual nature. He says that 'women murderers in particular are monsters of egocentric selfishness . . .'[10]

Predictably, a number of writers have asserted that the emancipation of women leads to a higher rate of offending by women.[11] We have found no convincing evidence to substantiate such claims.

Jan Jordan Robinson has identified the following broad categories in her summary of responses to the female offender: masculinisation (women criminals are seen as male-like); monsterisation (women are seen as far worse than their male counterparts); sexualisation (women's sexual desires underlie all female delinquency); victimisation (women offenders are forced into crime through circumstances beyond their control); psychiatrisation (women offenders are mentally ill); sociological (social environment causes women to offend); and the emancipation thesis (the female crime rate escalates as feminism liberates women).[12] We see a parallel between these ideas about female offenders and ideas about lesbians because all these categories have been used to describe and depict lesbians.[13]

Jordan Robinson points out:

'. . . any study of women and crime must be performed within a conceptual context which acknowledges the existence and significance of the sex role stereotypes underlying both the practical and theoretical responses to such crime.'[14]

A number of writers have now approached the study of women and crime from this perspective. Feminist scholar Ann Jones, although focusing on the United States, has provided a useful theoretical framework for the study of women who kill. Jones points out that 'dangerous people' may not be as 'extraordinary' as is thought. While the woman who takes an extreme solution may well do so because she feels trapped and is unable to conceive of a less destructive solution, she is often perceived not as 'futile' and 'ineffectual' but as terrifying in her evil or insanity. She comments that 'Society is afraid of both the feminist and the murderer, for each of them, in her own way tests society's established boundaries.'[15]

Jones deplores the paucity of serious studies on female offenders and notes that 'Academic criminologists ignore women while the popular crime writers describe "murderesses" in books with snappy titles like "Fatal Femmes" and "The Deadlier Species".'[16]

A number of other feminist scholars have considered the violent female offender. Chesney-Lind, for example, comments that women who kill are 'interesting precisely because of their rarity'[17] and goes on to say that:

'women's general conformity to social norms is neither mysterious nor a product of "femininity"; research indicates that women are closely monitored. The few women who escape domestic discipline find themselves confronting powerful correctional forces.'[18]

She concludes that 'Once a female offender is apprehended her behaviour is scrutinised for evidence that she is beyond the control of patriarchy and if this can be found she is harshly punished.'[19]

While some criminologists have asserted that women offenders are more leniently treated than men (the 'chivalry' argument), this has now been challenged and disproved. If 'chivalry' was ever shown by the criminal justice system to women, it was only toward the privileged.[20] As Anne Hiller, an Australian sociologist points out, research now shows that some female offenders are indeed more harshly treated:

'More rigorous analysis of arrest, conviction and sentencing statistics, introducing controls for type and seriousness of current offence and for previous criminal record, reveals in some cases no significant sex differences and in others harsher rather than more lenient treatment of females.[21]

Ann Jones quotes novelist Enid Bagnold as saying 'A murderess is only an ordinary woman in a temper'[22] and comments that 'Despite its flippancy, the remark suggests the truth that murder is often situational: given the same set of circumstances any one of us might kill. Women who kill find extreme solutions to problems that thousands of women cope with in more peaceable ways from day to day.'[23]

We applied these ideas to the Parker-Hulme case. What were the problems faced by Juliet and Pauline? They had experienced a series of threats to their relationship, largely from Honora; the threat of separation was the latest and most serious. Further, these threats to their relationship had occurred within the context of two families living in ways contrary to outside appearances. Juliet and Pauline would have experienced the stress which must have developed as a result of the secrets in both families. They lived within two interlocked family systems, both of which were under strain. We do not suggest that the western patriarchal nuclear family model would ever be stress-free since it functions as a mechanism to control women and children in order to benefit men and perpetuate male supremacy. The suggestion that some families are 'dysfunctional' implies the existence of a 'functional' family, a concept we reject.[24]

For Juliet and Pauline, the impending divorce and imminent departure of the Hulmes fractured these systems. They found an extreme solution to the problem they faced and stepped outside of expected gender patterns by using violence.

Children who kill

Juliet and Pauline were not only women who killed. They were, at the ages of fifteen and sixteen, also children who killed. In western societies children who kill are usually regarded as monstrous and deviant. In these societies, children are powerless, in that they are usually physically dependant on adults and there are no institutions within which children have power over adults. As a class, adults have power over children as a class.

The question of how to define 'child' is problematic. Various cultures at different times have used diverse criteria to establish when a person ceases to be a 'child' and is classed as an adult. Different legal systems set a range of points at which a person may have 'adult' privileges. In New Zealand in the early 1950s, the law allowed a person to leave school and to hold a driving licence at fifteen; to have sexual intercourse (females) at sixteen; to be conscripted (males) at nineteen; to vote, marry without parental consent, obtain credit, and purchase alcohol at twenty-one. The Capital Punishment Act 1950 specifically excluded persons under eighteen from the death penalty.

Child criminality is an extreme form of juvenile rebellion against adult authority and the structures which reinforce this. During the 1950s explanations for it ranged from socially constructed, external causes – for example, the parents were blamed for having lost control over their children, or the government was blamed for the availability of material which could give children criminal ideas. Or the cause was looked for within the individual child. The child could be depicted as monstrous and evil or perhaps as congenitally insane. Ideas of a biologically determined child criminality received some popular exposure: an example is the book *The Bad Seed*,[25] and the film based on it. This novel tells the story of a small girl who kills a number of people, including adults, for personal gain. She has apparently inherited her murderous tendencies. This range of explanations holds one particular factor in common. As is the case with women, children who are the perpetrators of violent offences are typically seen as special and unusual. They may be thought of as victims of unfortunate backgrounds, they may be pitied as mentally ill, or they may be seen as monstrously evil – all of these views regard them as special.

It is far more common that children are victims of crime than the perpetrators, especially with respect to murder. It is not usual that women kill, and it is even more unusual for children to kill.

As Murray Hahn and N. Dawson-Wheeler comment in a 1986 New Zealand study of young people who kill:

'We do not expect young people to kill another person, it is a crime which we associate more with those over seventeen years of age.'[26]

However, the number of children and young people who did kill during this period is larger than might be expected. From 1950 to 1969, of the fifty-six convicted murderers in New Zealand ten were fourteen to nineteen-year-olds, or eighteen per cent of the total.[27]

We read the available literature on children who kill even though we would dispute the assumptions in these studies about heterosexual family life, and note their cultural and gender bias. The ideas and assumptions about 'normality' are obviously not ones we would share. However, the factors which these writers discuss as being common to children who kill, we found useful. These studies do not make comprehensive comparisons between boys and girls.

First, the literature suggests that children, like adults, usually kill people who are known to them. In a 1971 study of murder, B. Cormier and associates placed murders on a continuum ranging from 'specific' to 'non-specific', depending on the relationship between the killer and the victim. Their study accepted that although some people kill persons who are complete strangers to them, and others kill persons of a certain age and type, most kill 'specific' persons – ones who are known to them. They consider that these killings occur where 'there are psychological ties' between the killer and the victim and the 'murder results from the conflict engendered in the relationship'.[28]

A recent New Zealand survey confirms this, showing that for the period from 1950-1985 over seventy-three per cent of victims were known to their murderers, with twenty-nine per cent being family or de facto partners.[29] An American survey also showed that in over sixty-five per cent of the cases studied a specific relationship existed between murderer and victim.[30]

In a 1976 American study of thirty young murderers, B. Corder and associates distinguished between those who killed their parents, those who killed other relatives or close acquaintances, and those who killed total strangers. They suggest that those who killed strangers were significantly more likely than the others to have a history of aggressive behaviour and poor impulse control. They were also more likely to have been identified as needing psychiatric treatment before the crime than those who had killed family members or acquaintances.[31] The implications here are that children who kill persons known to them are not children who have previously shown marked aggression to others. Nor have they been identified as children in need of psychiatric treatment. However, the size of the sample for this study must limit the accuracy of its conclusions.

A second important factor suggested by these studies is that a conflicted relationship usually exists between the child and the person killed. For many children, such a relationship occurs most readily within their immediate family – that is, the persons most important to them, and the closest to them. Naturally this does not apply to gang violence by young people. A 1966 Canadian study of matricide by C. McKnight and others comments:

> 'A number of surveys agree that the largest group of killings takes place within the family. The figures range from twenty-five per cent to sixty-six per cent of all homicides . . . Growdon (1950) reports that thirty-two per cent of the victims of fifty-four Ohio juveniles were family members and postulates that young murderers may kill a greater proportion of family members than older murderers.'[32]

A later writer, D. Chiswick, has pointed out:

> 'Family murder does not occur in a vacuum. It is a complex interaction of individual characteristics, precipitation by the victim, and environmental chance.'[33]

A comprehensive study by B. Cormier and others in 1978 of one hundred children (including Parker and Hulme) who had killed a member of their family concluded that: 'in dealing with violence against parents in a family, two factors are evident; an existing family relationship and, within this family conflictual psychological links between the parents and the chidren. A homicidal process occurs when the unresolved conflicts reach their peak.'[34] They suggested that 'the killing of the parents can be referred to as a family drama . . .'[35]

Some of these factors have parallels in the Parker-Hulme case. Juliet and Pauline killed a person known to them, the mother of one of them, who was well-known to the other. Juliet helped kill Pauline's mother at a time when her relationship with her own mother appears to have been difficult. The Parker and Hulme families contained many unresolved conflicts.

A third factor suggested in this literature is that although the conflict may be a long-standing one, a series of events which occurs shortly before the killing may act as a trigger for the final outcome. Often, observers from outside the situation mistake the trigger for the cause. A sequence of circumstances may become more and more uncomfortable, and killing, for some children, represents a resolution of events which have developed prior to the act. B. Cormier and associates suggest that feelings of ambivalence which could even be 'aggressive and deadly in content' start early in life. They point out that all children have death wishes and fantasies concerning their parents but that these homicidal moods co-exist with opposite feelings of being comfortable with the parents. They consider that when children actually do kill their parents it generally happens within very conflicted family relationships that 'cannot find their normal resolution.'[36] J.W. Duncan and G.M. Duncan, in 1971, also conducted a study of homicidal adolescents, looking at only five cases in which adolescents threatened to kill or did kill a parent. This small sample, they claim, supported other studies suggesting that 'in most cases the act of homicide represents a resolution of events that developed in the preceeding few days.'[37] They say that a sequence of circumstances progressively became more 'unbearable and less amenable to the adolescent's control. In the developing explosive circumstances, if alternatives to violence are not available or have been tried and have failed, the risk of a tragic outcome is greater.'[38]

It was certainly true in Pauline's case, and also in Juliet's, that tension within the family had been building up for some time before the murder. But in April 1954, the pace of events accelerated as events in the Hulme household and in Pauline's life changed everything. Pauline and Juliet searched for alternatives – going to a travel agency, selling Pauline's horse, and even considering shoplifting. But these alternatives were not thought through and they did not seem to consider more long-term alternatives – for example, Pauline getting a job and saving up for the fare. In this sense, their plans were immature. The conflict between Pauline and her mother was a long-standing one with a number of possible triggers in the months preceding the killing. Pauline chose to kill her mother as the solution to the conflicts. Juliet chose to help her, possibly as a substitute for killing her own mother, or perhaps simply to help Pauline.

A fourth factor suggested is that the child may feel that the only solution to the conflict with the parent is death. Cormier and associates describe a phenomenon they call 'lockage', where the killer feels unable to live with the relationship and at the same time, unable to live without it.[39] Suicide or homicide may be the outcome, or even homicide followed by suicide. Cormier and associates point out that suicide and attempted suicide is 'far from unknown' among adult murderers. Pauline Parker indicated several times in her 1954 diary that she felt depressed and had thought about suicide. Later, Pauline began to write of her plans to "moider mother". It is hard to decide simply from reading the diaries how serious she was about either suicide or murder – but we think her comments are significant given what happened. Her experience had similarities with those of other young people who have killed family members.

Fifth, a sense of relief and liberation may be experienced by adolescent killers following the killing. Cormier and associates say that this feeling of relief means that in comparison with adult murderers, suicide following the killing is rare.[40] They also suggest that the 'release of tension' which sometimes follows the killing occurs because the type of adolescent that they studied had been deprived of 'the ability to form a gratifying relationship with either or both parents.'[41] Therefore, the victim was not mourned by the killer in the same way as is often the case with a homicide among adults who are partners. Initially this seemed to be the case for both Juliet and Pauline.

The media commented on Juliet's and Pauline's apparent lack of remorse, which suggests to us that they might have felt a sense of relief and liberation following the killing. This was regarded either as callousness or madness. Later, the media headlined their apparent remorse with obvious satisfaction.

Sixth, 'overkilling', or violence beyond death, is a phenomenon not uncommon in adolescent killings. This has been discussed by J. Mohr and C. McKnight in 1971, particularly in relation to matricide, and also by B. Cormier and others in 1978. The latter attribute the phenomenon of overkilling to the fear and panic experienced by the killer that 'the omnipotent parental figure will get up and retaliate'. In their view such overkilling is not a result of explosive rage or brutality. They quote Mohr and McKnight's view that violence beyond death may be the result 'rather of panic and fear of not having completed the task'.[42]

In the Parker-Hulme case, the media reported the number of times Juliet and Pauline were said to have hit Honora and commented on the severity of their attack. Using Mohr and McKnight's analysis, Juliet and Pauline may have panicked when, contrary to their plan, Honora did not die after one blow. As Agnes Ritchie reported, they were certainly not calm when they reached the kiosk following her murder.

Seventh, the risk that adolescent murderers will kill again seems low. The Cormier study suggests that the 'process wherein murder is committed during adolescence is self-limiting and is not necessarily part of an ongoing delinquent or psychopathological process.'[43] However, they point out that other writers who have studied cases where the adolescent killers were in mental hospitals do not agree with this view. Their own cases were adolescent killers who were in prisons as they had been found legally sane, like Parker and Hulme. Duncan and Duncan say that 'experience in the field of corrections suggests that the person who has yielded to intense pressure and has killed a member of his [sic] family has by the act removed the cause of his [sic] difficulty and no longer is a danger,' though they note that some psychiatrists have said that 'once psychological barriers against murder are crossed, they no longer function to adequately restrain behaviour'.[44] However, they conclude that 'it appears that in cases where the murderer is sane, where the victim is the original hated parent and not a surrogate, and where immediate apprehension and control are established, then the chances that the offender will kill again are minimal.'[45] Neither Juliet or Pauline have killed again.[46]

Finally, other writers and researchers have been interested in attempting to attribute some responsibility to the victim for the murder by suggesting that it may in part have occurred in response to an unconscious death wish. Greggory Morris, a journalist who published a book called *The Kids Next Door* in 1985, cites a case where a toddler shot his father, using a loaded gun, and suggests that the availability of the weapon demonstrates some control of the situation by the adult victim over his child killer.[47] Adelaide Johnson's view is that a child complies with the wishes of the parental unconscious, in order to 'gratify the needed parent'.[48] Duncan and Duncan, however, suggest that a 'child complies not to gratify but to control the parent . . . by selectively acting out some but not all of the behaviour fostered by the parent.'[49]

Pauline and Juliet attempted to rationalise their actions by claiming that Honora 'wanted to die', and that she seemed pleased and happy about it.[50] We think it extremely unlikely that Pauline and Juliet were responding to some death wish by Honora. It is more likely that they were attempting to justify their actions to themselves and others, and also to mislead the defence psychiatrist.

When confronted with a murder by two young females whose victim was the mother of one of them, people reacted strongly. 'People who have adolescent children are asking such questions as: "Could this happen in my family?" "Why did it happen?" '[51] reported Christchurch psychiatrist, M Bevan-Brown, a friend of the Hulmes. Ian Hamilton, a social commentator sympathetic to Hulme and Parker, recorded with some disgust the feeling 'in the streets and in the offices': 'It's all this self-expression; get 'em sewing mailbags, that'll teach 'em.'[52]

One Christchurch parent worried:

> 'Our eldest girl was at school with those two girls, and I looked at her walking up the path in her school uniform and I thought oh no I can't believe that any girl could do such a thing.'[53]

Another woman felt that it was an 'awful murder' because Honora had trusted Pauline and Juliet and they had taken her to the park and killed her. 'I wonder how that woman must have felt at the first blow,' she said.[54]

Neither Juliet nor Pauline, as far as we know, had any previous personal experience of death. It is obvious that they had no real idea of what it would take to kill Honora. They were clearly shocked by the bloody episode. They probably had little idea of the permanence of death or what it meant, other than an immediate resolution to the conflict. In our view one of the tragedies of Honora Parker's murder is the likelihood that neither Juliet nor Pauline fully understood the permanent consequences of their actions.

A Maori interpretation

We discussed our research with Maori friends, some of whom were from the Puaui (Port Levy) area. When they read some of Pauline Parker's diary entries, especially those concerning her holidays in the area, they commented that there were a number of possible Maori interpretations and suggested that we should consult a Tohunga. The Puaui area was a pa site for six hundred years. There are several urupa and Wahi Tapu sites in the area which have considerable spiritual significance. We consulted a Tohunga from the Puaui area and asked for his opinion on the extracts.[55] His analysis involves an understanding of many key concepts and is highly complex.

First, there is the concept of Mauri. This is the physical life force or life principle which is fed from the solar system and controlled by Nga Kaitiaki. These Kaitiaki are imbued with Mana from their Atua and are therefore in a state of tapu. Mana means to be delegated spiritual power to act in this context. Tapu means that a person or an object are set aside for use of the Atua. The Kaitiaki is given that relationship to the Atua which is tapu and which generates certain psychological forces which bring about psychic power.

Then there is Ihi which is the inner force in a person which generates wehi from a person in proximity. Psychological and spiritual forces are all driven from a relationship with the Atua, via the Kaitiaki. The way of perpetuating the life-force, or Mauri, is by re-energising. Once a person knows where Mauri is, then Karakia can get them through to another dimension, as can Waiata Tawhito. Entry is sought and gained to accomplish this. Just before and just after certain planets come into alignment twice a year, it is possible to enter this dimension. Pauline and Juliet appear to have stumbled upon this accidentally.

It is also apparent from Pauline's diary that she was menstruating when she was at Puaui. That, coupled with the fact that they were both so young, would have made them especially vulnerable, said the Tohunga. Placation of the Atua/Kaitiaki was ritualistically accomplished, i.e. through blood sacrifice. This was in order to make a connection again to the spiritual powers and forces. Pauline's reference to 'Christ' in her diary may be interpreted as an allusion to a spiritual guardian.

In considering the Puaui extract the Tohunga noted the use of

Christian symbols – Saints, Easter and Jesus, for example, and pointed out that the passage contains a number of general symbols which have special meaning in Maori tradition, law and practice. He said that the saints and the use of the numbers seven and ten, could all be interpreted as gatekeepers to the Fourth World. He told us that there are ten parts to the Maori calendar year – ten worlds of which seven are male and three female. Easter is a time when the life-forces are fed – a gateway through the clouds may be interpreted as a way to ascend to other worlds. If a person knows the keys, he said, the gateway is possible – keys might be the pitch of words or incantations. The 'saints', or filmstars, the girls discussed could be gatekeepers – their experiments may have triggered a spiritual experience. Their frequent bathing, in such an interpretation, would have provided an opportunity for forces to go through them and to be received. Also, sexual symbolism can be an important part of the process and may have been a key aspect of what occurred.

He considered that Pauline and Juliet had been near several traditional spiritual Wahi Tapu. While there are spiritual guardians who protect those who are from Puaui, other knowledgeable people can also protect themselves by taking cooked food – at Puaui, probably cooked seafoods. Without the cooked foods, he said, a disaster could happen. The guardians, then, had to be placated with either cooked food or blood. If blood, the person killed would have to be someone of that person's own group. In this context, Honora's death could be interpreted as a sacrifice. However, he said, a Tohunga could have healed the girls by Karakia even though they had stumbled upon a powerful spiritual force.

The Tohunga also considered that it was highly significant that Pauline Parker had later studied Maori and said that the spiritual effect on the girls from the Puaui experience could have been the cause of many subsequent events, including the killing of Honora Parker.

We found this account compelling and helpful as it suggests a spiritual view of the case lacking in other accounts.

Conclusion

By finding Parker and Hulme guilty of this murder, the Court upheld the view that they had killed Honora because she was an obstacle to their relationship. This is simplistic. The Rieper and Hulme families must be understood in context. In the Hulme household the relationship between Juliet and Hilda contained conflicts typical of a culture which encouraged children to see the absence of a mother as neglect. The explanation for Juliet's participation in the killing was perhaps more complex than that of Pauline. She could have been engaged in killing a surrogate for her own mother. We think that Juliet's imminent departure was simply the trigger. This was intensely disturbing for Juliet and Pauline and they took practical steps to find a solution to the crisis. When these steps failed, they carried out an act which irrevocably altered what they experienced as an untenable situation. We also think that the killing was a consequence of long-standing domestic conflicts and complex circumstances within both families and that these originated largely in the prescriptions of the times.

The reason that Pauline and Juliet chose killing, rather than another solution, remains unclear. The Maori explanation suggests that the experiences of Juliet and Pauline at Port Levy accounted for their choice of violence as a solution, while the literature on women and children who kill suggests a variety of factors which may also have led to that choice.

There are a number of ways of looking at the case and a number of frameworks within which an analysis may be made. We think that each of the ones discussed gives a means to expand perspectives on the case and on the reasons for the killing. All of these go far beyond the simplistic 'mad' or 'bad' interpretations.

CHAPTER TEN

Lesbians in New Zealand

'There are the gangs of homosexuals who live together for the sake of perversion. You can see these warped-brain men – and women too – wandering about the streets or sitting idly in night cafes. Auckland has too many of them . . . Homosexuals have a strict code of ethics all of their own and on no account will they sexually associate with women. Oddly enough they fight among themselves like kilkenny cats. For this reason a group of homosexuals is always controlled by the "queen bee" whose word is absolutely final. Others in the sect are "marthas" who dress as women; "arthurs" who adopt the normal male role, and "butchs" who stand in either way . . . homosexuals, ambisexuals, lesbians and the like . . . are largely only a degrading menace, however undesirable, to themselves.'[1]

This was what the *N.Z. Pictorial* had to say in December 1955 about the few lesbians and gay men who could be found in public meeting places. The tone of this article was typical of the attitudes of the times – critical, judgemental and derogatory. It also indicated the prevailing ignorance about lesbians. It was in this hostile environment that Pauline and Juliet's relationship was judged.

We drew on our own personal knowledge and experiences of the 1950s in New Zealand and also spoke with a number of other lesbians and some gay men. The people we spoke with had experienced the 1950s in New Zealand and, not surprisingly, almost all did not wish to be named – a legacy of living and having to survive in a hostile anti-lesbian, anti-gay society.

Women who were attracted to other women at that time encountered many difficulties. The medical and psychiatric professions defined lesbianism as an abnormal condition, for which treatment was appropriate. Male homosexual behaviour was also regarded as deviant and was criminalised. References to homosexuality in the media were mostly about male homosexuals, usually in the context of criminal proceedings.[2] For some lesbians, the reports of the Parker-Hulme case were their first affirmation that there *were* other lesbians. (In the next chapter we have included some of their stories.)

Same-sex relationships between females were first explicitly criminalised in New Zealand in 1961. Section 139 of the Crimes

Act prohibited sex between a woman over the age of twenty-one years and a girl under the age of sixteen. Otherwise, it was and still is not illegal to actually live and identify as a lesbian.

In pre-European Maori societies same-sex relationships seem to have been a part of ordinary life. The 1988 Royal Commission on Social Policy noted that:

> 'Of specific concern to Maori lesbians ... is the claim ... that homosexuality was introduced by Pakeha and that it had no place in traditional Maori society. There is no evidence to support this claim. Kuia and Kaumatua have suggested to the Commission that on the contrary homosexuality – female and male – was not uncommon in pre-European times and that it was in fact more readily accepted than today.'[3]

The introduction of both Pakeha religions and a Pakeha legal system must have profoundly affected traditional Maori views about same-sex relationships.

For male homosexuals the situation was different. After the formal establishment of Pakeha government in 1840 in New Zealand a legal system based on English law was set up. In 1893 the Criminal Code Act was passed, based on the English Crimes Act of 1885, which criminalised male homosexual acts, including those in private, but did not mention sexual acts between women. This was followed by the Crimes Act 1908 which defined penalties for sodomy and 'indecency' between males. This Act was amended several times (1941 and 1954) and sentences were made less severe. By 1961 there were penalties of five and seven years' imprisonment for indecency and sodomy between males, while sodomy committed on a female, or a male under the age of sixteen was punishable by a maximum of fourteen years' imprisonment.

However, while there were no laws prohibiting lesbian sexual behaviour in the 1950s, lesbian identity and behaviour was proscribed by codes of ethics and sets of regulations which various occupations developed. These were used to justify the exclusion, disciplining, or dismissal of lesbians. Such occupations included the medical, legal, and teaching professions, the armed forces and the public service.

Lesbians in the armed forces could be discharged simply on the grounds that they were lesbian. Vaguely worded statutes allowed for the discharge of personnel who acted in an unbecoming manner. Lesbians in the police force faced similar regulations. Police Force Regulations of 1950 declared that candidates had to be of 'unexceptionable moral character.'[4] Once members, they could be disciplined or dismissed if they committed 'any offence for which they could be sentenced in a court of law.' This type of regulation was particularly problematic for gay men who were vulnerable to the restrictions of the Crimes Act. In one Wellington case during the 1950s where the homosexuality of a police officer was discovered, the man concerned committed suicide.[5] In 1957 there was the case of a police sergeant who was prosecuted and was found guilty on five charges of indecent assault against males. He was sentenced to three years' imprisonment. The sergeant had been arrested during a police raid on a Wellington house. Following his arrest he resigned from the force and during his trial he questioned 'why others in the police force whom he understood recently to have engaged in homosexual activities had not been prosecuted.'[6] Clearly, there were other police officers who were gay.

Other professions and occupations had also developed codes of ethics and defined standards of behaviour which could be used against lesbians in the 1950s. For example, the code of ethics adopted by the New Zealand Educational Institute (the primary school teachers' association) defined unprofessional actions in very broad terms, so simply identifying as a lesbian could be enough to bring disciplinary action and possibly dismissal.[7] In the same way, lesbians working in the public service were vulnerable.[8] Terms in the regulations such as 'disgraceful', 'improper', and 'seriously detrimental' could be broadly interpreted in the absence of any formal definition. Disciplinary action may not have involved actual dismissal. Lesbian employees could always be asked to resign, or if they refused to resign, could be transferred to unpleasant work or undesirable locations, or denied promotions.

Under these conditions, along with negative and antagonistic public attitudes, it is no wonder that there were few lesbians who were publicly identifiable. Despite the absence of a law proscribing lesbian behaviour, social attitudes towards lesbians were very negative and all homosexuality was seen as unnatural and as a threat to the order and stability of society. It was in this atmosphere that Honora Parker, Herbert Rieper and Henry

Hulme discussed the relationship which had developed between Juliet and Pauline. Like many other parents of the time, they wanted to break it up. Honora, seeing Pauline's relationship with Juliet as a medical problem, decided to take Pauline to their family doctor to discuss the situation. If she expected any enlightenment, she was bound to be disappointed.

Lesbianism and male homosexuality was defined by medical and psychiatric professionals as disease and deviation. Defence psychiatrist Medlicott, wrote a few years after the trial that 'Sexual deviation can be defined as any pattern of sexual behaviour which differs from normal coitus or foreplay to coitus.'[9]

Medical, psychiatric and educational professionals defined the parameters and boundaries of debate and discussions concerning sex and sexuality, while the media relayed some of these ideas and prescriptions to the public. Much of the medical and psychiatric literature concentrated on investigating the 'causes' of homosexuality and how homosexuality might be 'cured'. This view had existed since the medicalisation of homosexuality in the nineteenth century, substantially commencing with the German sexologists Krafft-Ebing and Ulrichs, and had continued into the later psychiatrisation of the subject with Sigmund Freud and his followers. French philosopher Michel Foucault has discussed the process by which homosexuality became medicalised – that is, the way in which it entered the domain of doctors, who could then describe and prescribe for it as they did for other 'diseases'. He says:

'The nineteenth century homosexual became a personage, a past, a case history, a childhood, in addition to being a type of life, a life form, and a morphology, with an indiscreet anatomy and possibly a mysterious physiology. Nothing that went into his [sic] total composition was unaffected by his [sic] sexuality . . . It was . . . less as a habitual sin than as a singular nature. We must not forget that the psychological, psychiatric, medical category of homosexuality was constituted from the moment it was characterised – Westphal's famous article of 1870 on contrary sexual sensations can stand as its date of birth . . . '[10]

What had previously been seen as sinful and a matter for priests or ministers was now, since the late nineteenth century, investigated, written about, and speculated upon by various medical 'experts'. By the 1950s, there was a considerable body of negative literature on homosexuality from a psychological perspective.

Most of this literature dealt with male homosexuality. However, many of these books and articles discussed lesbianism as Jeanette Foster, an important lesbian scholar, has documented.[11] Originally published in 1956, Foster's *Sex Variant Women in Literature* listed over three hundred items classified as 'scientific and psychiatric material' which dealt to some degree with lesbianism. However, many of these were not generally available in New Zealand during the 1950s.

Of the entire medical and psychiatric collection, there were few works which saw lesbianism as other than an abnormality. Kinsey's research, published as *Sexual Behaviour in the Human Female* in 1953, made it clear that many women had lesbian experiences and feelings which he considered part of a continuum of human sexuality. In contrast, writers like Frank Caprio viewed lesbianism as an abnormality. In 1957, in *Female Homosexuality*, Caprio wrote:

> 'Crime is intimately associated with female sexual inversion. Many crimes committed by women, upon investigation, reveal that the women were either confirmed lesbians who killed because of jealousy or were latent homosexuals with a strong aggressive masculine drive. Some lesbians manifest pronounced sadistic and psychopathic trends . . . The vast majority of lesbians are emotionally unstable and neurotic. Many of them become quite disturbed at the thought that psychiatrists regard them as "sick individuals" in need of treatment . . . Occasionally homosexual experiences may result in the precipitation of a psychosis. This also is reason enough why lesbians require psychiatric treatment.'[12]

Caprio also warned that 'Lesbianism is capable of influencing the stability of our social structure. Much of the incompatibility between the sexes is closely allied to this problem.'[13] Here, he at least grasped the political importance of lesbianism in power relations between men and women.

The medical and psychiatric literature, then, placed lesbianism and male homosexuality firmly in the categories of illness and abnormality, or as an immature phase which could be outgrown. At the same time, educationalists were either silent on the subject, or were condemnatory.

There was little information available to parents and nonprofessionals regarding lesbianism in New Zealand. In so far as sex education was concerned, male 'experts' and professionals defined the boundaries of debate and what information should be made known. This had been the case during the nineteenth and early twentieth century.[14] In the 1940s, qualified state support was given to the concept of sex education in schools. The 'facts of reproduction' were to be taught along with character development, and, in particular, 'the quality of self-discipline'.[15] A limited syllabus was outlined by the Education Department, but this was to be used only in secondary schools.[16] So far as primary schools were concerned, the Department decreed in 1948 that there was no place in the primary school curriculum for group or class instruction on this topic.[17] In any case, there was no mention of lesbianism. Instead, the state actively promoted narrowly defined sexuality and gender roles. In 1955 the Health Department published a series of information pamphlets aimed at parents which were republished ten years later. The ideal promoted was a heterosexual married couple with children.[18]

Another mid-1950s sex education pamphlet for parents was published by the British Medical Association and used by New Zealand doctors. It mentioned homosexuality only to warn parents that:

'. . . However much the modern attitude towards homosexuals may have shifted towards trying to cure rather than merely condemn, the fact remains that such men are on the hunt for boys and that there are many sensitive boys whose natures can be severely warped as a result. Again, older lads in almost any kind of job, and perhaps particularly in the Services, may come under superiors who have made such messes of their own lives that the only delight left to them is to try to drag others the same way.'[19]

The author did not mention lesbianism as such but linked all homosexuality to masturbation which he regarded as 'the immature self-interest of late childhood'.[20]

There were few resources about lesbianism – and certainly no positive information – that Honora and Herbert could have obtained during the 1950s. Material available to professionals at this time, and which the Hulmes might have read, was negative and destructive about lesbianism. Honora and Hilda might have read the columns in the popular *N.Z. Woman's Weekly*, which published a series about sex education in the early 1950s –

PSYCHOLOGIST'S CASEBOOK
BY DR. JOHN R. MARTIN

Can You Diagnose this Case?

TURN TO PAGE 61 FOR DR. MARTIN'S ANALYSIS.

1—Kay's childhood was unhappy because her parents were always bickering. Kay sided with her mother in these quarrels. She felt her father was cruel. Mother and daughter had no source of affection but each other, and grew extremely close.

2—When Kay went to college she felt at first that she could not bear being separated from her mother. But she found friendship and understanding in her room-mate, Sue. Kay became as dependent upon Sue as she had been upon her mother.

3—Kay preferred staying at home with Sue to going on dates. She tolerated Sue's leaving her to have dates, but when Sue returned and wanted to tell her all about her evening's fun, Kay always belittled the boy and hastily changed the subject.

4—One night Sue came home very late and told Kay how happy she was because she was going to be married. Kay couldn't sleep that night. The next day she wept bitterly and begged Sue not to leave her, saying that she could not get along without her.

Is Kay's attachment to Sue unhealthy? Or is she only trying to save her friend from unhappy marriage?

WHAT IS YOUR DIAGNOSIS?

1—Kay's distrust of her father has grown into distrust of all men, and she is mistakenly trying to save Sue unhappiness. ☐

2—Kay has learned to satisfy all of her need for love with her mother and has abnormally transferred this love to Sue. ☐

3—Kay's unreasonable outburst and failure to understand Sue's happiness show her total lack of feminine sexual desires. ☐

without mentioning lesbianism. But they could have tested themselves in a regular column entitled 'Psychologist's Casebook' where readers were presented with a 'case' and asked to choose a 'diagnosis' from a series of options. One such 'case', in February 1954, dealt with the relationship between two women – Kay and Sue.[21] Kay was depicted as having had an unhappy childhood because her parents were always 'bickering'. Kay 'sided with her mother in these quarrels' and the two who 'had no source of affection but each other' grew 'extremely close'. At college Kay finds 'friendship and understanding' in her room-mate, Sue, and becomes 'as dependent upon Sue as she had been upon her mother'. Kay prefers staying at home with Sue to going on dates.

> 'She tolerated Sue's leaving her to have dates, but when Sue returned and wanted to tell her all about her evening's fun, Kay always belittled the boy and hastily changed the subject. One night Sue came home and told Kay how happy she was because she was going to be married. Kay couldn't sleep that night. The next day she wept bitterly and begged Sue not to leave her, saying that she could not get along without her.'

The 'correct' diagnosis was:

> 'Individuals who have problems like Kay's are sick and unhappy people. They should be encouraged to seek professional help in the understanding and control of their emotional drives, so that they can achieve their measure of happiness and social effectiveness. To some extent each of us is both masculine and feminine. It is normal for each of us to display some of the mannerisms of the opposite sex. It is generous to reserve judgement of our fellows when we have no more than hearsay on which to base our opinions.'[22]

Perhaps the most publicised official statement made by the authorities on the subject of lesbianism and morals in general was the Mazengarb Report, which was published in 1954. It is difficult to assess the impact that it had upon the lives of young lesbians. However, we think that parents who read the Report and took the warnings it contained seriously would certainly have become more watchful and concerned about any indications of lesbianism among their children or their childrens' friends. The Mazengarb Committee found it necessary to remind parents that 'sexual misbehaviour can occur between members of the same sex'.[23]

Large numbers of women unquestioningly moved into heterosexuality during the early 1950s, some of whom became lesbians decades later when more options became possible.[24] For most women of the time, the possibility that lesbianism could be a choice never arose. The majority of women either remained ignorant about lesbianism, or if they did become aware of it, the fear of social punishment ensured that they did not step outside of the prescribed norms. Those who chose lesbianism and escaped the worst social consequences of their choice often internalised the negative social attitudes towards lesbianism. This sometimes resulted in alcoholism, suicide, mental breakdown and low self-esteem because of guilt and fear. Apart from the potential loss of employment, housing and connections with family and friends, there were more devastating possibilities. Parents and guardians could commit their lesbian and gay children under the age of twenty-one to psychiatric institutions as voluntary patients. Older lesbians and gay men could also be committed by their families with the collusion of doctors who believed that lesbianism and male homosexuality was indicative of insanity. Aversion therapy and electro-convulsive therapy were treatments used on lesbians at the time. We know of lesbians who received these treatments in the 1950s for their lesbianism.

Despite all this, lesbians resisted. Some women resisted openly. Others did so more discreetly.[25] We consider that whether or not women consciously saw themselves as resisting the pressures to conform to prescribed gender roles for women, they nevertheless placed themselves in a position of defiance to the prescribed ideal. In this sense we would define all lesbianism at that time as resistance.

For many Maori lesbians the experience was different. In *Tahuri*, her collection of stories, Ngahuia Te Awekotuku suggests that some Maori women who were in relationships together were often accepted by their communities.[26] Others were, however, less fortunate.

Lesbian resistance in the 1950s was not organised within lesbian political organisations. Present research indicates that there were no lesbian or gay organisations in New Zealand before 1963, when the Dorian Society, a social club for male homosexuals, was formed in Wellington. The Society refused to admit lesbians as members until the late 1960s.[27] The N.Z. Homosexual Law Reform Society was formed in 1967. Its main objective was to change the law relating to male homosexuality, but it included heterosexuals among its members. Its tactics were conservative and the organisation was not interested in the problems faced by lesbians. In Auckland in late 1970, the K.G. Club, a social club for lesbians, was started by a group of Maori, and some Pakeha working-class lesbians.

The Gay Liberation Front, initiated by Ngahuia Te Awekotuku and five others in Auckland in 1972, adopted more radical tactics and had a wider programme of social change than the Homosexual Law Reform Society. Separate lesbian political organisations were established soon after. The Sisters for Homophile Equality (S.H.E.) was started in Christchurch and Wellington in 1973, functioning as a national lesbian organisation until the mid-seventies and publishing a lesbian magazine called *The Circle* from December 1973 in Wellington. Another lesbian social club, named Club 41 after its street address, was started in Wellington by members from S.H.E. Christchurch. S.H.E. started the first women's refuge in that city.[28]

Outside New Zealand, organisations for homosexuals had started again after World War II, following the destruction by the Nazis of the European organisations in Germany and all occupied territories from 1933 onwards, including the Scientific Humanitarian Committee founded by Dr Magnus Hirschfeld in 1897. The post-war organisations included the C.O.C. (Cultuur en Ontspannings Centrum, or Centre for Culture and Recreation), Holland 1946; the Sex Education Society in Britain, in 1947; the Forbund af 1948, Norway and Denmark in 1948; the R.F.S.L. (National Society for Sexual Equality) in Sweden 1950; the Mattachine Society, USA 1951; One Inc, USA 1952; The Homosexual Law Reform Society, UK 1958; The Albany Trust, UK 1960, among many others world-wide.[29] All of these were primarily for male homosexuals, though they did admit lesbian members. Major lesbian organisations were The Daughters of Bilitis, USA 1956, and the Minorities Research Group, UK 1962. The focus for both lesbian and gay organisations of the post-war period up until the 1970s was on gaining social 'acceptance' and 'tolerance'. They all produced magazines or newsletters and it is possible that some lesbians in New Zealand may have been able to subscribe to them during the early 1950s, in spite of the difficulties of importing such material.

Most lesbians in New Zealand were unable to obtain any

information about lesbianism or lesbian relationships. The most serious problem was an absence of lesbian role models or positive images of lesbianism. This was difficult for lesbians who were aware of their sexuality – but for women generally it effectively meant that no alternative to the narrowly defined compulsory heterosexual model was visible. Some women of the time seemed never to have even heard the term 'lesbian'. Trade unionist Sonja Davies for example, recalled an incident during the mid-1940s where one nurse asked another 'What are lesbians?', while another wondered, 'Is it a political party?'[30] The situation had not changed by the 1950s.

Although there were no lesbian political organisations in New Zealand during the early 1950s, there were lesbian social networks. These varied according to the class, race, age and geographic location of the women. Most of the women in these groups were very careful, and among middle-class lesbians some women did not openly acknowledge their lesbianism even among themselves. Many of the women were married and maintained hidden relationships with other women, leading precarious double lives, though some husbands knew that their wives were lesbian. In one case a husband in New Plymouth during the later 1950s encouraged his wife to establish lesbian relationships, providing these 'did not become too serious' and that he could participate in the sexual encounters.[31] However, two married women who had a relationship with each other in the South Island during the early 1950s fled the area together when their husbands found out about the relationship and were scandalised and unforgiving.[32]

Within the female-intensive occupations of teaching and nursing contained small numbers of lesbians.[33] Within these occupations small networks of friends developed, consisting of perhaps two or three couples who met for an occasional evening together. These networks usually had little knowledge of other groups and the women were terrified that they might be exposed as lesbians. Such women, however, were aware that they were lesbian and did sometimes discuss it within their own circles.[34] Many women in these professions remained unmarried and some lived together. Because of the general ignorance about lesbianism at that time, some lesbians were able to live together without their families, colleagues or friends suspecting they were anything other than companions.[35]

These groups had their own special terms for themselves and for other lesbians, using expressions such as being 'like that' or 'she's one of the family'. Women who socialised with homosexual men used the term 'kamp'.[36] This term was used especially by working-class lesbians who had contact with 'ship-queens' – homosexual men working on board British ships which visited New Zealand at that time. The term 'gay', used in the USA to mean homosexual, was not used in New Zealand until the 1970s.[37]

Working-class lesbian networks existed in a number of occupational groups, including domestic workers in hotels or hospitals. Some of these women knew homosexual men from their workplaces and through them came in contact with overseas 'kamp' men at parties. Prostitutes and working-class heterosexual men were also part of these circles.[38] There were groups of both working-class and middle-class lesbians in the armed forces, and in the Post Office, which was another large employer of women. These women were cautious about accepting newcomers and socialised mainly within their own circles. Exposure as a lesbian could mean a dishonourable discharge from the military, and there were risks for other workers as well. In one case during the early 1960s, two lesbians in the armed forces were interrogated following an incident when they were seen kissing each other in a parked vehicle.[39] One of the women received a dishonourable discharge, while the other was able to convince her superiors that the incident had been quite innocent on her part.

Apart from occupational networks, there were also lesbian networks in women's sports, particularly women's cricket and hockey. These were mainly younger lesbians from varied class backgrounds. Nearly all of these women were extremely cautious about admitting their lesbianism.[40] There were also lesbians among theatrical and 'arty' circles. One lesbian who was thirty-three in 1954 and lived in Christchurch, working as a shorthand-typist, said that there were rumours about certain women, but that the word 'lesbian' was never mentioned. She recalled hearing about one notorious woman that 'There was something terrible about her, but no one said openly what it was or admitted it.' She also said:

> 'Special interest groups like repertory societies, music or ballet groups, or writing groups . . . all gave an excuse for mixing with people who were outside your family, neighbours or workmates. You could say that you met together because of these interests in common . . . The 1940s and 1950s in Christchurch were . . . awful. I left for Australia in 1958 and stayed there for the next twenty years.'[41]

She knew of other lesbians who had left for overseas because of the isolation they had felt.

Generally, it was extremely difficult for lesbians to make contact with other lesbians. There were hotels where male homosexuals could meet. However, the age restrictions and discrimination against women made it difficult for lesbians, especially young women, to meet in these places. Homosexual men also used public toilets, parks and particular streets as ways to make contacts.[42] Lesbians, however, did not make contacts in this way.

It is also likely that some lesbians during the 1950s in New Zealand cross-dressed and lived as men. Research from other countries, in particular the USA, has shown that this has been done by many lesbians. Dressing as men enabled women to gain access to male incomes and to avoid discrimination as lesbians, in spite of the risks involved in such a deception. The Lesbian Herstory Archives, New York, have a collection of documented histories of lesbians who cross-dressed in the 1950s. Female cross-dressing has occurred through the centuries. Dekker and van de Pol (1989) document female cross-dressers in the Netherlands from the sixteenth to the nineteenth centuries[43] and Gifford (1983), Katz (1978, 1983), and Faderman (1985), describe cross-dressers in the U.S.A. and Europe.[44]

For lesbians who wanted to find out more about lesbianism, sources of information were extremely limited in extent and content. This was partly as a result of censorship and partly as a result of the few positive images of lesbianism. The most prolific information sources were dominated by the distorted accounts of medical and psychiatric writers.

So far as novels were concerned, there were very few available in New Zealand at that time which dealt specifically with lesbianism. The novel *Olivia* by 'Olivia' (the pseudonym used by Dorothy Strachey) was available. Described as dealing with 'the ecstasy and despair of first love',[45] it deals with love between women at a French girls' boarding-school. Radclyffe Hall's book *The Well of Loneliness* (1928) presents a stereotyped view of lesbian relationships but did confirm for lesbian readers of the time that there were others like themselves. Some other novels which contained depictions of homosexual men or lesbians were also available through public libraries, for example, *Details of Jeremy Stretton* by Audrey Lindop (1955) which portrays an unhappy male homosexual, and Graham Greene's *Stamboul Train* which includes a lesbian character who loses her girlfriend to a man. Some local writers like Frank Sargeson, James Courage and Katherine Mansfield included homosexual or lesbian themes and subthemes in their work, for example Mansfield's 'Bliss', and Courage's 'A Way of Love'. These writers were themselves lesbian or gay, though this was not acknowledged. However, even though a library might possess a particular book, access to it could still be difficult. Some books were kept on 'closed shelves' and were available only on request from the librarian – and not all library-users were given access.[46]

During the 1950s in New Zealand, there were no films screened which dealt with lesbianism or male homosexuality.[47] Two films dealing with male homosexuality – 'Tea and Sympathy' and 'The Sergeant' – were screened in other countries during the 1950s.

As we have shown, the fifties were a difficult period for lesbians in New Zealand, even for those women who were part of a lesbian network. There were no feminist, lesbian, or gay social services, organisations, clubs, bookshops, magazines or radio pro-grammes. For lesbians who were not part of a network, the isolation could be devastating.

For young lesbians the situation was even more difficult. Discovery by parents or even teachers could result in punishment or medical treatment. Further, with the limited sources of information that were available, young lesbians were unlikely to have access to knowledge about lesbianism or other lesbians. It was also unlikely that young lesbians could have come into contact with any of the lesbian networks which have been mentioned, except perhaps the womens' sports networks. It is probable that the majority of older lesbians would have seen very young lesbians as a threat to their hidden networks. Some, having internalised negative social attitudes about themselves adopted a protective attitude to younger women, warning them away from lesbianism. We both have personal experience of lesbians doing this even into the late 1970s.

We think that for Pauline and Juliet, at the ages of fifteen and sixteen years, the possibility of making contact with lesbians in Christchurch in the early fifties was remote, even if they had wished to do so. Their access to books or to other sources of information about lesbianism was also negligible. However, there are two factors which cannot be dismissed. One is the library at Ilam. Although Pauline's diaries do not mention any books about lesbianism, this is not neccessarily conclusive evidence that neither she nor Juliet did not read or know of such books. One woman we interviewed said that the Ilam library was reported to have been extensive. The second, Hilda Hulme's involvement in marriage guidance, suggests that she might have possessed books about sexuality. Hilda had personal contacts with doctors and psychiatrists who could have given her such information, however negative. From reading Pauline's diaries, we think that Hilda probably gave Juliet some sex education. On 10 June, 1954, for example, Pauline reported that 'Mrs Hulme has told Deborah a great deal about the old subject and we have discussed it fully. We know a great deal more now.'[48] Other entries suggest that the 'old subject' refers to sex. If Juliet was given information it is likely that she would have shared it with Pauline. But it is most unlikely she got any information about lesbianism from Hilda.

However, we think that Pauline and Juliet had no accurate information about lesbians. Their knowledge most probably would have been restricted to their own experience. Nor were they in a position to make contact with other, older lesbians in Christchurch. We think that in these circumstances it was impossible for them to see their relationship in a wider, more positive, framework. Seeing themselves as special would have been one positive way to counter the hostile attitudes in their environment, but it would also have encouraged feelings of isolation and dependence on one another. Meanwhile, Honora took the central role in regulating a relationship which she could see only as undesirable.

CHAPTER ELEVEN

Impact of the Case on Lesbians

'Identity is what you can say you are according to how they say you can be.' (Jill Johnston in *Lesbian Nation*, 1974)[1]

The Parker-Hulme case had a significant effect on lesbians in New Zealand, especially before the mid 1970s. This happened in several ways: by associating lesbianism with violent death, criminality and insanity the case reinforced anti-lesbian attitudes; as well, it helped to construct new forms of anti-lesbianism. After the mid seventies more information about lesbians became generally available, particularly as a result of the Gay Liberation and Women's Liberation movements. Individual lesbians now had the backup of a developing political movement which emphasised lesbian pride and which helped counter the predominant negative views. The establishment of women's bookshops and publishing houses in New Zealand, as elsewhere, meant that there were sources of information which were pro-lesbian. Negative media reports in the context of criminal cases were no longer a dominant source of representations about lesbians. Also, lesbian magazines, radio programmes, centres and groups throughout the country transformed the environment for lesbians in New Zealand.

Immediately after the murder, people who had responsibility for young girls became watchful and fearful, in case girls formed same-sex attractions. People who had contact with declared lesbians treated them with suspicion, as if lesbianism and violence were inevitably linked. Also, girls and women who thought they might be lesbians internalised negative and stereotyped views of lesbianism which made identifying as a lesbian difficult, if not impossible. For those women who did identify as lesbian it was important for them to ensure that they were as unlike Parker and Hulme as possible in order to distance themselves in their own minds from these negative associations.

The interviews in this chapter are not based on a broad survey. They were collected by advertising through lesbian publications and through personal contacts. Some heterosexual women also discussed with us the effect the case had upon them – for many of these women it had played a central role in their lives because they turned away from lesbian attractions as a consequence of their fears of being like Parker and Hulme. However, we have not included these interviews here.

Personal accounts

The following five accounts are taken from written question-naires completed in 1987. The selection has been made on the basis of providing a diversity of experience, rather than repeating similar stories for confirmation. We did not include questions about race or class in this questionnaire so this information is not available.

Lesbian born in 1962

She first thought she might be lesbian in 1973 and had first heard about the Parker-Hulme case in 1972, when she was ten years old. Her mother told her about the case, saying that the two girls were friends, that they were strange and that they had attended the same Girls High School as her mother. She said that her mother did not mention the word lesbian. She said that she was shocked that a mother had been killed by her child and horrified that girls would kill. She wanted to know why they had killed her.

'I recall forming a picture in my mind of two women killing another and not being able to understand and being confused about the event. I think I felt this because of a lack of information – if I had known of these women's restrictions, I'd have understood their anger. My mother told me of the killing at a time when I was developing close friendships with other young women, perhaps to instill fear and distrust that she had of women. Because I now know the real story behind the killing, I'm pleased I never came out to my mother whilst I was a teenager because of how she had been introduced to lesbians. I feel the event did influence me subconsciously, it's been interesting exploring this by answering the survey.'

Lesbian born in 1963

She first thought she might be lesbian in 1969 and comments that 'of course, I didn't know the word lesbian then'. She first heard about the case in 1975, when she was twelve years old and living in Christchurch.

'My mother told me about the case. One day I wanted to go up to Victoria Park but my mother said no. When I asked why not she at first said it was because dirty old men went up there to look for young girls. I said I wasn't worried about that because I could look out for myself. Then she said that people got murdered up there. So I asked her who got killed and she told me of a mother who was murdered by her daughter and her friend; that they deliberately took her up there and smashed her head in with rocks and left her on one of the paths up there. She never said that the girls were lesbian although I do remember a feeling that there was something sick and evil between the two girls. This was probably due to the way my mother described them, i.e. they were unnatural, sick, evil, etc.'

She said that she was shocked that a mother had been killed by her child, because:

'I couldn't understand why someone would kill her own mother, and even more shocked that her friend helped her. My mother didn't tell me why the girls did it; so no wonder it seemed so odd and freaky, because to me it just looked like they did it because they were evil. If I had been told of all the circumstances (i.e. they loved each other and did it to stay together) I would have had a completely different view. Instead, I only had enough information to think the worst. I don't remember hearing anything else about the murder and I didn't go to Victoria Park that day or again for a very long time, till 1986 in fact. It just seemed like too eerie a place to visit once I'd heard that someone had been murdered there. Anyway, it was too far away from my suburb to go there much as it was. Eventually I didn't think about it. I've had no long-term effects other than not going to the park, and I decided to complete the survey since I am Christchurch-born and bred (though living in London at present). Having heard of the story, I feel concerned about having the story put right.'

Lesbian born in 1949

She first thought she might be a lesbian sometime between twelve and fifteen years old, in 1962-65. She first heard about the case in 1966 when she was seventeen at a girls' school in Hamilton and read about it in a book of 'famous murders'. She thinks that the book said they had 'a close and intense friendship' which was 'unhealthy/unnatural'. The book may or may not have said 'lesbian' – she said that she 'knew it anyway'. She said that:

'I was shocked that a mother had been killed by her child – slightly. I was pleased that there were other lesbians. I was disappointed that they had been caught and separated. I couldn't imagine killing my mother, I felt very isolated and different. I understood how they felt about each other. I didn't tell anyone about reading the book. I have never forgotten reading it. I remember the circumstances of finding and reading the book in quite good detail even though it was twenty-one years ago – so it must have had a great impact. I can't remember the name of the book or any of the other cases – not even if they were all N.Z. cases or worldwide. I don't remember hearing or seeing anything else about it till I read your article when I recognised it immediately. I found the case absolutely fascinating in a macabre sort of way. The relationship more than the murder, I think.'

Lesbian born in 1942

She first thought she might be lesbian in 1952 at the age of ten, when she 'loved another girl and wanted to be a boy'. However, she did not 'discover the label homosexual' and realise 'that was me' until 1956, at the age of fourteen. She first heard about the Parker-Hulme case in 1975, when she was thirty-three years old, when she was 'sharing a house', and was told about the case 'by a prison officer'. She said that she was:

'Told that the mother did not like their relationship (too close, maybe unnatural). Felt that I was told in order to get at me. I felt upset that their mother was not accepting and that they had no one to turn to . . . I felt this because my own mother thought my lesbianism was good for me and was very accepting towards my lover and friends.'

As a long term effect of hearing about the case she thinks that 'I have become interested in helping parents of lesbians understand our lives.'

Lesbian born in 1951

She came out in 1979 at the age of twenty-eight. She reported that in 1967, at the age of sixteen, she 'fleetingly' considered lesbianism, but was 'very threatened by the thought'. She first heard about the Parker-Hulme case in 1960, when she was a nine-year-old child living with her parents. Her mother told her about the case, and she heard that 'the girls had a close and intense friendship, as well as an unhealthy and unnatural relationship.' She reported that she was shocked that a mother had been killed by her child, 'but also rather thrilled that there were daughters who had power over their mothers'. She said that:

'I know that my mother was drawing some kind of parallel between them and my intense relationship with my "best" friend P – we were inseparable from six to seventeen. My mother was obviously somewhat threatened that a "good girl" could turn on her mother as a result of a relationship like ours. P and I sexually experimented off and on from six to puberty, usually at my instigation. This stopped at puberty which is when my mother talked quite a lot about the girls – in the early sixties. There were other similarities. I was an only child, we were working-class whereas P's parents were both doctors, and they were wealthy, intellectual etc. My life was schizophrenic, as I spent about equal amounts of time at each house. My parents were awed and rather scathing about P's parents and their life.'

So far as long-term effects resulting from the case are concerned, she said that:

'I think it was another factor in influencing my parents and public opinion that lesbians were bad, crazy etc. My mother fought all these attitudes in herself when I came out later. I think it made it that much harder to come out to yourself in the fifties and sixties. The manipulation of their case was a powerful ideology.'

She said of Parker and Hulme that 'they were sad, mystical (important though I didn't know why) figures in the background of my childhood.'

The following experiences are from interviews with lesbians made between 1987 and 1991.

Pakeha lesbian, born in 1937
'When it happened I was fascinated – one of the most interesting things – I felt I knew them. I really identified with the fantasy world. A girlfriend and I used to write to each other, pretending we were boyfriends. Also, I used to make up stories for my younger sister for years and years.'

'I followed the case in the newspapers – they were both very intelligent – I was interested in things like telepathy and other things to do with the mind and was trying those kinds of things out with my own friends.'

'I thought it was awful that they'd killed a mother, but seeing the two girls, I wondered what the mother could have done to cause them to do that. They seemed very intense. A lot depends on who you meet. They almost became one. They had the same fantasy world.'

'I think I understood they were having a relationship. That made it fascinating, the intensity of their feelings.'

'I can still remember the photograph with Pauline looking downcast in a long coat – Juliet seemed to be more powerful.'

'Also, I wrote a diary and poetry and stories, so I felt close to them. What struck me was that thing of fate – that could make you do the same thing yourself.'

'I came out as a lesbian when I was forty years old, after being married for twenty years.'

Pakeha lesbian, born in 1941
'Between 1957 and 1958 I was at a girls' boarding school. I was involved in an intense and important sexual relationship with another boarder. We used to take walks together to a deserted part of the grounds and make love. I distinctly remember sitting at the table at home during the holidays and reading a newspaper report of the Parker-Hulme case. I felt sick and horrified because I realised that the relationship I was involved in was like theirs. I finished my relationship with my friend and never saw her again. I went on to University and got involved with men as soon as I could. I had sex with a man in order to prove that I wasn't abnormal – having sex with men in 1959 was not the ordinary thing to do. I married an older man and stayed married for fifteen years. After this I lived with a younger man for five years. I finally came out as a lesbian at the age of forty-one, in 1982. When I came out, I remember talking and crying about my first lover and about the Parker-Hulme case to a friend. It was really traumatic for me. What I don't understand, is that I know the case happened in 1954 – but I read about it in 1958. I have blocked off some parts of this memory from myself, obviously. It is a very frightening memory. Perhaps I found an old newspaper, or perhaps there was a later

report in the press. I don't remember. One thing that made me frightened was that I hated my mother and wanted to kill her. The other thing was that I realised from the newspaper that there was something very wrong and insane about lesbianism. What I regret is that it took me so many years to come out. Also that I have never seen my first lover again. I just abandoned her. I heard that she married early. I would like to find her but I have no idea where to look.'

Pakeha lesbian, born in 1943
'It would have been in 1961-62 when I was seventeen or eighteen, that I was engaged in that relationship. I was at secondary school in Christchurch and I got involved with K. My mother found letters under my mattress from K and I got rushed off to a psychiatrist and we were forbidden to see one another and even had the threat of police put onto us, you know, if we were going to engage in seeing one another . . . during all that my mother brought up about the two girls Parker-Hulme had murdered their mother and they were Girls High pupils . . . Girls High was meant to be a good school. And my mother was quite frightened that because my parents had forbidden K and I to see one another that my mother might be in for the same treatment – that K and I could actually murder her which is just too bloody ridiculous. That made me feel very frightened too, because it was like a trust thing, you know, if I was anywhere with my mother, just the two of us, I felt what was she thinking? K and I each saw a psychiatrist for about six months, and it was a wee bit after that that my mother mentioned about these two girls who had murdered their mother and that she felt quite frightened too. So you can imagine, I love walking up Victoria Park, up that track, even now it goes through my mind though. I've grown out of it now, I spend quite a lot of time with my mother, through lots of good communication I have let her know about my involvement with women. That doesn't bother her or me now, obviously, but it certainly did, and you can imagine how horrible that was for me when I was only seventeen or eighteen growing up with that.'
Question: When the case itself happened did you read about it independently or did your mother tell you about it later?
'My mother told me. I didn't even know what a lesbian was when I had this mad desire to be close to another girl at school. I mean

I didn't know I was doing, well, wrong in their eyes, so until I was taken to the psychiatrist I didn't know the word lesbian and I didn't know anything about these two girls Parker and Hulme. And I truly don't think my mother and father knew how to handle finding out their daughter was a lesbian and just shot us off to a psychiatrist. My mother did say that I would go mad if I continued my life living with women and having relationships with women – that was something else that freaked me out too, so probably the idea was I was to go mad and then bop her on the head.'

Question: What about the woman that you had the relationship with and her parents?

'There were just phone calls made between sets of parents forbidding us to see one another so I am not too sure whether they were clued up, aware of the murder. But you can see why my mother and father probably would have thought that, because I mean weren't Parker and Hulme forbidden to see one another? Or one was going away overseas? . . . I've had a lot of counselling in recent years with a psychologist who has made me discuss all this business of K again with my mother which has been quite difficult because I found that whenever I mentioned K's name my mother freaks out and avoids the conversation. I think she is terrified still that K and I will get back together. K is in a settled marriage, she married shortly after our affair finished, she's got two grown-up children. My mother said about two years ago that she would be frightened that I would ruin her marriage – how ridiculous. K has been here for lunch and we have been able to talk all the past through as the psychologist suggested. I've had a lot of depression and anxiety in my life and the psychologist thinks it might be because I've never worked through my relationship with K properly. That relationship was stopped between K and I by my parents and her parents so he's trying to get it all unravelled if you can see what I mean, and work through it properly with my mother. My father died so I can't consider him. Then I've gone back and talked to the psychologist. I felt really good, it's cleared a lot of fog and freed things up a bit. When a relationship is terminated by parents I think that affects later relationships. I think it's affected my relationships with other women because I have had very short term relationships and haven't seen anything through.'

Question: Some feeling that somebody else is going to finish the relationship for you?
'Exactly.'

Pakeha lesbian, born in 1946
'I lived in Ashburton . . . What I remember most is that my first knowledge of the word lesbian was shock and fear because of the way that my parents, aunt, grandparents talked about the case while it was going on in Christchurch. I can remember snippets – one of them being that one of the girls must have hated her mother – and I felt frightened, because somehow, I identified with that.

'The other thing I remember was that they were allegedly very intelligent which I also identified with (rightly or wrongly) and that made me scared too. I don't know to what extent the case coloured my attitude to lesbianism but I feel that it probably affected my parents. They had good reason to believe I was a lesbian when I was thirteen, and what I remember was the fear that my parents conveyed to me.'

Maori lesbian, born in 1938
'I was sixteen when the case happened. There were articles about it in *Truth*, but I was forbidden to read them. However, my friends and I got hold of *Truth* and read about it behind the bus-shed. I didn't quite understand what had happened at the time. I thought it was wrong of them to kill the mother. I thought their relationship was strangeish, but three years later, in 1957 when I was nineteen and interested in another girl I connected it to the case and thought back on it. The newspapers had all implied that Juliet and Pauline were "sick" – I wondered what this meant, whether it had something to do with the relationship. However there was a photograph of them and one had pock-marked skin. I thought that this must be the "sickness".'

Pakeha lesbian, born in 1942
She was twelve years in 1954 and was living on a farm. She said that she was 'very interested in the case' though 'cannot remember why'. When she asked her mother 'Why would girls kill their mother?' her mother told her that:
'Mothers were just like cats, dogs and horses – they were all

different. Something very terrible must have happened to the girls – not all mothers were good mothers. The girls must have been hurt.'

She said that her mother told her not to believe everything that is written in the newspapers. Her mother explained that very little was known about why the girls did it, a lot was being kept hidden, and nothing was reported about how the girls felt or why they did it. She said that in the following months she kept enquiring about where they were now, and 'who was looking after them now since they haven't a mummy'.

She said that she asked her mother about her responses to the case again in 1987, in order to check her memory of what her mother had said before she talked to us. Her mother confirmed the explanation she had given to the twelve-year-old and added that the case 'had seemed to worry her considerably'.

Pakeha lesbian, born in 1940
'I was fourteen when the case happened. I remember reading about it and hearing about it. I was very excited by the case, because they were two girls in love with each other. I was sorry they were caught. I understood perfectly well why they had killed the mother because I wanted to kill my mother too. After they were caught though, I thought that they were very lucky, because they wouldn't have to live at home any more. They would be able to live in a prison together, with a whole lot of other girls. I was sorry when I heard that they would be separated. I began having lesbian affairs from my late teens, but was emotionally interested in other girls for a long time before that.'

Pakeha lesbian, born in 1935
'When the case happened in 1954, I was nineteen years old and on the verge of getting married. For some reason, I was fascinated by the case. I felt that they had done something really important, something that I should be thinking about. One part of me knew that I was interested in other women. Killing the mother, and being involved together, going to prison for it seemed to be making a statement, striking out in some way. I was married for over twenty years, and first came out as a lesbian when I was over forty years old. Perhaps I should have thought more about it all at that time and broken off the marriage.'

Maori lesbian, born in 1956
'I heard about those girls that they were "like that" and that they had killed the mother of one of them. I must have been seven or eight years old when I heard this in about 1963-64. I think I overhead a conversation between my mother and my aunt. I kept hearing about the event through my teenage years. I got a sense of some need to cover it up, not to talk about it and especially not to talk about them being "like that" – a feeling, really, that the whole thing was perverse, not that the word was actually said, more implied. There was a whole atmosphere around the event of something very wrong which should be kept hidden.'

Pakeha lesbian, born in 1950
'I don't remember the case happening, of course. But when I was about twelve years old we were living in Christchurch, and I remember my grandmother taking me for a drive in her car. We drove by Victoria Park, and she told me about the case and how the two girls had murdered the mother. I was doing well at school and knew I would be going on to University. I came from a family who encouraged this. I thought to myself when my grandmother told me about the case that if you did anything like that it would really spoil everything for you – you'd have to go to prison, and wouldn't be able to go to University.'

Pakeha lesbian, born in 1941
'I heard about the case on the radio. I would have been about thirteen years old. I wanted to kill my father very badly, so I could identify with them really easily. I thought how lucky they were that they could really do it. I had a sense of "good on them". I can see myself standing in the kitchen thinking "good, really good". I had an incredibly intense hatred of my father. This lasted until I had a dream about being in prison, and going to be hung next day for a crime I hadn't committed. In my dream an angel came and told me to fear not, and then I was taken out to the hanging place, with everyone condemning me for this crime very unjustly. I woke up feeling cleansed and released and at that point I knew that to hate my father so much was to destroy myself. I have never hated anyone to that degree ever again. My first lesbian feelings would have been at the age of thirteen to fifteen. My parents got very anxious around the time of my first crush, and stopped the

relationship for me. I didn't know why, or what that was about until I was in my late twenties. I saw Parker and Hulme as adolescents like myself who had annihilated something and someone who was destructive to them.'

Maori lesbian, born in 1947
'A local women's group was holding a lunch-time meeting, and the female sixth formers were all taken along to listen to the guest speaker. I went along with the other two young women who were in the sixth form at the time, this was 1965. We were escorted by a woman teacher. A women's prison officer, was the speaker at the meeting. She talked at great length about the school and about the Borstal, she called it a school and talked about the number of Maori girls there and predictably I was the only Maori girl at this meeting. She paid particular attention to me. She was an absolutely fascinating woman. After she had talked about what happens to young women when they run foul of the law, we all ate cucumber sandwiches and sipped little cups of tea, and somehow she managed to isolate me and we talked. During our conversation, which my teacher was watching from a very worried distance, the prison officer brought out some letters that the girls had written her and asked me if I knew any of them and what I thought of the letters. Its quite strange really, because at that time I had just realised my lesbianism, and I knew that that was what I wanted to be.

'We talked about these letters, and what I remember most about them was the way the women writing to her talked about their "darls". She asked me if I knew what a darl was. I didn't, but I pretended that I did because I assumed it meant someone that you did it with, and we giggled and twitched and looked at each other. Then along came the teacher and said it was time to go home.

'So off we all went in her funny little car, there were four of us, two other girls in the back seat, and the teacher in the front with me. We dropped the other girls off which I thought was peculiar because they should have been dropped off after me – she did this big circle around the town and took them home first.

'Then she took me home, and I'll never forget, it was really strange. We were driving along and she put her hand on my knee and then she asked me if I had had thoughts about other girls –

at which point, very po-faced I said "oh goodness no", during which time my head was still spinning from the letters by the "darls".

'Then she launched into this great rave about two young girls in Christchurch, and what they had done to their mother, or what one of them had done to one of their mothers – she had her hand on my knee and proceeded to describe with, I think, a rather gruesome relish how this young woman had put a brick in her stocking and smashed her mother over the head with it. I couldn't really figure out why she was telling me this, so I sat there and I looked at her and the old hand was sort of you know . . .

'I had another experience with her a few weeks later in the infirmary, when she continued her tale about these two young girls up in the Cashmere Hills bashing the head of their mother with a brick, and I couldn't understand why she was telling me this . . . I realise now, of course, that she was warning me, that that was the message. If you have these unnatural desires, if you do feel like that about other girls, you might end up committing a similar, revolting crime.

'The confusion I felt came from the excitement of her hand on my leg, which was really strange and yet the morbidity and detached dreamy melancholy with which she described what had happened there . . .

'During the car ride when we pulled up and stopped she said "I really do think you should think about what I have just told you, it's very important that you think about it." . . . and to this day I've been thinking about it, and the only conclusion I can come out with is that she was warning me, and yet looking back, why did she feel me up in the car.

'Worse still was the time in the infirmary . . . I had a swelling in my groin and I couldn't play sport, I needed to see this teacher and get a note to be excused from sport. She took me to the infirmary and quite literally laid me down, I was sort of stretched out there, and she sort of, I suppose she indecently assaulted me really. She didn't actually do any sexual stroking, she just sort of had a look and she was getting her rocks off . . . I slammed my knees together and sat up and said "Well you've seen it now haven't you, I need the note." She said yes and wrote it for me, and then sort of hung about.

'Then she said "Have you thought much about what I told you

when I ran you home." And I said "Yes, well I've tried to bring it up with my mother."

'My mother was fascinating, she'd lived around lesbians all her life, but she couldn't make the connection, she couldn't figure out why this teacher had brought up this particular issue, though she was fairly conscious of my leanings at that time.

'The teacher never came back to me about the issue . . . I think she was afraid she might have gone too far . . . and she did, though it didn't affect my sexuality at all.

'I actually read the book about the case though, *Obsession*, but I didn't identify with them, that wasn't me. For a start they were pakeha, they were rich, you know, their parents had cars, they were at university, they were totally different from me, I was living within a very working-class Maori environment. There was no connection, I mean they were white girls, pakeha, in Christchurch which was foreign land, it was completely alien from the pa that I was brought up in, so that there was no immediate recognition or self-identification at all.

'The book didn't impact on my life, it was something out there. But another lesbian book, *Women's Barracks*, that scene was much more me because it was about rough coloured women that belted each other up and drank lots of booze, sort of ran around getting each other off, it was much more immediate . . .'

Question: . . . and they didn't murder mothers?

'No they didn't murder mothers, they murdered each other and they murdered husbands . . .'

'In 1971 I was in Christchurch and some local lesbians drove me around the Cashmere Hills and sort of showed it to me as part of the lesbian herstory of the area. I thought it was very, very morbid.

'The thing for me about the case is that it focuses upon the violence in our relationships, not only with each other, but with those who reject us or who in some way endanger us either spiritually or emotionally and it's a really good, for me looking at it now, it's a superb illustration of how we respond under stress, what we do . . . something so primeval, a primeval act of absolute despair and what horrifies me I think is that they're still paying, that we bring the case up with straights and they still can't see beyond their own grisly and fettered limitations. I mean, how many heterosexuals kill each other off!'

Pakeha lesbian, born 1939

'I was fifteen when the murder happened. We all talked about it at school, trying to figure out what it was about – what was all this stuff about the diaries. I was really scared that my own diary would be discovered like theirs, because it was full of sexual fantasies. I suspected that they were in a sexual relationship but didn't dare to discuss this with my friends.

'I thought it was OK that they had killed the mother – she was obviously nasty and could be killed off.

'I thought there was something terribly exciting about the sexual stuff and that interested me more than the murder. One of my schoolmates actually gave a speech about the Christchurch murder case in the school oratory competitions that year . . . we were at a provincial co-ed school. She spoke about the case with some compassion and an attempt to understand them. I think she won the competition.

'I talk to many women in my work, and I can tell you that I believe it is every adolescent's fantasy, it is the ultimate freedom, to get rid of your mother. And I think most mothers experience an urge to annihilate their kids at some stage, too. I think that the imagination of people was gripped by the case because here are some people who have really done it. It is actually very satisfying that someone else acts out your fantasies for you. I also think that there is an impact on everyone when this happens because you can move on in your life and don't need to fantasise any more. Most girls do think about killing their mothers, I think. But they know they can't and won't. When the Parker murder happened it showed that it could be done, and this gave a sense of "freedom" – in a way Parker and Hulme became hidden heroines for many of us. Also I do think that girls knowing about them being lesbians meant that more girls felt able to become lesbians themselves, just knowing that the possibility was there for us.'

The next account is taken from *Broadsheet*[2] magazine and is an interview with two lesbians, D. and M., who met in 1951 and lived together for twenty-seven years. When they met they were both nurse trainees and they soon became close friends.

D.: 'We spent hours and hours and hours talking. But then, being in a nursing situation everybody knew but us. We didn't know. Parker and Hulme were the only two people I'd heard of and they had a *folie à deux* – a mental condition that's aggravated by one another, and one of them killed one of their mothers. That was all that I'd heard of . . . One night we were doing our usual talking and talking and talking, M. and I, it did evolve into a sort of physical response to one another . . . So we lay awake all that night thinking that there was something terribly wrong with us. We were both totally confused as to what had happened. Once we'd started that we wanted to repeat it. We didn't know what to do. We both left nursing in any case. M went to Hawkes Bay. I got taken to my doctor and sent to a psychiatrist. That was a terrible experience because he gave me an internal examination which was a hell of a shock to me, to be in that situation. He was such a horrible man and he said "Did you do so and so and so" and he went through this list of things . . . I knew there was something awfully wrong with me, and I was miserable and confused and it was horrible. All I could think of was that I really wanted to be with M. and of course then Parker and Hulme kept coming into my mind and their madness.'

The interview with D. and M. is illustrated by some photographs of each of the women on their own. There is no photograph of the two women together as they had always avoided having one taken. This was because they had felt so horrified by the photographs of Parker and Hulme in the newspaper reports of the case that they resolved never to be photographed together themselves.

The examples which have been included here have been related by a small group of lesbians. We do not claim that these are representative of all lesbians or that the experiences which are described constitute all of the possible responses which lesbians could have had to the case. Nevertheless, we think that they begin to give a picture of some of the impact which the case has had on lesbians.

None of the women who gave us these accounts seemed particularly outraged by the murder. Although many lesbians were frightened and revolted by the killing, others saw Pauline and Juliet as hidden heroines who defied the codes and protected their own interests. Some saw the killing as an act they had wanted to carry out themselves. One woman saw prison as a desirable alternative to an unhappy home. Some lesbians became aware that there were other lesbians. For these girls and women, lesbianism became a possible option.

Most of the women giving these accounts did not want us to identify them. For some, the air of secrecy and mystery which surrounded their introduction to the case continued, even many years later. The feeling that lesbians were not fit subjects for discussion persisted.

Noteworthy in the experiences related here, are the responses of the adults. There was a lack of any informed support for the girls and the associations of lesbianism with murder and insanity seemed to have been accepted unquestioningly by these adults – even though this association was disputed by the prosecution at the trial and the *folie à deux* explanation rejected. Instead, the case was used as a tool by these adults to police girls in their relationships. In some instances they blatantly broke up lesbian relationships, with the Parker-Hulme case as justification. No doubt, there are many other examples during this period.

Clearly the Parker-Hulme case created a public association of lesbianism and murder. This contributed to the difficulties faced by lesbians in New Zealand. Yet, as one lesbian questioned 'How many heterosexuals kill each other off?' Heterosexuality and murder are not automatically linked as a result. It is clear to us, though, that in a society where heterosexuality is the prescribed 'norm' there could never be an association of heterosexuals and murder. Lesbians are a threat to society because we challenge this prescription simply by existing at all. Our existence demonstrates that alternatives to the unequal power relations between men and women are not only possible but are a reality. This real threat which lesbians pose is obscured when particular lesbians are portrayed as bizarre, monsters, or special individuals, capable of violence, murder and mayhem. Because Parker and Hulme were objectified and marginalised the murder they committed could be more easily associated with lesbianism in general. This frightened many women away from considering the relevance of lesbianism for themselves. It also frightened many lesbians.

Conclusion

The Parker-Hulme case occurred in a particular time and place. We have described some of the aspects of this context in order to create a framework from which an alternative analysis of the murder, the events leading up to it, and the impact of it could be made.

Some events assume a significance out of proportion to what actually happened. The tragic reality of this case was that a daughter assisted by a close friend committed a domestic murder, killing her mother. This murder might seem almost unremarkable in that a woman of little social prominence was killed in a provincial city in a small country. Yet the murder received international attention and was extensively written about in newspapers, magazines and books. Most of these accounts are sensational and contain a sexist and heterosexist bias.

Diana Trilling, commenting on the Scarsdale murder said that some cases 'bring into conjunction our private and public dilemmas'.[1] This is true of the Parker-Hulme case. It also brought together some key issues, and exposed contradictions, in public facades and private worlds in New Zealand during the early 1950s.

The private worlds of the Riepers and of the Hulmes reveal a complex intersection of themes important to early 1950s society. The Riepers lived together without being married and Herbert had left his first family to live with Honora. Their four children were technically illegitimate; the first child had died shortly after birth, and the youngest child had Downs Syndrome. Some people believed that breaking social codes brought about retribution; the circumstances of the Parker/Rieper family were presented as proof of some 'hereditary taint' within the family.

The behaviour of the Hulme household also was not acceptable according to the dominant social codes. Hilda had a relationship with Walter Perry, and furthermore had met Perry while counselling him about his own marital breakup. Although he lived in a separate flat in the Ilam residence, to some people this close proximity was tantamount to Hilda living with him in the family home. Henry, instead of taking up a position as the moral guardian of the home, had in some people's minds condoned the situation. The relationship between Juliet and Pauline was depicted as a sexual perversion which attacked and undermined both the prescribed moral codes and expected gender roles. They were pictured at the trial and in the media as adolescents out of control. Their attempts at shop-lifting and their boasts of breaking all of the ten commandments were given as proof of their juvenile delinquency. That 'sexual perverts' who might be either 'mad' or 'bad' could become killers was not an unexpected outcome for those who believed that all sexual perversion would lead to destruction and should therefore be severely regulated. The participants in the case broke fundamental social rules – a daughter had killed her mother, girls were involved in a lesbian relationship, a wife had deviated from her role, a seemingly 'respectable' family was exposed as one in which the parents were unmarried and the children were technically 'illegitimate'. To some observers, the violent outcome of such 'chaos' must have seemed inevitable. In the post-war period, the dominant culture emphasised 'family values', following the disruptions of the war years. Women were expected to devote their energies to being good wives and mothers and there were many warnings about the harmful effects of working mothers, 'broken' homes, and neglect of children. 'Juvenile delinquency' was said to be in part a consequence of ignoring the prescriptions of correct mothering and family controls. But the realities of many lives were different and beneath surface respectability there were many contradictions.

The treatment of the Parker-Hulme case is typical of other cases where women or children have killed. The monsterisation, sexualisation, and psychiatrisation factors discussed by Robinson[2] were used by the defence and prosecution, and by later writers to depict Parker and Hulme as 'mad' or 'bad'. They were described on the one hand as '*folie à deux* homosexual paranoics of the elated type', and on the other as 'highly intelligent and perfectly sane but precocious and dirty-minded girls'. The murder was described as one of the worst crimes of the twentieth century and Pauline Parker's diaries as 'one of the strangest and most terrible exhibits in criminal history'.

In all this, the people involved, including the victim and the other family members, were lost in the sensational stories. Yet there are other possible perspectives on the case. The feminist and Maori interpretations allow explanations of the case to go far beyond the simplistic 'mad' or 'bad' accounts.

We think that the causes of domestic murder lie in the frustrations and dynamics surrounding the relationship between killer and victim. Such murders are the culmination of long-standing conflicts. We think the origins of this murder lie in the dynamics of both households and in the mother-daughter conflicts, not in any special or unusual abnormalities. In our view such conflicts and tensions are an integral part of the post-war western nuclear family with its rigid gender roles and expectations. Domestic violence is a feature of this model although murder is infrequent and the killers are not usually the children of the family. In our view, a violent outcome in the Parker-Hulme case was not inevitable. The conflicts produced by the complex sets of circumstances could have been resolved in other ways. The violent outcome was tragic for all concerned.

We have discussed the situation for lesbians in New Zealand in some detail, as the relationship between Pauline and Juliet was a major aspect of the case. An important interaction occurred in that the relationship was seen as perverse because of negative social attitudes towards lesbians, and in turn the case helped to construct a new myth of lesbianism in New Zealand, connecting lesbians with murder and insanity. The publicity surrounding the case had a strong impact on lesbians, both at the time and subsequently. The reports of the case made some women afraid of their lesbian feelings, while others felt those feelings were affirmed because it was clear that lesbian relationships were possible. At least public discussions about homosexuality took place, even though these were negative. However, the case became a cautionary tale, warning girls and women away from breaking prescribed codes of morality.

The Parker-Hulme case encapsulated key social issues in a public drama. It was more comfortable for many people to think of the case as an isolated and unusual occurrence, rather than to place the events in a social context. The media played a clear role not only in taking the medical, psychiatric and legal accounts from the courtroom and reporting these to their readers, but also in transforming and extending the original details of the murder.

Writing about the events of 1954 more than thirty-five years after they happened, we have provided some new interpretations of the case. We have described the context and the events from a lesbian perspective. This has enabled us to break the narrow pattern of previous accounts and to open up new areas for discussion.

NOTES

Chapter One: The Place

1. Ian Hamilton, 'The End of the Affair', *Here and Now*, October 1954, p.9.
2. New Zealand Tourist Publicity and Advertising Agency, *Christchurch, City of Beautiful Gardens and Parklands*, Christchurch, 1950, p.11.
3. Pauline O'Regan, *Aunts and Windmills*, Wellington,1991, pp.4-5; see also Stevan Eldred-Grigg, *A New History of Canterbury*, Dunedin, 1982, pp.22-24.
4. S. Eldred-Grigg, *A New History of Canterbury*, 1982, p.20.
5. *Christchurch Star-Sun*, 28 January 1954.
6. Friends of Christchurch Cathedral, *Guide to Christchurch Cathedral*, Christchurch, 1954.
7. W. J. Gardner, E. T. Beardsley, and T. E. Carter, *A History of the University of Canterbury*, Christchurch, 1973, p.17.
8. New Zealand Tourist Publicity and Advertising Agency, *Christchurch, City of Beautiful Gardens and Parklands*, p.11.
9. Eldred-Grigg, *A New History of Canterbury*, p.12.
10. Bill Pearson, 'Fretful Sleepers', *Landfall*, p.218, September 1952.
11. Eldred-Grigg, *A New History of Canterbury*.
12. G. Dunstall, 'The Social Pattern', in W. H. Oliver, with B. R. Williams, eds. *The Oxford History of New Zealand*, Oxford and Wellington, 1981, p.406.
13. Maude Eaton, *Girl Workers in New Zealand Factories*, Wellington, 1947, p.103.
14. Interview with classmate of Parker and Hulme, August 1987 (1987-4).
15. Interview with classmate of Parker and Hulme, February 1987 (1987-3).
16. *New Zealand Official Year Book*, 1958, p.47.
17. *New Zealand Official Year Book*, 1958, p.47.
18. *New Zealand Population Census*, X, 1956, pp.80-84.
19. *New Zealand Official Yearbook*, 1958, p.44.
20. *ibid*, p.xviii.
21. *NZ Herald*, 30 September 1954.
22. New Zealand Tourist Publicity and Advertising Agency, *Christchurch, City of Beautiful Gardens and Parklands*, p.11.
23. Pauline Parker, Diary, 1953 and 1954.
24. Personal communication from ex-private school pupil (1960s) to AJL, May 1987.
25. *New Zealand Post Office Directory*, 1953.
26. Pauline Parker, Diary 1953 and 1954.
27. J. H. Robb and A. Somerset, *Report to Masterton: results of a social survey*, 1957.
28. Parker, Diary, 23 May 1953.
29. Personal knowledge, AJL; also, see J. Phillips, *A Mans' Country?*, Auckland, 1987, for discussion of post-war Pakeha male culture.
30. Bill Pearson, 'Fretful Sleepers', *Landfall*, September 1952, p.215.
31. Personal knowledge, AJL; also see J. Phillips, *A Mans' Country?*.
32. *NZ Freelance*, 19 July 1950, p.8.
33. *NZ Woman's Weekly*, 27 July 1950, p.54.
34. Hamilton, 'The End of the Affair', p.8.
35. Fay Weldon, Interview with Kate Coughlin, *Dominion Sunday Times*, 31 May 1987.

Chapter Two: The Families

1. Personal details of Herbert Rieper, Honora Parker and their children are largely derived from birth, death and marriage certificates, Registrar-General, Lower Hutt.
2. Interview, July 1987 (1987-15).
3. Interview with eyewitness, June 1987 (1987-2).
4. Department of Justice, Transcripts of the

Supreme Court trial Regina v Pauline Yvonne Parker and Juliet Marion Hulme, 23-28 August 1954 (this includes statements made by Parker and Hulme, Coroner's Report, and the full transcripts of the trial proceedings), Notes of Evidence, p.8.

5. *ibid*, p.14.

6. Department of Justice, Transcripts, Notes of Evidence, p.10.

7. R. W. Medlicott, 'Paranoia of the Exalted Type in a Setting of *Folie a Deux* : A Study of Two Adolescent Homicides', in W. A. M. Black and A. J. W. Taylor (eds), *Deviant behaviour : New Zealand Studies*, Auckland, 1979.

8. Department of Lands and Survey, Christchurch, Certificate of Title, 1946:252/49.

9. Dunstall, 'The Social Pattern', pp.403-405.

10. *NZ Observer*, 6 February 1952.

11. Interview with classmate of Parker and Hulme, August 1987 (1987-4); Interview with Christchurch Girls High School teacher of the time, June 1987 (1987-6).

12. Interview with classmate of Parker and Hulme, August 1987 (1987-4).

13. *ibid*.

14. Department of Justice, Transcripts . . ., Notes of Evidence, p.10; Parker, Diary, 1953.

15. Interview with R. W. Medlicott, Wellington, May 1987 (1987-12).

16. Parker, Diary, 1954; Medlicott, 'Paranoia of the Exalted Type . . .'.

17. Parker, Diary, 1953; Medlicott, 'Paranoia of the Exalted Type . . .', pp.111-112.

18. Parker, Diary, 1953.

19. Department of Justice, Transcripts, Notes of Evidence, p.43.

20. *NZ Listener*, 19 June 1953.

21. R. Winterbourn, *Caring for Intellectually Handicapped Children*, Wellington, 1962, p.38.

22. M. Kennedy and H. C. D. Somerset, *Bringing up Crippled Children*, Christchurch, 1951, p.21; R. Winterbourn, *Caring for Intellectually Handicapped Children*, p.34.

23. Department of Health, *Mental Breakdown: A Guide for the Family*, Wellington, 1965, pp.6-7.

24. Ann Gath, *Down's Syndrome and the Family, the early years*, London, 1978, p.5.

25. *Appendices to the Journals of the House of Representatives*, 1952, H-22.

26. E. Beaglehole, *Mental Health in New Zealand*, Wellington, 1950, p.4; Janet Frame, *Faces in the Water*, Christchurch, 1961, p.50; Theodore G. Gray, *The Very Error of the Moon*, Devon, 1948, p.94.

27. Interview with classmate of Parker and Hulme, August 1987 (1987-4).

28. Parker, Diary, 1954.

29. Parker, Diary, 1953.

30. *ibid*.

31. *ibid*.

32. Personal communication from Methodist Church member to AJL and JVG, May 1987.

33. Parker, Diary, 1953; Parker, Diary, 1954.

34. Gardner et al, *A History of the University of Canterbury*, pp.319-320.

35. *Who's Who*, London, 1951, p.117.

36. Christchurch Marriage Guidance Council, Minutes, 1948-1954.

37. *ibid*.

38. *NZ Listener*, 6 July 1951.

39. Department of Justice, Transcripts, Notes of Evidence, p.17; Medlicott, 'Paranoia of the Exalted Type . . .', p.112.

40. Medlicott, *ibid*., p.112.

41. Department of Justice, Transcripts, Notes of Evidence, p.17; Medlicott, *ibid*., p.112.

42. G. W. Parkyn, *Children of High Intelligence: A New Zealand Study*, 1953, p.9.

43. Parker, Diary, 1953.

44. Department of Justice, Inmate Files for Juliet Hulme and Pauline Parker, 1954-1966, Report, September 1954.

45. Department of Justice, Transcripts, Notes of Evidence, p.18; Parker, Diary, 1953.

46. Interview with I. Ramsden, 1990.

47. Several contemporaries of Henry Hulme told us that the relationship between Hilda Hulme and Walter Perry had developed through their involvement with the Christchurch Marriage Guidance Council – Hilda as a counsellor, and Walter Perry as a client. (Interview June 1987, (1987-7) and Interview, June 1987 (1987-1); R. W. Medlicott, May 1987 (1987-12), considered that Henry knew of their relationship.

48. Christchurch Marriage Guidance Council, Minutes.

49. Gardner et al, *A History of the University of Canterbury*, p.361.

50. Interview with contemporary of Henry Hulme, May 1987 (1987-7).

51. *Who's Who*, London, 1987.

52. *NZ Truth*, 8 September 1954.

53. *Who's Who*, London, 1987.

54. *NZ Truth*, 22 September 1954.

55. Parker, Diary, 31 March 1954 and 30 April 1954.

56. Parker, Diary, 21 February 1954.

57. Parker, Diary, 29 May 1953.

58. Parker, Diary, 1953; Parker, Diary, 1954.

59. Department of Justice, Transcripts, Notes of Evidence, p.14.

Chapter Three: The Time

1. Quoted in *People's Voice*, 18 March 1953.

2. Jane Kelsey, 'Legal Imperialism and the Colonisation of Aotearoa', in *Tauiwi – Racism and Ethnicity in New Zealand*, Palmerston North, 1984; see also Donna Awatere, *Maori Sovereignty*, Auckland, 1984.

3. *NZ Listener*, 15 September 1950, p.13.

4. *NZ Listener*, 14 July 1950.

5. *Landfall*, September 1958, pp.233-246.

6. Dunstall, 'The Social Pattern', p.403.

7. Angela Ballara, *Proud to be White?*, Wellington, 1986.

8. Donna Awatere, *Maori Sovereignty*, p.87.

9. *NZ Woman's Weekly*, 1 February 1951, p.14.

10. *NZ Woman's Weekly*, 7 April 1949, p.10.

11. G. A. F. Knight, *The Jews and New Zealand*, Christchurch, 1948ca.

12. *Evening Post*, 22 April 1987, p.24.

13. *NZ Woman's Weekly*, 15 June 1950, p.37.

14. *People's Voice*, 27 February 1952.

15. *People's Voice*, 20 October 1954.

16. *People's Voice*, 27 February 1952; 7 October 1953; 14 October 1953; 3 March 1954; 20 September 1954; 26 April 1955.

17. *NZ Listener*, 14 July 1950.

18. Customs Department, C1 Registered Files, Series 36/959.

19. Customs Department, C1 Registered Files, Series 24/43/107.

20. A. C. Burns, 'Some Aspects of Censorship: A survey of censorship law and practice in New Zealand from 1841 to 1963 mainly concerning the control of indecent publications', Victoria University of Wellington, MA thesis, 1968, p.95.

21. Customs Department, C1 Registered Files, Series 24/43/300.

22. Customs Department, C1 Registered Files, Series 36/959; *NZ Libraries*, December 1950, p.275.

23. Customs Department, C1 Registered Files, Series 36/959.

24. Department of Internal Affairs, Annual Report, 1955.

25. L. Constable, 'Controversy in the Air', *Landfall*, X(3), 1956, pp.242-245.

26. *NZ Listener*, 10 April 1952.

27. *NZ Listener*, 21 September 1951, p.5.

28. P. Hyman, 'Tables on Women's Employment in New Zealand', unpublished paper, Victoria University of Wellington, 1988.

29. S. Middleton, 'Feminism and Education in Post-War New Zealand: An Oral History Perspective', in R. Openshaw and D. McKenzie (eds), *Reinterpreting the Educational Past*, Wellington, 1977.

30. *New Zealand Offical Year Book*, 1958, pp.1012-1029ff.

31. *Appendices to the Journals of the House of Representatives*, 1956, H-14, p.13.

32. Middleton, 'Feminism and Education . . .', p.4.

33. *New Zealand Nursing Journal*, May 1948.

34. *New Zealand Nursing Journal*, 15 December 1948.

35. See for example, *NZ Woman's Weekly*, 10 January 1952; 31 January 1952; and 10 August 1954.

36. C. Simmons, 'Companionate Marriage and the Lesbian Threat', *Frontiers: A Journal of Women's Studies*, 4(3), 1979, pp.54-59.

37. Leslie M. Hall (pseud), 'Women and Men in New Zealand', *Landfall*, 12(1), 1958, pp.47-57.

38. *NZ Woman's Weekly*, 9 August 1951.

39. H. Cook, 'Images, illusions of harmony: the 1950s wife and mother', *New Zealand Women's Studies Journal*, 1(2), 1985, pp.83-108.

40. *NZ Pictorial*, 3 May 1954.

41. *NZ Woman's Weekly*, 13 April 1950.

42. W. Glass, 'Unmarried Mothers in New Zealand', D.P.H. thesis, London University, 1959, p.13.

43. *ibid*, p.17.

44. *Taranaki Herald*, 9 September 1954.

45. Christchurch Marriage Guidance Council, Minutes.

46. Interview, June 1987 (1987-1).

47. Jennifer M. Daly, *MG Reflecting: A Portrait of the New Zealand Marriage Guidance Council 1949-1989*, Wellington, 1990, p.9.

48. *ibid*, p.10.
   49*ibid*, p.20.

50. Interview with former member of Marriage Guidance Council, June 1987 (1987-14).

51. Interview, June 1987 (1987-1).

52. R. Phillips, *Divorce in New Zealand: A Social History*, Auckland, 1981.

53. W. Glass, 'Unmarried Mothers in New Zealand', p.3.

54. See for example *People's Voice, Landfall, Here and Now*, for the period; also, A.E. Manning, *The Bodgie: A Study in Abnormal Psychology*, Wellington, 1958, documents lesbianism, and other sexual rebellions, in a mid-1950s survey of a small group of teenagers.

55. O.C. Mazengarb, *Report of the Special Committee on Moral Delinquency in Children and Adolescents*, Wellington, 1955, pp.7-8.

56. *ibid*, p.25.

57. *ibid*, p.15.

58. Roger Openshaw, 'Hooligans at Hastings: Reactions to the Hastings Blossom Festival Affray, September 1960', unpublished paper, 1988.

59. *ibid*, p.2.

60. R. Phillips, *Divorce in New Zealand*.

Chapter Four: The Relationships

1. Interview with Christchurch Girls High School teacher of the time, June 1987 (1987-5).

2. R. W. Medlicott, 'Paranoia of the Exalted Type . . .', 1979.

3. Parker, Diary, 3 April 1953.

4. Parker, Diary, 9 September 1953.

5. Parker, Diary, 12 June 1954.

6. Parker, Diary, 13 June 1954.

7. Parker, Diary, 16 June 1954.

8. Parker, Diary, 17 June 1954.

9. Parker, Diary, 9 October 1953.

10. A. Rich, *Compulsory Heterosexuality and Lesbian Existence*, London, 1981.

11. J. Zita, 'Historical Amnesia and the Lesbian Continuum', *Signs*, 7(1), 1981, pp.172-186.

12. A. Ferguson, 'On Compulsory Heterosexuality and Lesbian Existence: defining the issues', *Signs*, 7(1), 1981, pp.158-172.

13. Interview with lesbian, April 1987 (1987-11).
14. Interview with lesbian concerned, July 1987 (1987-17).
15. Personal communication from lesbian to AJL, July 1987.
16. Department of Justice, Transcripts, Notes of Evidence, p.97.
17. Parker, 16 April 1954.
18. Parker, 1 May 1954.
19. Department of Justice, Transcripts, Notes of Evidence, pp.22-23.
20. Department of Justice, Transcripts, Notes of Evidence, p.23.
21. Parker, April 1954.
22. Parker, 6 April 1953.
23. Department of Justice, Transcripts, Notes of Evidence, p.21 and p.23; Parker, Diary, 1953.
24. Department of Justice, Transcripts, Notes of Evidence, p.22.
25. Parker, Diary, 30 August 1953.
26. Department of Justice, Inmate Files, Report on progress, 29 September 1954.
27. Interview with classmate of Parker and Hulme, August 1987 (1987-4).
28. R. W. Medlicott, 'Paranoia of the Exalted Type . . .', p.121; R.W. Medlicott, 'Some Reflections on the Parker-Hulme, Leopold-Loeb Cases with Special Reference to the Concept of Omnipotence', *New Zealand Law Journal*, 37(22), 1961, pp.343-348.
29. Parker, Diary, 1953 and 1954.
30. Medlicott, 'Paranoia of the Exalted Type . . .', p.115.
31. *ibid.*
32. Parker, Diary, 1953 and 1954.
33. Interview with classmate of Parker and Hulme, August 1987 (1987-4).
34. Interview with classmate of Parker and Hulme, February 1987 (1987-3).
35. Interview with classmate of Parker and Hulme, August 1987 (1987-4).
36. Interview with classmate of Parker and Hulme, February 1987 (1987-3).
37. Medlicott, 'Paranoia of the Exalted Type', p.111.
38. Interview with classmate of Parker and Hulme, February 1987 (1987-3).
39. *ibid.*
40. Interview with classmate of Parker and Hulme, August 1987 (1987-4).
41. *ibid.*
42. Interview, June 1987 (1987-16).
43. Interview with classmate of Parker and Hulme, February 1987 (1987-3).
44. Interview with classmate of Parker and Hulme, August 1987 (1987-4).
45. Interview with classmate of Parker and Hulme, February 1987 (1987-3).
46. Telephone interview, June 1987 (1987-9).
47. Christchurch Girls High School, Class Records, 1953-1954.
48. Parker, Diary, 14 March 1954.
49. *ibid.*
50. Parker, Diary, 19 March 1954.
51. Parker, Diary, 21 April 1954.
52. Medlicott, 'Paranoia of the Exalted Type . . .'.
53. Department of Justice, Transcripts, Notes of Evidence, p.18 and p.22.
54. Interview, June 1987 (1987-5).
55. Department of Justice, Transcripts, Notes of Evidence, p.14.
56. *ibid*, p.86.
57. *ibid*, p.12.
58. Parker, Diary, 23 April 1954.
59. Parker, Diary, 24 April 1954.
60. Parker, Diary, 13 February 1954.

Chapter Five: The Diaries

1. Tom Gurr and H. Cox, *Famous Australasian Crimes*, London, 1957, pp.148-156.
2. *Daily Mail*, 30 August 1954; Interview June 1987 (1987-1); Transcripts, Notes of Evidence, p.80.
3. Deborah Sosin, 'The diary as a transitional object', *Adolescent Psychiatry, Developmental and Clinical Studies*, XI, 1983, p.93.

4. *ibid*, p.93.
5. *ibid*, p.96.
6. *ibid*, p.99.
7. *ibid*, p.99.
8. *ibid*, p.100.
9. *ibid*, p.97.
10. *ibid*, p.96.
11. *ibid*, p.98.
12. *ibid*, p.101.
13. Parker, Diary, 14 January 1953.

Chapter Six: The Trial

1. *NZ Truth*, 1 September 1954.
2. *The Press*, 18 June 1957.
3. *Evening Post*, 12 August 1986.
4. *The Press*, 1 July 1987.
5. *New Zealand Law Journal*, 18 December 1956, pp.358-359; *Auckland Star*, 15 November 1967.
6. *Who's Who*, 1950.
7. *Who's Who*, 1950.
8. *The Press*, 24 August 1954; *New Zealand Official Year Book*, 1958, p.248; the National Council of Women's was mentioned by Elizbeth Orr, Women's Studies lecture, 27 March 1991, Victoria University of Wellington.
9. *Dominion*, 24 September 1954.
10. *The Press*, 24 August 1954.
11. *Daily Express*, 22 July 1954.
12. Department of Justice, Transcripts, Notes of Evidence, pp.31-32.
13. Rita Simon, *The Jury and the Defense of Insanity*, Boston, 1967, p.23.
14. W.J. Winslade and J.W. Ross, *The Insanity Plea*, New York, p.12; H. Jenner Wily and K. R. Stallworthy, *Mental Abnormality and the Law*, Christchurch, 1962.
15. Interview, June 1987 (1987-1).
16. *The Press*, 25 August 1954.
17. F. O. Bennett, *Hospital on the Avon*, Christchurch, 1962.
18. Christchurch Marriage Guidance Council, Minutes.
19. Interview, June 1987, (1987-1).
20. *ibid*.
21. *People's Voice*, 13 October 1954.
22. Interview, June 1987, (1987-1).
23. *NZ Truth*, 1 September 1954.
24. *People's Voice*, 13 October 1954.
25. Interview, March 1987, (1987-8).
26. *The Press*, 1 July 1987.
27. M. Bevan-Brown, *Mental Health and Personality*, Christchurch, 1961, p.218.
28. Department of Justice, *Crime in New Zealand*, Wellington, 1968, p.4, 24.

Chapter Seven: The Punishment

1. *Dominion*, 31 August 1954.
2. *ibid*.
3. *Taranaki Herald*, 1 September 1954.
4. *People's Voice*, 13 October 1954, p.5; *The Standard*, 15 September 1954.
5. Hamilton, 'The End of the Affair', p.9.
6. *NZ Truth*, 25 February 1958.
7. *NZ Truth*, 8 September 1954.
8. Department of Justice, *A Penal Policy for New Zealand*, Wellington, 1954.
9. Department of Justice Statistics, 1954.
10. D.F. McKenzie, *While We Have Prisons*, Auckland, 1980, p.15.
11. *ibid*, pp.13-14.
12. *ibid*, p.47.
13. *ibid*, p.22.
14. *ibid*, p.73.
15. *ibid*, p.73.
16. *ibid*, p.76.
17. *NZ Truth*, 8 September 1954.
18. Department of Justice, *A Penal Policy for New Zealand*, p.12.
19. *ibid*.
20. Mackenzie, *While We Have Prisons*, p.15.
21. *NZ Truth*, 8 September 1954.
22. *ibid*.
23. Department of Justice, Inmate Files, 1954-1959. Further, Barnett may have known Hilda Hulme. He had attended the inaugural meeting of the National Marriage Guidance Council in Christchurch in November 1949 as an observer for the Department of Justice.

He remained involved with the work of the Council and later played a central role in expanding its services in New Zealand. (See J. Daly, *MG Reflecting. . .*, 1990.)

24. MacKenzie, *While We Have Prisons.*
25. *ibid*, p.15.
26. *ibid*, p.15.
27. Department of Justice, *A Penal Policy for New Zealand.*
28. *Sydney Morning Herald*, 12 December 1954.
29. *The Sun*, 10 December 1954.
30. Interview, June 1987 (1987-1).
31. *Sydney Morning Herald*, 12 December 1954.
32. Department of Justice, Inmate Files, Report, 31 August 1954.
33. Department of Justice, Inmate Files, File Note, 13 December 1954; Report on Progress, 21 September 1955; File Note, 21 October 1957.
34. Department of Justice, Inmate Files.
35. *ibid*, Report, 14 January 1956; Report 22 July 1956.
36. *ibid*, Telegram to Prime Minister from K. Earles, 4 December 1959.
37. Department of Justice, Inmate Files.
38. Janet Frame, *Faces in the Water*, Christchurch, 1961; also, R. W. Medlicott, 'The Place of Electronarcosis in Psychiatric Treatment: A Clinical Assessment based on the Treatment of Four hundred Patients', *New Zealand Medical Journal*, LIII, 1954.
39. Jill Julius Matthews, *Good and Mad Women*, Sydney, 1984.
40. Department of Justice, *Inmate Files . . .*, Letter, 11 December 1963.
41. *ibid*, File Note, 12 November 1957.

Chapter Eight: The Stories

1. Personal communication from contemporaries to AJL and JVG, May 1987.
2. The literature on the relationship between the news media and society is extensive. See, for example, Stanley Cohen and Jock Young (eds), *The Manufacture of News: Social Problems, Deviance and the Mass Media*, California, 1981.
3. *Dominion*, 28 August 1954.
4. *Zealandia*, 26 August 1954.
5. *The Press*, 4 September 1954.
6. Hamilton, 'The End of the Affair', p.9.
7. *ibid.*
8. *Time*, 6 December 1954.
9. *ibid.*
10. *London Evening Standard*, 12 November 1964.
11. R. Furneaux, *Famous Criminal Cases*, London, 1955, pp.33-47.
12. Gurr and Cox, *Famous Australasian Crimes*, pp.148-166.
13. *ibid*, p.158.
14. *ibid*, p.166.
15. *ibid.*
16. R. G. Jones (ed), *Killer Couples*, London, 1989, pp.249-268.
17. T. Gurr, *Obsession*, London, 1958.
18. C. Franklin, *The World's Worst Murderers*, London, 1965, pp.283-313.
19. L. Gribble, *The Hallmark of Horror*, London, 1973.
20. *ibid.*
21. Gerald Sparrow, *Queens of Crime*, London, 1973, pp.114-121.
22. *ibid*, p.120.
23. *ibid*, p.118.
24. *ibid*, p.119.
25. *ibid*, p.118.
26. *ibid*, p.121.
27. See for example, Phyllis Chesler, *Women and Madness*, New York, 1972; Mary Brown Parlee, 'Review Essay: Psychology and Women', *Signs*, 5(1), 1979; Jill Julius Matthews, *Good and Mad Women*, Sydney, 1984.
28. Matthews, *Good and Mad Women*, p.24.
29. R. W. Medlicott, 'Concepts of Normality and Moral Values', *New Zealand Sexologist*, March 1986.

30. Medlicott, 'Paranoia of the Exalted Type . . .', pp.111-123.
31. *ibid*, p.120.
32. *ibid*, p.123.
33. *ibid*, p.120.
34. *ibid*, p.121.
35. *ibid*, p.123.
36. See, for example, Joanna Rohrbaugh, *Women: Psychology's Puzzle*, London, Sphere Books, 1981.
37. Medlicott, 'Paranoia of the Exalted Type . . .', p.119.
38. *ibid*, pp.119-120.
39. *ibid*, p.123.
40. *ibid*, p.117.
41. *ibid*, p.121.
42. *ibid*, p.114.
43. *ibid*, p.115.
44. *ibid*, p.115.
45. See for example, Joanna Russ, *How to Suppress Women's Writing*, London, 1984.
46. Medlicott, 'Paranoia of the Exalted Type . . .', p.111.
47. *ibid*, p.111.
48. *ibid*, p.112.
49. *ibid*, p.112.
50. *ibid*, p.123.
51. Medlicott, 'Some Reflections . . .', pp.343-348.
52. *ibid*.
53. Medlicott, R.W. 'An examination of the necessity for a concept of evil: some aspects of evil as a form of perversion' in British Journal of Medical Psychology, 43, 1970, pp.271-280.
54. *ibid*, p.271.
55. *ibid*, p.274.
56. *ibid*, p.276.
57. *ibid*, p.277.
58. *ibid*, p.277.
59. *ibid*, p.277.
60. *ibid*, p.278.
61. *ibid*, p.278.
62. *ibid*, p.280.
63. Medlicott, 'Concepts of Normality . . .', p.6.
64. *ibid*.
65. Discussion papers circulated to staff by Dr Medlicott.
66. Bevan-Brown, 'Mental Health and Personality', p.214.
67. *ibid*, p.219.
68. *ibid*, p.209.
69. *ibid*, p.212.
70. C. Kitzinger, *The Social Construction of Lesbianism*, London, 1987.

Chapter Nine: Why was Honora Parker killed?

1. Jeffner Allen, *Lesbian Philosophy: Explorations*, Palo Alto, 1986, p.38.
2. C. Lombroso and W. Ferrero, *The Female Offender*, London, 1895.
3. *ibid*, pp.187-188.
4. *ibid*, pp.147-148.
5. Carol Smart, *Women, Crime and Criminology*, London, 1976, p.40.
6. *ibid*, p.41.
7. *ibid*, p.45.
8. O. Pollak, *The Criminality of Women*, New York, 1961.
9. Gerald Sparrow, *Women Who Murder*, London, 1970, p.7.
10. *ibid*, p.21.
11. See R. Simon, *The Contemporary Woman and Crime*, Maryland, 1975; R. Simon, *Women and Crime*, 1975; F. Adler, *Sisters in Crime*, New York, 1975.
12. Jan Jordan Robinson, 'Of Diverse Persons, Men and Women and Whores: Women and crime in nineteenth century Canterbury', MA thesis, University of Canterbury, Christchurch, 1983, pp.26-80.
13. See for example F. Caprio, *Female Homosexuality*, New York, 1957.
14. Jordan Robinson, 'Of Diverse Persons . . .', p.26.
15. A. Jones, *Women Who Kill*, New York, 1980, p.13.

16. *ibid*, p.xv.

17. M. Chesney-Lind, 'Women and Crime: The Female Offender', *Signs*, 12(1), 1986 p.83.

18. *ibid*, p.96.

19. *ibid*.

20. N. Rafter and E. Natlaizia, 'Marxist Feminism: Implications for Criminal Justice', *Crime and Delinquency*, 27, 1981, p.92.

21. A. E. Hiller and A. Mandish, 'Women, Crime and Criminal Justice: The state of current theory and research in Australia and New Zealand', *Australia and New Zealand Journal of Criminology*, 15, 1982, pp.73-74.

22. Jones, *Women Who Kill*, p.14.

23. *ibid*.

24. See Lois Braverman ed, *A Guide to Feminist Family Therapy*, New York, 1988; also, Anna Lee, 'Therapy, the Evil Within', *Trivia*, 9, Fall 1986.

25. W. March, *The Bad Seed*, New York, 1954.

26. M. Hahn and N. Dawson-Wheeler, 'Adolescents Who Kill: What should we do with them?', New Zealand Psychological Society Annual Conference, paper, 1986, p.2.

27. Department of Justice, *Submission to the Committee of Inquiry into Violence*, Wellington, 1986, p.114.

28. B. M. Cormier et al, 'The Psychodynamics of Homicide Committed in a Specific Relationship', *Journal of Criminology and Correction*, 1, 1971, pp.1-2.

29. Department of Justice, *Submission . . .* , p.117.

30. C. Sheppard, 'Towards a Better Understanding of the Violent Offender', *Canadian Journal of Criminology and Corrections*, 13(1), 1971, p.61.

31. B. F. Corder et al, 'Adolescent Parricide: A Comparison with other Adolescent Murder', *American Journal of Psychiatry*, 133(8), 1976, p.959.

32. C. K. McKnight et al, 'Matricide and

Mental Illness', *Canadian Psychiatric Association Journal*, 11(2), April 1966, p.99.

33. D. Chiswick, 'Matricide', *British Medical Journal*, 283, 14 November 1981, p.1279.

34. B. M. Cormier et al, 'Adolescents Who Kill A Member of the Family', *Family Violence: An International and Interdisciplinary Study*, 1978, p.468.

35. *ibid*, p.471.

36. *ibid*, p.469.

37. J. W. Duncan and G. M. Duncan, 'Murder in the Family: A study of some homicidal adolescents', *American Journal of Psychiatry*, 127(11), 1971, p.77.

38. *ibid*.

39. Cormier et al, 'Adolescents Who Kill . . .', p.469.

40. *ibid*, pp.475-476.

41. *ibid*, p.475.

42. J. W. Mohr and C. K. McKnight, 'Violence as a Function of Age and Relationship with Special Reference to Matricide', *Canadian Psychiatric Association Journal*, 16, 1971; Cormier et al, 'Adolescents Who Kill . . .', p.470.

43. *ibid*, pp.475-476.

44. Duncan and Duncan, 'Murder in the Family . . .', pp.77-78.

45. *ibid*.

46. Interview with R. W. Medlicott, May 1987 (1987-12).

47. Greggory Morris, *The Kids Next Door: Sons and Daughters Who Kill Their Parents*, New York, 1985.

48. Cited in Duncan and Duncan, 'Murder in the Family . . .', p.77.

49. *ibid*.

50. Medlicott, 'Paranoia of the Exalted Type . . .', p.120.

51. Bevan-Brown, 'Mental Health and Personality', p.209.

52. Hamilton, 'The End of The Affair', pp.7-9.

53. Interview with eyewitness, May 1987 (1987-2).

54. Interview with contemporary, December 1990 (1990-1).

55. Consultations with Tohunga, May 1989 and March 1991.

Chapter Ten: Lesbians in New Zealand

1. *NZ Pictorial*, 12 December 1955.
2. The *NZ Herald* and *Auckland Star* in May 1944 reported the acquittal of a male nineteen year old New Zealand soldier on a charge of murdering a male twenty-five year old American soldier who had made sexual advances to him (described by Phil Parkinson, 'A Soldier's Tale', *Pink Triangle*, 61, Spring 1986; *NZ Truth* 1950-1959 reports a number of cases of criminal proceedings against gay men – see, for example, *NZ Truth*, 30 July 1957, 'Ex-Police Sergeant and Associates Sent to Prison'; *NZ Truth*, 28 July 1959, ' "Marilyn" Was Frank When Interviewed'; *NZ Truth*, 6 October 1954 gives an account of a preliminary hearing where a boy of 15 years was charged with the murder of an eight year old boy. There was some evidence that a sexual assault had taken place. Lesbians and gay men were also included in A. E. Manning's survey *The Bodgie . . .*, 1958, which recorded interviews with lesbians and gay teenagers. This work received some media coverage when published (see *Evening Star*, 17 July 1958).
3. Royal Commission on Social Policy, Wellington, II, 1988, p.167.
4. NZ Police, Black Book (The Police Force Act, 1947 and Regulations made thereunder and General Instructions for the guidance of the Police Force of New Zealand), 1950ca.
5. Interview with member of police force, 1987.
6. *NZ Truth*, 30 July 1957.
7. *National Education*, 3 September 1951, p.289.
8. Public Service Manual, Wellington, 1955ca.
9. R. W. Medlicott, 'Sociopathic Personality Disturbance', in *Mental Health and the Community*, Christchurch, 1963, p.373.
10. M. Foucault, *A History of Sexuality Volume One*, New York, 1978, p.101.
11. J. Foster, *Sex Variant Women in Literature*, Baltimore, 1975.
12. F. Caprio, *Female Homosexuality*, pp.302-305.
13. *ibid*, p.viii.
14. Eldred-Grigg, 'Pleasures of the Flesh . . .'; *Education Gazette*, December 1921, p.5 and November 1922, p.119.
15. Department of Education, *The Post Primary School Curriculum* (Thomas Report), Wellington, 1959, p.54. Originally published in 1944.
16. Department of Education, *The Primary School Curriculum, Revised Syllabuses*, Wellington, 1955, p.8.
17. *ibid*.
18. For example, Department of Health, *Sex and the Adolescent Girl*, Wellington, 1965, p.9.
19. R. Pilkington, *Facts of Life for Parents*, British Medical Association, 1955ca, p.3.
20. *ibid*, p.17.
21. *NZ Woman's Weekly*, 18 February 1954.
22. *ibid*.
23. O.C. Mazengarb, *Report of the Special Committee on Moral Delinquency in Children and Adolescents*, p.16.
24. Interviews with lesbians, 1987.
25. E. Philipp, 'Homosexuality as Seen in a New Zealand City practice', *New Zealand Medical Journal*, 67(430), March 1968, mentions two lesbians who were married and had children. In each case their husbands knew of their lesbianism, but both families kept up a conventional heterosexual family front; L. K. Gluckman, 'Lesbianism: A Clinical Approach', *New Zealand Medical Journal*, 65(407), July 1966, reports on his private psychiatric practice in which he saw one

hundred lesbian clients, over a period of fourteen years. He reports that some lesbians married for 'social and economic reasons and for reasons of security and status'; also, see A. Rich, 'Compulsory Heterosexuality . . .', 1981, for discussion on lesbian resistance.

26. Ngahuia Te Awekotuku, *Tahuri*, Auckland, 1989.

27. Personal knowledge, AJL.

28. Personal communication from lesbian founder member of S. H. E. Christchurch, to JVG, September 1990; see also *Lesbian-feminist Circle*, 1973-1983 and Ngahuia Te Awekotuku, 'Dykes and Queers', in *Broadsheet*, 168, May 1989, for beginnings of gay liberation in New Zealand.

29. See J. Katz, *Gay American History*, New York, 1978; J. Katz, *The Gay/Lesbian Almanac*, 1978; J. Weeks, *Coming Out: Homosexual Politics in Britain from the nineteenth century to the present*, London, 1977.

30. Sonja Davies, *Bread and Roses*, Masterton, 1986, pp.47-48.

31. Personal communication from lesbian concerned to AJL, information given in 1962.

32. Personal communication from one of the women concerned to AJL, information given in 1962.

33. Personal communications from lesbians nurses and teachers to AJL and JVG, 1987; L. K. Gluckman, 'Lesbianism: A Clinical Approach', describes lesbians from various backgrounds and occupations, including teaching and nursing; E. Philipp, 'Homosexuality . . .', mentions a lesbian nurse.

34. Personal communications from lesbian nurses and teachers to AJL and JVG, 1987, and at Hamilton, 1990, regarding lesbian nurses at Waikato Hospital in the early 1960s.

35. Personal knowledge, AJL.

36. Interview with lesbian, August 1987 (1987-10); also, Personal knowledge, AJL.

37. Interview with lesbian, August 1987 (1987-10); also, Personal knowledge, AJL.

38. Personal knowledge, AJL.

39. Interview with lesbian, member of armed forces at the time, August 1987 (1987-10).

40. Personal communication from lesbian researcher, Lynne Gifford, to AJL and JVG, February 1988. She carried out research on lesbian sports networks, but this work was not completed.

41. Interview with Christchurch lesbian, April 1987, (1987-11).

42. Various gay men have told us that this was how they had made contacts with other men.

43. R. M. Dekker and Lotte C. van de Pol, *The Tradition of Female Transvestism in Early Modern Europe*, London, 1989.

44. See for example Lynne Gifford, ' "Butch" We Win, "Femme" You Lose: The Myth of Lesbian Impunity', *Women's Studies Conference Papers*, New Zealand Women's Studies Association 1983; J. Katz, *Gay American History*, New York, 1978; J. Katz, *The Gay/Lesbian Almanac*, New York, 1983; Lillian Faderman, *Surpassing the Love of Men*, New York, 1981.

45. *NZ Libraries*, 1949, p.236.

46. *NZ Libraries*, 1949, p.34.

47. Office of the Chief Film Censor, Records of film censor's classifications, 1930-1965.

48. Parker, Diary, 10 June 1954.

Chapter Eleven: Impact of the case on lesbians

1. Jill Johnston, *Lesbian Nation*, New York, 1974, p.68.

2. Pat Rosier, 'The Only Ones', *Broadsheet*, 153, November 1987.

Conclusion

1. Diana Trilling, *Mrs Harris: The Death of the Scarsdale Diet Doctor*, London, 1982, p.66.

2. Jan Jordan Robinson, 'Of Diverse Persons. . .'.

Bibliography

UNPUBLISHED SOURCES

Christchurch Girls High School, Class Records, 1952-1954.

Christchurch Marriage Guidance Council, Minutes, Christchurch, 1948-1954.

Customs Department. C1: Registered Files: Series 36/959
                                                  24/43/1
                                                  24/43/107
                                                  24/43/300

Department of Justice. Regina vs Pauline Yvonne Parker and Juliet Marion Hulme, Transcripts of Supreme Court proceedings, 1954.

Department of Justice. Prison Inmate Files for Juliet Hulme and Pauline Parker, 1954-1966.

Department of Justice. Registrar of births, deaths and marriages, Lower Hutt.

Department of Lands and Survey. 'Certificate of Title', 1946: 252/49, Christchurch, 1946.

Faed, Julia. 'Narrowly Missed Mothers', unpublished paper, Cherry Farm Hospital, 1987.

Hyman, P. 'Tables on Women's Employment in New Zealand', unpublished Women's Studies paper, Victoria University of Wellington, 1988.

New Zealand Police. Black Book (The Police Force Act, 1947 and Regulations made thereunder and General Instructions for the guidance of the Police Force of New Zealand), 1950ca.

New Zealand Police. File 54/669, New Zealand Police College, Porirua.

Office of the Chief Censor, Records of film censor's classifications, 1930-1965.

Parker, Pauline. Diary, 1953 and 1954.

State Services Commission. *Public Service Manual*, Wellington, 1955.

PUBLISHED SOURCES
Newspapers

New Zealand Newspapers
  Christchurch Star, 1987.
  Dominion, 1950-55, 1958-60.
  Evening Post, 1950-54, 1958-60.
  New Zealand Herald, 1950-54.
  New Zealand Times, 1986.
  NZ Truth, 1950-59.
  Otago Daily Time, 1950-1954.
  People's Voice, 1950-54.

Taranaki Herald, 1950-54.
The Christchurch Star-Sun, 1954.
The Dominion Sunday Times, 1969, 1987.
The Press, 1950-54, 1958-59.
The Standard, 1954.
The Star, 1982.
Zealandia, 1950-54.
Australian Newspapers
Sydney Morning Herald, 1954.
The Sun, 1954.
British Newspapers
Daily Express, 1954, 1955, 1957, 1959, 1967.
Daily Mail, 1954.
Daily Mirror, 1954.
Daily Sketch, 1954.
Daily Telegraph, 1954.
Evening News, 1954.
London Evening Standard, 1964.
The Sunday Express London, 1954, 1959.
Times London, 1954.

Official Publications

Appendices to the Journals of the House of Representatives, New Zealand, 1956.
New Zealand Official Year Book, 1950-1959.
New Zealand Parliamentary Debates, 1949-1954.
New Zealand Population Census, 1951, 1956.
New Zealand Post Office Directories, 1920-1954.
New Zealand Statutes.

Periodicals

Comment, 1960-1967.
Landfall, 1947-1959.
Lesbian-Feminist Circle, 1973-1983.
Lesbian Herstory Archives News, New York, 1980-1988.
National Education, The Journal of the New Zealand Educational
   Institute, 1919-1954.
New Zealand Freelance, various.
New Zealand Law Journal, 1965.
New Zealand Libraries, 1938-1955.
New Zealand Medical Journal, 1945-1955.
New Zealand Nursing Journal, 1945-55.
New Zealand Observer, various.
New Zealand Pictorial, 1955.
New Zealand Women's Studies Journal, 1981-1987.
New Zealand Weekly News, various.
New Zealand Woman's Weekly, 1949-54.

Psychology of Women Quarterly, 1982, 1986.
Signs, various.
Sinister Wisdom.
Time, 1954.

Articles, Books, Pamphlets, Theses

Adler, F. *Sisters in Crime*, New York, McGraw-Hill, 1975.

Allen, Jeffner. *Lesbian Philosophy: Explorations*, Palo Alto, Institute of Lesbian Studies, 1986.

Altmann, Dennis. *Coming Out in the Seventies*, Alyson, 1981.

Altmann, Dennis. *The Homosexualization of America*, Beacon, 1982.

Anglo, Michael. *Nostalgia: Spotlight on the Fifties*, London, Jupiter Books, 1977.

Ausubel, David. 'Race Relations in New Zealand', *Landfall*, 12(3), 1958.

Awatere, Donna. *Maori Sovereignty*, Auckland, Broadsheet, 1984.

Ballara, Angela. *Proud to Be White?*, Auckland, Heinemann, 1986.

Bardsley, Barney. *Flowers in Hell: An Investigation into Women and Crime*, London, Pandora, 1987.

Beaglehole, E. *Mental Health in New Zealand*, Wellington, New Zealand University Press, 1950.

Beeby, C. E. *Books You Couldn't Buy*, Price Milburn, 1981.

Bennett, F. O. *Hospital on the Avon*, Christchurch, North Canterbury Hospital Board, 1962.

Bevan-Brown, M. 'Adolescent Murder', in M. Bevan-Brown, *Mental Health and Personality*, Christchurch, Dunford, 1961. Originally written in 1955.

Black, W. A. M. and A. J. W. Taylor. *Deviant Behaviour, New Zealand Studies*, Auckland, Heinemann, 1979.

Bowles, Gloria and Renate Duelli Klein. *Theories of Womens Studies*, London, Routledge and Kegan Paul, 1985.

Braverman, Lois, ed. *A Guide to Feminist Family Therapy*, London, Harrington Park Press, 1988.

Bromby, R. *An Eyewitness History of New Zealand*, Victoria, Currey O'Neil Ross, 1985.

Browne, Susan E., Debra Connors and Nanci Stern. *With the Power of Each Breath: A Disabled Women's Anthology*, San Francisco, Cleis Press, 1985.

Bullough, V. *Sexual Variance in Society and History*, Chicago, University of Chicago Press, 1976.

Bunkle, P. and B. Hughes, eds. *Women in New Zealand Society*, Auckland, Allen and Unwin, 1980.

Burns, A. C. 'Some Aspects of Censorship: A survey of censorship law and practice in New Zealand from 1841 to 1963, mainly concerning the control of indecent publications', Wellington, MA thesis, Victoria University of Wellington, 1968.

Campbell, A. E. *The Fielding Community Centre*, Christchurch, New Zealand Council for Educational Research, 1945.

Campbell, A. *Girl Delinquents*, Oxford, Basil Blackwell, 1981.

Caprio, Frank. *Female Homosexuality*, New York, Citadel, 1957.

Chesler, Phyllis. *Women and Madness*, New York, Avon, 1972.

Chesney-Lind, M. 'Women and Crime: The Female Offender', *Signs*, 12(1), 1986.

Chiswick, D. 'Matricide'. *British Medical Journal*, 283, 14 November 1981.

Cohen, Stanley and Jock Young, eds, *The Manufacture of News: Social Problems, Deviance and the Mass Media*, California, Sage, 1981.

Commission of Inquiry Into Equal Pay. *Equal Pay in New Zealand*, Wellington, Government Printer, 1971.

Congalton, A. A. *Hawera – A Social Survey*, Hawera, Hawera Star Publishing, 1954.

Congalton, A. A. *Social Class Consciousness in Adolescents*, Wellington, Department of Psychology, Victoria University College, 1952.

Constable, L. 'Controversy in the air', *Landfall*, X(3), 1956.

Cook, H. 'Images, illusions of harmony: the 1950s wife and mother', *New Zealand Women's Studies Journal*, 1(2), 1985.

Cooper, D. *Death of the Family*, Harmondsworth, Middlesex, Penguin, 1971.

Corder, B. F. et al, 'Adolescent Parricide: A Comparison With Other Adolescent Murder', *American Journal of Psychiatry*, 133, 8, August 1976.

Cormier, B. M. et al, 'Adolescents Who Kill a Member of the Family', *Family Violence: An International and Interdisciplinary Study*, 1978.

Cormier, B. M et al, 'The Psychodynamics of Homicide Committed in a Specific Relationship', *Journal of Criminology and Correction*, No 1, 1971.

Courage, James. *A Way of Love*, London, Cape, 1959.

Cox, S. *Public and Private Worlds: Women in Contemporary New Zealand*, Wellington, Allen and Unwin, 1987.

Craven, C. et al. *Women's Studies Handbook*, Auckland, New Women's Press, 1986.

Cruikshank, Margaret. *Lesbian Studies: present and future*, New York, The Feminist Press, 1982.

von Dadelszen, Jane. *Sexual Abuse Study*, Department of Social Welfare, Wellington, 1987.

Daly, Jennifer M. *MG Reflecting: a portrait of marriage guidance in New Zealand 1949-1989*, Wellington, New Zealand Marriage Guidance, 1990.

Dalziel, Margaret. 'Comics in New Zealand', *Landfall*, March 1955.

Dann, C. *Up From Under: Women and Liberation in New Zealand 1970-1985*, Wellington, Allen and Unwin, 1985.

Darty, T. and S. Potter. *Women-Identified Women*, Palo Alto, Mayfield, 1984.

Davies, Sonja. *Bread and Roses*, Masterton, Fraser Books, 1986.

Davis, M. and E. L. Kennedy. 'Oral history and the study of Sexuality in the lesbian community: Buffalo, New York, 1940 – 1960', *Feminist Studies*, Spring 1986.

Dekker, R. M. and Lotte C. van de Pol. *The Tradition of Female Transvestism in Early Modern Europe*, London, MacMillan Press Ltd, 1989.

Department of Education. *Primary School Syllabuses: Health Education*, Wellington, Government Printer, 1958.

Department of Education. *The Education (Post-primary Instruction) Regulations: Syllabuses of Instruction and Prescriptions for the School Certificate Instruction*, Wellington, Government Printer, 1955.

Department of Education. *The Post Primary School Curriculum (Thomas Report)*, Wellington, Government Printer, 1959, originally published in 1944.

Department of Education. *The Primary School Curriculum: Revised Syllabuses*, Wellington, Government Printer, 1948.

Department of Health. *Mental Breakdown: A Guide for the Family*, Government Printer, Wellington, 1965.

Department of Health. *Parents, the Adolescent and Sex: The Parents Role*, Wellington, Government Printer, 1965.

Department of Health. *Sex and the Adolescent Boy*, Wellington, Government Printer, 1965.

Department of Health. *Sex and the Adolescent Girl*, Wellington, Government Printer, 1965.

Department of Health. *Sex and the Parent*, Wellington, Government Printer, 1965.

Department of Health. *Sex and the Young Child*, Wellington, Government Printer, 1965.

Department of Internal Affairs. *Annual Report*, Wellington, Government Printer, 1955.

Department of Justice. *A Penal Policy for New Zealand*, Wellington, Government Printer, 1954.

Department of Justice. *Crime in New Zealand*, Wellington, Government Printer, 1968.

Department of Justice. *Submission to the Committee of Inquiry into Violence*, Wellington, Government Printer, 1986.

deRahm, E. *How Could She Do That? A Study of the Female Criminal*, New York, Clarkson N. Potter, 1969.

Dexter, L. and David Manning, eds. *People, Society, and Mass Communications*, London, Free Press of Glencoe, 1964.

Dodge, J. S. and J. M. Dodge. *The Community Care of the Disabled*, Dunedin, University of Otago, 1979.

Duncan, J. W. and G. M. Duncan 'Murder in the Family: A study of some homicidal adolescents', *American Journal of Psychiatry*, 127(11), 1971.

Dunstall, G. 'The Social Pattern', in W. H. Oliver with Bridget Williams, eds. *The Oxford History of New Zealand*, Oxford, Clarendon Press, 1981.

Eaton, Maude. *Girl Workers in New Zealand Factories*, Wellington, Industrial Psychology Division, Department of Scientific and Industrial Research, 1947.

Ebbett, E. *When the Boys Were Away: New Zealand Women in World War Two*, Wellington, Reed, 1984.

Edmond, L. *Women in Wartime; New Zealand Women Tell Their Story*, Wellington, Government Printer, 1986.

Edwards, S. S. M. 'Neither Bad Nor Mad: The female violent offender reassessed', *Women's Studies International Forum*, 9(1), 1986.

Edwards, S. S. M. *Women on trial*, Manchester, Manchester University Press, 1984.

Eekelaar, J. M. and Katz, S. N. *Family Violence: An International and Interdisciplinary Study*, Toronto, Butterworth, 1978.

Ehrenreich, B. and D. English. *For Her Own Good: 150 Years of the Expert's Advice to Women*, New York, Doubleday, 1979.

Eisenstein, Hester. *Contemporary Feminist Thought*, London, Unwin Paperbacks, 1984.

Eldred-Grigg, S. *A New History of Canterbury*, Dunedin, McIndoe, 1982.

Eldred-Grigg, S. *Pleasures of the Flesh – Sex and Drugs in Colonial New Zealand 1840-1915*, Wellington, A. H. and A. W. Reed, 1984.

Faderman, L. *Surpassing the Love of Men*, New York, William Morrow and Co. Inc, 1981.

Ferguson, Ann. 'On "Compulsory Heterosexuality and Lesbian Existence": defining the issues', *Signs*, 7(1), 1981.

Finkelhor, D. et al. *The Dark Side of Families*, Beverly Hills, Sage Publications, 1981.

Foster, Jeanette. *Sex Variant Women in Literature*, Baltimore, Diana Press, 1975. Originally published in 1956.

Foucault, M. *A History of Sexuality: Volume One*, New York, Pantheon Books, 1978.

Frame, J. *An Angel at My Table: An Autobiography: Volume Two*, Auckland, Hutchinson, 1984.

Frame, J. *Faces in the Water*, The Pegasus Press, Christchurch, 1961.

Franklin, C. *The World's Worst Murderers*, London, Odhams Books, 1965.

Franklin, C. *Woman in the Case*, London, Robert Hale, 1967.

Friday, Nancy. *My Mother, Myself*, New York, Fontana, 1979.

Friends of Christchurch Cathedral, *Guide to Christchurch Cathedral*, Christchurch, 1954.

Fry, R. *It's Different for Daughters: A History of the Curriculum for Girls in New Zealand Schools*, Wellington, NZCER, 1985.

Furneaux, R. *Famous Criminal Cases*, London, Wingate, 1955.

Gardiner, Muriel. *The Deadly Innocents: Portraits of Children Who Kill*, London, Hogarth Press, 1977.

Gardner, W.J., E. T. Beardsley and T. E. Carter. *A History of the University of Canterbury, 1873-1973*, Christchurch, University of Canterbury, 1973.

Gath, Ann. *Down's Syndrome and the Family, the early years*, London, Academic Press, 1978.

Gaute, J. H. H. and Robin Odell. *The Murderer's Who's Who*, London, Harrap, 1979.

Gifford, Lynne. 'Butch We Win, Femme You Lose: The Myth of Lesbian

Impunity', Women's Studies Association New Zealand, *Women's Studies Conference Papers 1983*, 1983.

Glass, W. 'Unmarried Mothers in New Zealand', D.P.H. thesis, London University, 1959.

Glazebrook, S. G. M. 'The Mazengarb Report:Impotent Victorianism', Auckland, MA thesis, University of Auckland, 1978.

Gluckman, L. K. 'Lesbianism: A Clinical Approach', *New Zealand Medical Journal*, 63(407), July 1966.

Grahn, J. *Another Mother Tongue: Gay Words, Gay Worlds*, Boston, Beacon Press, 1984.

Gray, Theodore G. *The Very Error of the Moon*, Arthur Stockwell, Devon, 1948.

Green, C. 'Matricide by Sons', *Med.Sci.Law*, 21(3), 1981.

Greene, Graham. *Stamboul Train*, London, Heinemann, 1974. Originally published 1932.

Gribble, L. *The Hallmark of Horror*, London, Long, 1973.

Gunn Allen, Paula. 'Beloved Women: Lesbians in American Indian Cultures', *Conditions Seven*, New York, 1981.

Gurr, T. and H. H. Cox. *Famous Australasian Crimes*, London, Muller, 1957.

Gurr, T. and H.H. Cox. *Obsession*, London, Muller, 1958.

Hahn, M. and N. Dawson-Wheeler. 'Adolescents Who Kill: What should we do with them?', New Zealand Psychological Society Annual Conference paper, August 1986.

Hall, Leslie M. (pseud). 'Women and Men in New Zealand', *Landfall*, 12(1), 1958.

Hall, Radclyffe. *The Well of Loneliness*, London, Corgi, 1972. Originally published in 1928, London, Cape.

Hamilton, Ian. 'The End of the Affair', *Here and Now*, October 1954.

Harre, J. *Maori and Pakeha: A study of mixed marriages in New Zealand*, Wellington, A.H. and A.W. Reed, 1966.

Hartman, M. S. *Victorian Murderesses*, London, Robson Books, 1977.

Hill, Michael et al, eds. *Shades of Deviance*, Palmerston North, Dunmore Press, 1983.

Hiller, A. E. and A. Mandish, 'Women, Crime and Criminal Justice: The state of current theory and research in Australia and New Zealand', *Australia and New Zealand Journal of Criminology*, 15, 1982.

Houston, Stewart, ed. *Marriage and the Family in New Zealand*, Wellington, Sweet and Maxwell, 1970.

Hyde, H. Montgomery. *The Other Love*, London, Mayflower Books, 1972.

Johnston, Jill. *Lesbian Nation*, Simon and Schuster, New York, 1974.

Jones, A. *Women Who Kill*, New York, Holt, Rinehart and Winston, 1980.

Jones, R. G. *Killer Couples: Terrifying True Stories of the World's Deadliest Duos*, London, W. H. Allen and Co, 1989.

Katz, J. *Gay American History*, New York, Thomas Crowell, 1978.

Katz, J. *The Gay/Lesbian Almanac*, New York, Harper and Row, 1983.

Kelsey, J. 'Legal Imperialism and the Colonisation of Aotearoa, in P.

Spoonley et al, eds. *Tauiwi – Racism and Ethnicity in New Zealand*, Palmerston North, Dunmore Press, 1984.

Kennedy, M. and H.C. D. Somerset. *Bringing Up Crippled Children*, Christchurch, New Zealand Council for Educational Research, 1951.

Keohane, N. O., M. Z. Rosaldo and B. C. Gelpi. *Feminist Theory: A Critique of Ideology*, Great Britain, The Harvester Press, 1982.

Kinsey, Alfred C. et al. *Sexual Behaviour in the Human Female*, Philadelphia, W. B. Saunders, 1953.

Kitzinger, Celia. *The Social Construction of Lesbianism*, London, SAGE Publications, 1987.

Knight, G. A. F. *The Jews and New Zealand*, Presbyterian Bookroom, Christchurch, 1948ca.

Koopman-Boyden, Peggy ed. *Families in New Zealand Society*, Wellington, Methuen, 1978.

Koopman-Boyden, Peggy, G. and Claudia D. Scott. *The Family and Government Policy in New Zealand*, Sydney, George Allen and Unwin, 1984.

Laurie, A. J. 'Lesbian-Feminism: A Re-View', *Sites*, 15, Spring 1987.

Laurie, A. J. 'Lesbian Worlds', in S.Cox, ed. *Public and Private Worlds: Women in Contemporary New Zealand*, Wellington, Allen and Unwin, 1987.

Lawrence, P. J. ed. *Mental Health and the Community*, Christchurch, Canterbury Mental Health Council, 1963.

Lee, Anna. 'Therapy, the Evil Within', *Trivia*, 9, Fall 1986.

Leitch, Shirley. *NewsTalk, Media Stories on Unemployment*, Palmerston North, New Zealand, Dunmore Press, 1990.

Levin, Meyer. *Compulsion*, New York, Simon and Schuster, 1956.

Lindop, Audrey Erskine. *Details of Jeremy Stretton*, London, Heinemann, 1955.

Lombroso, C. and W. Ferrero. *The Female Offender*, London, Fisher Unwin, 1895.

MacClure, V. *She Stands Accused*, Connecticut, Hyperion Press, 1975.

MacKay, I. K. *Radio Broadcasting in New Zealand*, New Zealand, 1953.

MacKenzie, D. F. 'Homosexuality and the Justice Department', *New Zealand Medical Journal*, Special Number, 1967.

MacKenzie, D. F. *While We Have Prisons*, Auckland, Methuen Publications, 1980.

McKnight, C. K et al. 'Matricide and Mental Illness', *Canadian Psychiatric Association Journal*, 11(2), April 1966.

McLintock, A. H. *Encyclopaedia of New Zealand*, Wellington, Government Printer, 1966.

Maharey S. and M. O'Brien. *Alternatives – Socialist Essays for the 1980s*, Massey, Department of Sociology, Massey University, 1986.

Manning, A. E. *The Bodgie: A Study in Abnormal Psychology*, Wellington, A.H. and A.W. Reed, 1958.

Mansfield, Katherine. *Bliss and other stories*, Auckland, Century Hutchinson, 1988. Originally published 1920.

March, W. *The Bad Seed*, New York, Hamish Hamilton, 1954.

Marohn, R. et al. 'Juvenile Delinquents and Violent Death', *The Acting-Out and Violent Adolescent*, 10, 1982.

Matthews, J. J. *Good and Mad Women*, Sydney, George Allen & Unwin, 1984.

Mazengarb, O. C. *Report of the Special Committee on Moral Delinquency in Children and Adolescents*, AJHR 1954, H-47.

Medlicott, R. W. 'An examination of the necessity for a concept of evil: Some aspects of evil as a form of perversion', *British Journal of Medical Psychology*, 43, 1970.

Medlicott, R. W. 'Concepts of Normality and of Moral Values', *N.Z. Sexologist*, March 1986.

Medlicott, R. W. 'Paranoia of the Exalted Type in a Setting of *Folie a Deux*: A Study of Two Adolescent Homicides', in Black and Taylor, eds, *Deviant Behaviour: New Zealand Studies*, 1979.

Medlicott, R. W. 'Sociopathic Personality Disturbance', in P. J. Lawrence, ed. *Mental Health and the Community*, Canterbury Mental Council, Christchurch, 1963.

Medlicott, R. W. 'Some Reflections on the Parker-Hulme, Leopold-Loeb Cases with Special Reference to the Concept of Omnipotence', *New Zealand Law Journal*, 37(22), 1961.

Medlicott, R. W. 'The Place of Electronarcosis in Psychiatric Treatment: A Clinical Assessment based on the Treatment of Four Hundred Patients', *New Zealand Medical Journal*, LIII, 1954.

Mental Deficiency Sub-Committee, New Zealand Branch, British Medical Association. *The Mental Deficiency Services: An analysis of existing policy and the community's requirements*, Wellington, Commercial Print, 1955ca.

Middleton, S. 'Feminism and Education in Post-War New Zealand: An Oral History Perspective', in R.Openshaw and D. McKenzie (eds), *Reinterpreting the Educational Past*, Wellington, NZCER, 1987.

Middleton, S. *Women and Education in Aotearoa*, Wellington, Allen and Unwin/Port Nicholson Press, 1988.

Moffat, M.J. and C. Painter, *Revelations: Diaries of Women*, New York, Vintage Press, 1975.

Mohr, J. W. and C. K. McKnight. 'Violence as a Function of Age and Relationship with Special Reference to Matricide', *Canadian Psychiatric Association Journal*, 16, 1971.

Montgomerie, Deborah. 'War and Women: Work and Motherhood', *New Zealand Women's Studies Journal*, 3(2), 1988.

Morris, Greggory. *The Kids Next Door: Sons and Daughters Who Kill Their Parents*, New York, William Morrow, 1985.

Naffine, Ngaire. *Female Crime: The construction of women in criminology*, Sydney, Allen & Unwin, 1987.

Nash, J. R. *Look for the Woman*, London, Harrap, 1984.

Nicholas, M. *The World's Wickedest Women*, London, Octopus Books, 1984.

Nixon, A. J. *Divorce in New Zealand*, Auckland, A.U.P., 1954.

New Zealand Tourist Publicity and Advertising Agency. *Christchurch City of Beautiful Gardens and Parklands*, Christchurch, 1950.

O'Donoghue, A. F. *The Rise and Fall of Radio Broadcasting in New Zealand*, Auckland, A. F. O'Donoghue, 1968.

O'Regan, P. *Aunts and Windmills*, Wellington, Bridget Williams Books, 1991.

Ogilvie, G. *The Port Hills of Christchurch*, Wellington, A. H. and A. W. Reed, 1978.

Old Timer. 'Sex and Education', *National Education*, November 1, 1954.

Oliver, W. H. with Bridget Williams, eds. *The Oxford History of New Zealand*, Oxford, The Clarendon Press, 1981.

Olivia. *Olivia*, London, The Hogarth Press, 1951.

Olssen, E. and A. Levesque. 'Towards a history of the European family in New Zealand', in P. Koopman-Boyden, ed, *Families in New Zealand Society*, Wellington, Methuen 1978.

Openshaw, Roger. 'Hooligans at Hastings: Reactions to the Hastings Blossom Festival Affray, September 1960', unpublished paper, 1988.

Openshaw, R. and D. McKenzie, eds *Reinterpreting the Educational Past*, Wellington, NZCER, 1987.

Parkinson, Phil. 'A Soldier's Tale', *Pink Triangle*, 61, Spring 1986.

Parkyn, G. W. *Children of High Intelligence: A New Zealand Study*, N.Z.Council for Educational Research, 1953.

Parlee, Mary Brown. 'Psychology and Women', *Signs*, 5(1), Autumn, 1979, pp.121-3.

Pearson, B. 'Fretful Sleepers', *Landfall*, 6(3), September 1952.

Pearson, B. 'The Banning of The Butcher Shop', in J. Devanny, author, *The Butcher Shop*, Auckland, A.U.P., 1981.

Perry, S. *The Indecent Publications Tribunal*, Christchurch Whitcombe and Tombs, 1965.

Philipp, E. 'Homosexuality as Seen in a New Zealand City Practice', *New Zealand Medical Journal*, 67(430), March 1968.

Phillips, J. *A Man's Country? The Image of the Pakeha Male : A History*, Auckland, Penguin Books, 1987.

Phillips, R. *Divorce in New Zealand: A Social History*, Auckland, Oxford University Press, 1981.

Pilkington, R. *Facts of Life For Parents*, British Medical Association, 1955ca.

Pitt, D., ed. *Social Class in New Zealand*, Auckland, Longman Paul, 1977.

Pool, D. Ian. *The Maori Population of New Zealand 1769-1971*, Auckland, Auckland University Press, 1977.

Pollak, O. *The Criminality of Women*, New York, A. S. Barnes, 1961.

Rafter, N. and E. Natlaizia. 'Marxist Feminism: Implications for Criminal Justice', *Crime and Delinquency*, 27, 1981.

Raymond, Janice G. *A Passion for Friends: Toward a philosophy of female affection*, London, The Women's Press, 1986.

Rich, A. *Compulsory Heterosexuality and Lesbian Existence*; London, Onlywomen Press, 1981.

Rich, A. *Of Woman Born*, New York, Bantam, 1976.

Rich, A. *On Lies, Secrets, and Silences*, Norton, 1979.

Robb, J.H. and A. Somerset. *Report to Masterton: Results of a social survey*, Masterton, Robb and Somerset, 1957.

Robinson, Jan Jordan. 'Of Diverse Persons, Men and Women and Whores: Women and crime in nineteeth century Canterbury', University of Canterbury, Christchurch, M.A. Thesis, 1983.

Rohrbaugh, Joanna B. *Women: Psychology's Puzzle*, London, Sphere Books, 1981.

Rosier, Pat. 'The Only Ones', *Broadsheet*, 153, November 1987, pp.24-29.

Roth, H. *Trade Unions in New Zealand*, Wellington, A. H. and A. W. Reed, 1973.

Royal Commission on Social Policy. *The April Report*, II, 'Future Directions', Wellington, The Commission, 1988.

Russ, Joanna. *How to Suppress Women's Writing*, London, The Women's Press Ltd, 1983.

Sainsbury, A. *Misery Mansion: Grim Tales of New Zealand Asylums*, Otahuhu, 1946.

Saphira, M. *The Sexual Abuse of Children*, Auckland, Papers Inc., 1981.

Sargent, D. 'Children who kill – A family conspiracy?', *Social Work*, 7, 1962

Sayers, Janet. *Biological Politics: Feminist and Anti-Feminist Perspectives*, London, Tavistock, 1982.

Schur, E. M. *Labelling Women Deviant: Gender, Stigma and Social Control*, New York, Random House, 1984.

Sheppard, C. 'Towards a Better Understanding of the Violent Offender', *Canadian Journal of Criminology and Corrections*, 13(1), 1971.

Simmons, C. 'Companionate Marriage and the Lesbian Threat', *Frontiers:A Journal of Women's Studies*, 4(3), 1979.

Simon, Rita James. *The Contemporary Woman and Crime*, Maryland, National Institute of Mental Health, Center for Studies of Crime and Delinquency, 1975.

Simon, Rita James. *The Jury and the Defense of Insanity*, Boston, Little Brown and Company, 1967.

Simon, Rita James. *Women and Crime*, Massachusetts, Lexington Books, 1975.

Sinclair, K. *A History of New Zealand*, Auckland, Penguin Books, 1980.

Smart, C. *Women, Crime and Criminology*, London, Routledge and Kegan Paul, 1976.

Smith, L. L. 'The problem of abortion in New Zealand in the nineteen-thirties', University of Auckland, Auckland, M.A. essay, 1972.

Smith, Valerie. 'Social History of Comunity Care of the Disabled', in J. S. and J. M. Dodge, *The Community Care of the Disabled: Proceedings of a Seminar held in Dunedin on October 11th-13th 1978*, University of Otago, Dunedin, 1979.

Society for Research on Women. *The Unmarried Mother; Problems Involved in Keeping her Child*, Johnsonville, S.R.O.W., 1980.

Sosin, Deborah Ann. 'The diary as a transitional object in female adolescent development', *Adolescent Psychiatry, Developmental and Clinical Studies*, XI, 1983.

Sparrow, Gerald. *Queens of Crime*, London, Arthur Barker, 1973.

Sparrow, Gerald. *Women Who Murder*, London, Arthur Barker, 1970.

Spoonley, P. et al, eds. *Tauiwi – Racism and Ethnicity in New Zealand*, Palmerston North, Dunmore Press, 1984.

Stace, Michael. 'Legal form and moral phenomena: A study of two events', Doctor of Jurisprudence thesis, Osgoode Hall Law School, York University, Toronto, 1980.

Stanley, Julia and S. Wolfe, eds. *The Coming Out Stories*, Persephone, 1980.

Stanley, L. and A. Wise. *Breaking Out: Feminist Consciousness and Feminist Research*, London, Routledge & Kegan Paul, 1983.

Sutch, W. B. *The Quest for Security in New Zealand 1840 to 1966*, Wellington, Oxford University Press, 1966.

Tait, Gordon. *The Bartlett Syndrome*, Christchurch, Freedom to Read, 1979.

Tate, A. B. 'The Parker-Hulme Murder', *The Australian Police Journal*, July 1955.

Taylor, Nancy M. *The Home Front*, Wellington, Historical Publications Branch, Department of Internal Affairs, 1986.

Te Awekotuku, Ngahuia. 'Dykes and Queers', *Broadsheet*, May, 168, 1989.

Te Awekotuku, Ngahuia. *Tahuri*, Auckland, New Women's Press, 1989.

Thomas, W. I. *The Unadjusted Girl*, New York, Harper and Row, 1967.

Thorne, B. and M. Yalom. *Rethinking the Family: Some Feminist Questions*, New York, Longman, 1982.

Totman, Jane. *The Murderess: A Psychosocial Study of Criminal Homicide*, San Francisco, R and E Research Associates, 1978.

Trilling, Diana. *Mrs Harris: The Death of the Scarsdale Diet Doctor*, London, Hamish Hamilton, 1982.

Tuttle, Lisa. *Encyclopoedia of Feminism*, London, Arrow Books, 1987.

Webb, S. D. and J. Collette. *New Zealand Society – Contemporary Perspectives*, Sydney, John Wiley and Sons Australasia, 1973.

Weeks, J. *Coming Out: Homosexual Politics in Britain from the nineteenth century to the present*, London, Quartet Books, 1977.

Wolff, Charlotte. *Love Between Women*, London, Duckworth, 1971.

Who's Who, London, 1950, 1951, and 1987.

Wilkins, E. H. 'Sex Education', *Education Gazette*, 1 December 1921.

Wilkins, E. H. 'Sex Education', *Education Gazette*, 1 November 1922.

Wilson, Colin and Patricia Pitman. *Encyclopaedia of Murder*, London and Sydney, Pan Books, 1984.

Wilson, P. *Murderess*, London, Michael Joseph, 1971.

Wily, H. Jenner and K.R. Stallworthy, *Mental Abnormality and the Law*, Christchurch, N. M. Peryer Ltd, 1962.

Winslade, W. J. and J. W. Ross, *The Insanity Plea*, New York, Charles Scribner's Sons, 1983.

Winterbourn, R. *Caring for Intellectually Handicapped Children*, Wellington, New Zealand Council for Educational Research, 1962.

Zita, Jacquelyn. 'Historical Amnesia and the Lesbian Continuum', *Signs*, 7(1), 1981.

INDEX

Other titles from Firebrand Books include:

Artemis In Echo Park, Poetry by Eloise Klein Healy/$8.95

Before Our Eyes, A Novel by Joan Alden/$8.95

Beneath My Heart, Poetry by Janice Gould/$8.95

The Big Mama Stories by Shay Youngblood/$8.95

The Black Back-Ups, Poetry by Kate Rushin/$9.95

A Burst Of Light, Essays by Audre Lorde/$9.95

Cecile, Stories by Ruthann Robson/$8.95

Crime Against Nature, Poetry by Minnie Bruce Pratt/$8.95

Diamonds Are A Dyke's Best Friend by Yvonne Zipter/$9.95

Dykes To Watch Out For, Cartoons by Alison Bechdel/$8.95

Dykes To Watch Out For: The Sequel, Cartoons by Alison Bechdel/$9.95

Eight Bullets by Claudia Brenner with Hannah Ashley/$12.95

Exile In The Promised Land, A Memoir by Marcia Freedman/$8.95

Experimental Love, Poetry by Cheryl Clarke/$8.95

Eye Of A Hurricane, Stories by Ruthann Robson/$8.95

The Fires Of Bride, A Novel by Ellen Galford/$8.95

Food & Spirits, Stories by Beth Brant (*Degonwadonti*)/$8.95

Forty-Three Septembers, Essays by Jewelle Gomez/$10.95

Free Ride, A Novel by Marilyn Gayle/$9.95

A Gathering Of Spirit, A Collection by North American Indian Women
edited by Beth Brant (*Degonwadonti*)/$12.95

Getting Home Alive by Aurora Levins Morales and Rosario Morales/$9.95

The Gilda Stories, A Novel by Jewelle Gomez/$10.95

Good Enough To Eat, A Novel by Lesléa Newman/$10.95

Humid Pitch, Narrative Poetry by Cheryl Clarke/$8.95

Jewish Women's Call For Peace edited by Rita Falbel, Irena Klepfisz, and
Donna Nevel/$4.95

Jonestown & Other Madness, Poetry by Pat Parker/$7.95

Just Say Yes, A Novel by Judith McDaniel/$9.95

The Land Of Look Behind, Prose and Poetry by Michelle Cliff/$8.95

Legal Tender, A Mystery by Marion Foster/$9.95

Lesbian (Out)law, Survival Under the Rule of Law by Ruthann Robson/$9.95

A Letter To Harvey Milk, Short Stories by Lesléa Newman/$9.95

Letting In The Night, A Novel by Joan Lindau/$8.95

Living As A Lesbian, Poetry by Cheryl Clarke/$7.95

Metamorphosis, Reflections on Recovery by Judith McDaniel/$7.95

Mohawk Trail by Beth Brant (*Degonwadonti*)/$7.95

Moll Cutpurse, A Novel by Ellen Galford/$7.95

The Monarchs Are Flying, A Novel by Marion Foster/$8.95

More Dykes To Watch Out For, Cartoons by Alison Bechdel/$9.95

Movement In Black, Poetry by Pat Parker/$8.95

My Mama's Dead Squirrel, Lesbian Essays on Southern Culture by Mab
Segrest/ $9.95

New, Improved! Dykes To Watch Out For, Cartoons by Alison Bechdel/$8.95

Normal Sex by Linda Smukler/$8.95

Now Poof She Is Gone, Poetry by Wendy Rose/$8.95

The Other Sappho, A Novel by Ellen Frye/$8.95

Out In The World, International Lesbian Organizing by Shelley Anderson/$4.95

Politics Of The Heart, A Lesbian Parenting Anthology edited by Sandra Pollack and Jeanne Vaughn/$12.95

Post-Diagnosis by Sandra Steingraber/$9.95

Presenting...Sister NoBlues by Hattie Gossett/$8.95

Rebellion, Essays 1980–1991 by Minnie Bruce Pratt/$12.95

Restoring The Color Of Roses by Barrie Jean Borich/$9.95

A Restricted Country by Joan Nestle/$9.95

Running Fiercely Toward A High Thin Sound, A Novel by Judith Katz/$9.95

Sacred Space by Geraldine Hatch Hanon/$9.95

Sanctuary, A Journey by Judith McDaniel/$7.95

Sans Souci, And Other Stories by Dionne Brand/$8.95

Scuttlebutt, A Novel by Jana Williams/$8.95

S/he by Minnie Bruce Pratt/$10.95

Shoulders, A Novel by Georgia Cotrell/$9.95

Simple Songs, Stories by Vickie Sears/$8.95

Sister Safety Pin, A Novel by Lorrie Sprecher/$9.95

Skin: Talking About Sex, Class & Literature by Dorothy Allison/$13.95

Spawn Of Dykes To Watch Out For, Cartoons by Alison Bechdel/$9.95

Speaking Dreams, Science Fiction by Severna Park/$9.95

Stardust Bound, A Novel by Karen Cadora/$8.95

Staying The Distance, A Novel by Franci McMahon/$9.95

Stone Butch Blues, A Novel by Leslie Feinberg/$12.95

The Sun Is Not Merciful, Short Stories by Anna Lee Walters/$8.95

Talking Indian, Reflections on Survival and Writing by Anna Lee Walters/$10.95

Tender Warriors, A Novel by Rachel Guido deVries/$8.95

This Is About Incest by Margaret Randall/$8.95

The Threshing Floor, Short Stories by Barbara Burford/$7.95

Trash, Stories by Dorothy Allison/$9.95

We Say We Love Each Other, Poetry by Minnie Bruce Pratt/$8.95

The Women Who Hate Me, Poetry by Dorothy Allison/$8.95

Words To The Wise, A Writer's Guide to Feminist and Lesbian Periodicals & Publishers by Andrea Fleck Clardy/$5.95

The Worry Girl, Stories from a Childhood by Andrea Freud Loewenstein/$8.95

Yours In Struggle, Three Feminist Perspectives on Anti-Semitism and Racism by Elly Bulkin, Minnie Bruce Pratt, and Barbara Smith/$9.95

You can buy Firebrand titles at your bookstore, or order them directly from the publisher (141 The Commons, Ithaca, New York 14850, 607-272-0000).

Please include $3.00 shipping for the first book and $.50 for each additional book.

A free catalog is available on request.